REGENSBURGER BEITRÄGE
ZUR GENDER-FORSCHUNG
Band 8

Herausgegeben von
Rainer Emig
Anne-Julia Zwierlein

SARAH SCHÄFER-ALTHAUS

The Gendered Body

Female Sanctity, Gender Hybridity and the Body in Women's Hagiography

Universitätsverlag
WINTER
Heidelberg

Bibliografische Information der Deutschen Nationalbibliothek
Die Deutsche Nationalbibliothek verzeichnet diese Publikation in der Deutschen Nationalbibliografie; detaillierte bibliografische Daten sind im Internet über *http://dnb.d-nb.de* abrufbar.

Zugl.: Paderborn: Univ., Diss., 2015

ISBN 978-3-8253-6680-3

Imprimé en Allemagne · Printed in Germany
Umschlaggestaltung: Klaus Brecht GmbH, Heidelberg, Umschlagbild: fotolia
Druck: Memminger MedienCentrum, 87700 Memmingen

Gedruckt auf umweltfreundlichem, chlorfrei gebleichtem und alterungsbeständigem Papier

Den Verlag erreichen Sie im Internet unter:
www.winter-verlag.de

Acknowledgements

During the time of writing, revising and publishing this book, I have benefited greatly from a number of scholars, colleagues and mentors who helped and supported me along the way.

First of all, I owe a sincere and earnest debt of gratitude to my supervisor Prof. Dr. Merle Tönnies, whose continual and unconditional support, empowerment and encouragement as well as her personal and professional guidance from the early stages of my research has helped me to become an independent scholar. I furthermore want to thank my second supervisor, Prof. Dr. Christoph Ehland, for his critical and in-depth assessment of my work, as well as the other members of the defense committee, Prof. Dr. Christoph Ribbat and Dr. Sara Strauß, for their time and commitment. I also owe a particular debt to Prof. em. Dr. Rolf Breuer, who, with his excellence in teaching, introduced me to the field of medieval studies during my time as a graduate student at the University of Paderborn, and to Prof. Dr. Susan Kim, whose class on medieval gender studies during my time at Illinois State University (2009) has greatly influenced my own work.

Over the years I have been generously provided with fellowships and research grants from the University of Paderborn, for which I am particularly thankful as without them this study could have been neither started nor completed. In this respect I am truly grateful to the university for a six-month fellowship ("Förderlinie I", 2010-2011) and for a three-year full-time doctoral fellowship ("Promotionsstipendium im Bereich der Genderforschung", 2011-2014) as well as to the Fakultät für Kulturwissenschaften for two conference travel grants (2013).

I have in addition profited immensely from the many opportunities I have had to discuss some of the ideas of this study at various conferences – especially at the annual Gender and Medieval Studies Conference held by the Gender and Medieval Studies Group (2012-2014), the International Congress on Medieval Studies at Western Michigan University, Kalamazoo (2013) and the International Medieval Congress at the University of Leeds (2013, 2014). At this point I also want to thank the lively and encouraging online communities of the Society for Medieval Feminist Scholarship and the Hagiography Society for discussing difficult matters and thus helping me to progress in the final stages of this project.

Furthermore, I wholeheartedly want to thank both editors of this series, Prof. Dr. Anne-Julia Zwierlein and Prof. Dr. Rainer Emig, for their interest in my work and the possibility to publish my dissertation within the realms of the *Regensburger Beiträge zur Gender-Forschung*, as well as Dr. Andreas Barth, Ralf Stemper and the entire team at Winter for the close collaboration in the publication process.

My sincere thanks goes to the group of colleagues and friends who have constantly supported my project and encouraged me to pursue the path I have chosen. They include Prof. Dr. Greta Olson, my inspiring mentor and patient listener; Dr. Mareike Tüllmann and Dr. Sara Strauß, whose thoughtful suggestions and corrections were valuable in different stages of this project; and my dear friends and colleagues Mirja Gehring, Anna Krumm and Dr. Antonio Roselli for their late-night talks, the uncountable coffee dates and their undemanding support when I needed it the most. I also want to express my sincere appreciation to Tim Feeney, whose careful reading and impressive, magical editing skills were extremely helpful and improved the final version of this book. Needless to say, all remaining errors are entirely my own responsibility.

Above all, no words can express the gratitude I owe to my husband, Daniel, for his strong encouragement, his unflagging interest, his continual support and his loving care over the last years. Without him, his love and his unconditional belief in me and my work, this book would not have been completed. To him this book is dedicated.

Introduction

> Warum müssen wir uns mit dem Körper des Menschen im Mittelalter beschäftigen? Weil er zu den größten Forschungslücken in der Geschichtsschreibung gehört.
>
> Jacques Le Goff and Nicolas Truong[1]

In their study *Die Geschichte des Körpers im Mittelalter* (2007), the French historian and sociologist Jacques Le Goff and journalist Nicolas Truong illustrate that the human body, with its various limbs, fluids and functions, was a highly controversial and much debated topic in the Middle Ages, a time period traditionally located between the sixth and late fifteenth centuries. The body constantly had to negotiate its place between glorification and crucifixion, between superiority and subordination. It was seen as a symbol of constant decay and mirrored human imperfections, but at the same time, the body was worshipped and praised, and many social, cultural and gender-related implications were closely connected to it (Le Goff and Truong 14). The body was an all-encompassing metaphor, describing society and institutions, symbolising unity and conflict, order and disorder, and most of all, organic life in all of its facets (14). Unfortunately, among cultural historians the body belonged for a long time to nature rather than culture, an assumption which led to the fact that no other aspect of medieval cultural history has been more neglected within scholarship than the body, leaving a research gap in chronicles of cultural history and in the modern understanding of the past (18, 23). However, as the medieval era has shaped the present like no other time period preceding it – it is a period seen as "crucial in the development of Western attitudes" (Bullough and Brundage, *Sexual Practices* xi; see also Le Goff and Truong 33), a period whose mentalities, customs and attitudes affect humanity up to the present day – the question arises of whether the body does not have a history of its own. Is the body not able to shape culture to various degrees – economically, socially and mentally, but also sexually, and in relation to gender (Le Goff and Truong 18)?

Therefore, the initial research interest of this thesis lies in the question of how women, femininity and in particular the female body were constructed and treated in medieval literature and culture. In this respect, female saints' legends prove to be the most promising source for further investigations of early attitudes and phenomena concerning medieval femininity and femaleness for a variety of reasons. First, saints

[1] Unless specifically noted, all translations are the author's. Trans.: "Why do we have to deal with the body of the Middle Ages? Because it belongs to the greatest research gaps in history". Jacques Le Goff and Nicolas Truong, *Die Geschichte des Körpers im Mittelalter* (Stuttgart: Klett-Cotta, 2007), p. 9. Originally published as Jacques Le Goff and Nicolas Truong, *Une Histoire du Corps au Moyen Âge* (Paris: Levi, 2003). All direct citations within this study are taken from the German edition (2007) and translated.

were considered to be the "superheroes and the celebrities" (Salih, *Companion* 1) of the Middle Ages, as Sarah Salih writes in her introduction to *A Companion to Middle English Hagiography* (2003):

> They pervaded the landscape: their names, images and narratives were attached to buildings, geographical features, parishes, guilds and towns. Saint-cult was multimedia and interactive. Every church displayed paintings and sculptures of the saints; their feast days were celebrated with liturgies, readings, plays, processions and feasts. (1)

Saints' legends were the "fabric of everyday life" (3), and hagiography, the study of saints' lives, was identified as the most frequently read genre of medieval times. Hagiographies such as the *Legenda Aurea* by Jacobus de Voragine (1260) would nowadays be considered influential bestsellers, and the *Legenda* in particular is claimed to be the second-most read book during the European Middle Ages (Long 54). Even though hagiographical narratives often lack historical authenticity,[2] the numerous *passiones* and *vitae* can nevertheless function as representations of culture, common knowledge and conventional motifs and as such arguably fit into "a surprisingly wide array of purposes, intended audiences, notions of decorum and kinds of religious and socio-political teachings" (Reames, "Artistry" 178).

Second, saints' legends are body-centred texts. Saints and their bodies are interconnected and interdependent, and the length of the individual *life*,[3] especially in descriptions of martyrdoms, increases with the number of sentences focusing on the body and its torture. As Stavroula Constantinou remarks, "the longer the body remains unharmed [by tortures], the larger the tormenter's desire to harm it" (40). Consequently, the longer a narrative focuses on the body as a stylistic device and offers detailed descriptions of various, usually negative treatments of the body and individual body parts, the longer the body functions as a metaphor and the more successful the legends were in their public reception and reproduction.

Third, next to the popularity of saints' legends in general, female saints' legends in particular offer unique insights into this body-focused genre, with its indoctrinated, almost exclusively male[4] descriptions of women's bodies. On the one hand the function of masculinity, which commonly appears in the form of male authorship of and male heathen torturers in the legends, allows a rather traditional, male-dominated reading of the *vitae*, and even the "selection of saints in Legendaries", as Robert Bartlett points out, has always been "masculine and archaic" (555). On the other hand, however, the majority of women saints presented in this study challenge the traditional gender hierarchy and thus question not only traditional presumptions about women, but also the narrowness of the common binaries: sex and gender. Legends featuring female cross-

[2] For a discussion of the genre of hagiography, its author-text relation and its influence in the medieval era, see chapter 1.

[3] "Life" has two meanings here: the length of the saint's *vita* and the length of her biological life.

[4] For example, Jacobus de Voragine, Alban Butler, or Ælfric. As Jane Tibbetts Schulenburg notes, with the exception of two *vitae*, all of the lives of women saints with identifiable authors in the *Bibliotheca Hagiographica Latina* are written by men. Jane Tibbetts Schulenburg, *Forgetful of Their Sex: Female Sanctity and Society, ca. 500-1100* (Chicago: U of Chicago P, 1998), p. 31.

dressers, bearded women or uncommonly outspoken female protagonists are thereby examples of "a discourse which frames [a] construction of gender which may not be entirely familiar to the modern reader" as it describes "individuals [who] could move on occasion between genders or adopt the attributes of another gender" (Riches and Salih 4). This possibility to transcend their female sex and the repeatedly displayed permeability of sex and gender roles set female saints "apart from ordinary women and singled them out as candidates for sainthood" (Schulenburg 1). However, as saints' legends in general and women saints' in particular were intended to serve as role models, as sources of inspiration and imitation,

> this heroic and strong, or "virile" behaviour which was encouraged in certain cultural contexts proved to be problematic in others. Seen as a serious threat to male order or authority, actions which had once won the approbation of the Church and society came to be perceived as extreme and dangerous. Instead of attracting praise and elevation to sainthood, the transcendence of the limitation and temptations of female sexuality and their proper gender roles [...] brought suspicion and contempt to women. Viewed as exercising profoundly threatening, transgressive, or disturbing roles, such women were seen as the dangerous "other"; they needed to be contained, marginalized, or punished. (2)

Hence, at "a time when there is far less certainty regarding spiritual orthodoxy and sexual normality than ever before", female saints' legends "challenge us to ask new questions" and to investigate these "controversial or unusual historical artifacts from new perspectives" (Friesen 7).

Therefore, the aim of this study is the exploration of these complex historical, cultural, sociological and gendered constructions of the medieval female body in popular female saints' legends. By focusing on frequently recurring body parts in women's hagiography, such as the breast, hair(styles) and the tripartite construction of mouth, teeth and tongue, this study will critically reflect on the gendered treatment of these body parts against the ideological and religious background of this masculine genre and the role of women at that time. It will show that the treatment of specific body parts often mirrors male anxieties about the female body and women in general and frequently highlights sexual and even sadistic fantasies. Furthermore, even though female saints were supposed to be consistently orthodox in ideological, instructive terms, many of them are depicted as what Judith Butler has called "incoherently sexed" ("Sexual Inversions" 67), as transvestites or eunuchs, and thus as (bodily) gender hybrids, creating a "screen for potentially dangerous ideas" (Reames, "Artistry" 199) and turning them into a "serious threat to male order or authority" (Schulenburg 2).

In order to examine these different aspects, the legends will be approached with the help of context and content-oriented methodologies. Next to a comparative, intertextual and close reading of the narratives, this study will embed the *vitae* in their literary and cultural history, treating the legends as a reflection and product of their social reality. In this way, the thesis will combine the analytical methods and approaches of gender studies with those of cultural studies in a broader sense and provide additional interdisciplinary insights into sociology, body theory, theology, art history, medicine and other fields relevant for the ensuing interpretation of the literary works in general and the female body in particular.

In the process of selecting female saints' legends for further analyses, the first stages of research commenced with a census of European women saints in popular reference works for hagiographers, such as the previously mentioned *Legenda Aurea*, also known as the *Golden Legend* (1260), by Jacobus de Voragine, translated by William Granger Ryan (2 vols., 1993, rpt. 1995);[5] Alban Butler's *Lives of the Saints* (1756-1759), edited, revised and supplemented by Herbert Thurston and Donald Attwater (4 vols., 1956);[6] David Hugh Farmer's *Oxford Dictionary of Saints* (1982; 5th ed., 2004); Ælfric's *Lives of Saints*, edited and translated by Walter Skeat (2 vols., 1881-1900); and Leslie A. Donovan's *Women Saints' Lives in Old English Prose* (1999).

Of the collective numbers, approximately eighty female saints' legends, whether historically authentic or completely fictional, could be singled out in which the body, its description and commonly also its destruction played a significant role for the individual saint's life, her martyrdom and her endeavour to achieve sainthood in medieval times through today – the latter criterion being applied in order to ensure that the saint and the focus on certain body parts are linked with apodictic certainty and can be considered standard elements in the respective traditions.

In selecting saints, this study was "more inclusive than exclusive in this exercise" (Schulenburg 11) and purposely expanded its research to the large number of marvellous individuals whose lives are not historically authentic, but rather completely fictional or improbable. "After the triumph of Christianity in the fourth century", as Bartlett asserts, "the genre of martyrdom accounts took wing, and purely legendary and fantastical Passions of the martyrs were composed, even if, on occasion, the martyr who was the subject was indeed a real historical person" (505). Consequently, as the discussion of the genre of hagiography in the first chapter will show, saints' legends are often constructed, adapted and modified by their authors and compilers to suit the tastes of employers and sponsors and to represent their ideological beliefs. As Bartlett notes, "hagiographers often wrote in their prefaces that the work had been imposed on them by the order of superiors" (513) and in many "occasions it is clear that hagiographic writers had been formally missioned to undertake their work by members of another

[5] However, it is the edition by Theodor Graesse from the nineteenth century which is seen as the standard Latin version on which most of the twentieth-century translations, such as Ryan's, are based. See Jacobi a Voragine [Jacobus de Voragine], *Legenda aurea vulgo Historia lombardica dicta*, ed. Theodor Graesse, 2nd ed. (Lipsiae [Leipzig]: Librariae Arnoldianae, 1850; rpt. Osnabrück: Zeller, 1969). As the majority of the saints' legends analysed in this study appear in the *Legenda Aurea*, de Voragine's work will be used as the predominant primary source. The following study will take the translation of Graesse's edition by William Granger Ryan as the basis for further analysis; see Jacobus De Voragine, *The Golden Legend: Readings on the Saints*, 2 vols., ed. and trans. William Granger Ryan (Princeton: Princeton UP, 1995), from now on referenced as "de Voragine" unless otherwise noted. Direct quotes are furthermore supplemented with the Latin taken from Graesse's edition of the *Legenda Aurea*, from now on referred to as "Graesse". Both texts can be found under de Voragine in the bibliography. Other editions of the *Legenda Aurea* such as the *Gilte Legende* or William Caxton's translation are not considered herein, as de Voragine's version is widely acknowledged as the standard text for medieval saints' lives. Furthermore, the entries in both the *Gilte Legende* and Caxton's work do not include substantial modifications of the texts which would alter the arguments made in this study.

[6] All references to Butler's *Lives of the Saints* are to the edition by Thurston and Attwater (1956).

community" (514). This explains why especially in the cases of saints whose lives are entirely constructed by authors, with sometimes only the name of the saint being historically accurate, long descriptions of bodily tortures are featured, which strongly reflect patriarchal attitudes towards the female body. Hence, it is reasonable to argue that the body parts mentioned are placed within the narratives on purpose to manifest theological ideology on the one hand and gender ideology on the other.

The first census showed that within female saints' legends the focus is arguably set on the upper female body, though sometimes implying analogies to the lower, unmentionable, mysteriously private female parts.[7] Whereas some body parts, such as the breast, hair and hairstyles in various lengths, and the gorge and its components (teeth, tongue, throat) are frequently featured in women's hagiography, others, such as arms or legs, are barely mentioned and still others, such as the genital area, are not mentioned at all. In addition, an unexpectedly high number of legends describe women who either cross-dress and disguise themselves as men and as such neglect their assigned sex and expected gender behaviour or who transcend their female sex in other ways and move into the territory of men by, for example, shortening their hair or miraculously growing a beard. Within the scope of this study, the focus will consequently be set on these frequently recurring body parts – the breast, hair(styles) and the mouth and its components (teeth and tongue) – the latter being grouped together because of their closely related symbolism and cultural history.[8]

As a result, the finalized corpus of saints' *vitae* selected for this study includes about twenty medieval women saints. Among them are the popular European virgin martyrs Agatha, Agnes, Lucy and Cecilia, whose names were "familiar throughout the medieval West" as they were "mentioned in every Latin Mass" (Bartlett 114) and whose *vitae* have long and diverse narrative traditions. Other saints studied in detail include repentant prostitutes such as the saints Mary Magdalene and Mary of Egypt, admired transvestite saints such as Eugenia and Euphrosyne, controversial and obscure women saints such as the bearded Saint Wilgefortis and late-medieval women mystics such as Clare of Assisi and Catherine of Siena.[9]

Regarding the primary sources used for textual references, the *Legenda Aurea* is utilized throughout because of its inclusion of the majority of saints selected for this

[7] For example, see chapter 4 about the analogies between mouth and vagina, teeth and hymen, tongue and clitoris.

[8] As particular hagiographical legends describing the martyrdom of a saint commonly include more than one body part, a general claim that one body part is exclusively featured per saint cannot be made, even though this is the case in some *vitae*, such as in the legend of Saint Agatha (breasts) or Saint Wilgefortis (beard). For many saints more than one body part is affected, which resulted in their significance for several chapters and interpretations in this study. For example, Saint Christina has her head shaved, her breasts pierced with hot tongs and her tongue cut out. Furthermore, in this study a saint was taken into consideration for further analysis only if either more than one version of her legend included the description of a specific body part and her legend still includes these descriptions in modern compilations of saints' lives, or if her life is inseparably connected to a specific bodily feature (for example, Saint Agatha and the breast; see chapter 2).

[9] Another saint who is discussed extensively is Saint Christina. The remaining saints and their *vitae* appear in supporting capacity of the arguments made.

study. In addition, other major collections of primary sources for the study of medieval saints, such as the *Acta Sanctorum* or the *Patrologia Latina*, were consulted, as well as a number of individually edited or translated texts, such as the *Damasi Epigrammata* (Saint Agnes) or the *Dialogues* of Gregory the Great (Saint Galla). The *Acta* was particularly helpful in providing medieval textual evidence and in-depth detail for the three late-medieval saints Wilgefortis (dates unknown), Clare (1194-1253) and Catherine of Siena (1347 (1333?)-1380), whose literary traditions originate in the fourteenth to early sixteenth century. As "saint's Lives did not remain static but changed with ecclesiastical and societal perceptions and needs, scholars should study and compare, when possible, a series of subsequent Lives for the same saint" (Schulenburg 51). Therefore, earlier Latin and Old English accounts, such as Bede's *Martyrologium* or Ælfric's *Lives of Saints*, are used mainly for comparative purposes and to indicate the development of particular, significant details or influential coexisting literary traditions and alterations.[10] Even though most of the versions overlap in their representations and descriptions of saints' *vitae*, each compilation seems "to favour" some saints and to "neglect others", as Jane Tibbetts Schulenburg notes (10), yet all of them in combination provided beneficial and unique additions and perspectives to the study.[11]

At this point it has to be noted that the cults of the saints and their praise and worship are often phenomena beyond any geographical and time-specific boundaries. As Bartlett notes:

> One striking thing about the Christian cult of the saints is how adaptable and malleable it has been. It arose in the cities of the ancient Greek and Roman world but spread in its early centuries deep into the deserts of Egypt and the Middle East and then westwards to the cool, wet landscapes of Gaul and Britain, reaching the Atlantic coasts of Ireland, a country never subdued by Rome, in the fifth century. It has remained a central part of Christian worship and devotion ever since, in the monasteries of Germany and Greece, the trading towns of the Italian Renaissance, the baroque churches of Austria and Mexico, in Russia, Armenia and Georgia, in the industrial cities of modern France, and the Catholic and Orthodox congregations of North America. (637)

Thus, saints were and still are of global significance, particularly once they are officially venerated by the Catholic Church and included in the official martyrologies, such as the *Martyrologium Romanum*. Saints are "both universal and local [...] they were present but also transcended time, and they were often imagined as a glorious company in

[10] The exception is the analysis of the transvestite saint Euphrosyne. Direct quotes are predominately taken from Ælfric's more popular *Natale Sancte Eufrasiæ* with the earlier Latin *Vita Sanctæ Euphrosinæ* from the *Patrologia Latina* used in supporting capacity. Unless otherwise noted, all subsequent (direct) references to Ælfric's *Lives of Saints* will be referenced as Skeat. However, the work is listed under Ælfric's name in the bibliography.

[11] An example of a minor, yet significant alteration is for example visible in the legend of Saint Agatha, a young virgin martyr who in the course of her martyrdom has her breasts torn off her body. Whereas the *Legenda Aurea* and Ælfric's *Natale Sancte Agathe* speak of one breast being detached, Bede's martyrology and Aldhelm's *Carmen de Virginitate* include the mastectomy of both breasts. For a closer analysis consult chapter 2.

heaven" (Bartlett 637) and as such they "have shaped the lives and imaginations of millions, and still do" (637). Thus, the female saints' legends analysed in the following are not specifically Anglo-Saxon, British or Italian even if they enjoyed an active cult in the respective countries or were known to Anglo-Saxon authors such as Bede or Aldhelm, medieval English authors such as Geoffrey Chaucer[12] or Italian hagiographers such as Jacobus de Voragine, as the "fame and name of a saint could be universal, spreading far beyond the revered tomb that formed the original focus of a cult" (637). Similarly, these legends cannot be claimed to be exclusively medieval. Even though most of the saints analysed in the course of this study appear in Jacobus de Voragine's *Legenda Aurea* or other medieval sources, demonstrating their circulation and popularity in the Middle Ages, most of the legends were composed earlier and are, in their origin, heroic accounts of early Christianity.[13] Consequently, the majority of the legends in question are "about women from Rome and Egypt in the early Christian period" (Frantzen 70) rather than being narratives of medieval women acting in a closely defined geographical and time-specific frame. However, these legends are nevertheless a valuable source for "examin[ing] early Christian attitudes" (70) as they "represent cultural codes" (71) towards femininity, sexuality and the female body. Saints' lives in medieval Europe are "complex registers of a culture's structure of gender relations" (71) and as such "invite us to wonder how women [in medieval times] responded to such narratives, especially since violence towards women (torture, martyrdom) is prominently featured in them" (70). Therefore, as Allen Frantzen summarizes, "Narratives change in the telling [...] they never represent only the past but also represent the present in which they are retold" (70).

To further clarify the theoretical framework for the upcoming analyses and interpretations, the study will first explain the reception and popularity of saints' cults throughout the Middle Ages and will provide an introduction to the multilayered complexity of hagiography as a genre and its significant author-text relation. The second part of the first chapter will elaborate on the discourse about the human body from theoretical, historical, metaphorical, symbolic and of course religious angles. It will define the concept of the body for the further analyses and will examine the differences between human and saintly bodies. In addition, the chapter will question how femininity and femaleness were constructed and in how far the growing Christian community influenced medieval ideas about sexuality, moral codes and attitudes towards the body.

The breast, the most obvious marker of femininity, will be the focus of the second chapter. In hagiography this dominant symbol of femininity is frequently challenged, threatened and tortured, and just the fact of possessing a breast and thus of being a woman causes dangers of various degrees for an individual saint's life. As the chapter

[12] See for example Chaucer's *The Second Nun's Tale*, which deals with the legend of Saint Cecilia.

[13] Except for minor exceptions, such as the legend of Saint Wilgefortis or Saint Catherine of Siena, who did not appear until approximately the fourteenth century, most of the other female saints' legends analysed in this study are older or even premedieval in their origin and setting. The oldest to be examined is the legend of Saint Mary Magdalene, whose *vita* is set in the first century.

will show, the breast functions primarily as a locus for negation – either of the presumed roles of women in society or of theological statements. In addition, whereas Saint Agatha is brutally mastectomized, others such as Saint Eugenia disguise their femininity in masculine clothing to avoid marriage, and still others, such as Saint Christina, excrete wondrous fluids from their breast wounds, raising the question of whether the maltreatment of the female breast is supposed to prove the weakness of the female sex. In addition, the chapter will provide an excursus into the discourse of *imitatio Christi* and gender-related torture and discuss how the removal of the breast can be perceived as a form of male sexual aggressiveness.

What happens when a holy woman challenges, changes and subverts the social reality will be explored in the third chapter, which examines the symbolic significance of hair and hairstyles. Among the female saints only three types of hairstyles are emphasized: long hair, as described in the legends of Saint Mary Magdalene and Saint Agnes; short hair, as in the legends of Saint Euphrosyne and Saint Eugenia; and the bearded female, as in the legends of the saints Wilgefortis, Galla and Paula. The chapter will argue that hair in women's hagiography influences the way these saints are perceived, treated and remembered within and beyond their legends. Hair connects sinner with saint, helps to progress spiritually, and purifies and protects and is thus "attached to a complex system of gender specific interpretations" (Walter 311),[14] as the analyses will show.[15]

The fourth chapter will investigate the intersections between the historical understanding of tongues and throats in relation to the physical silencing of rhetorically advanced women on the one hand (Saints Lucy and Cecilia) and the symbolic defloration of the virgin saints on the other (Saint Christina). The analysis will demonstrate that the mouth and its tripartite components are not only treated as a "door" through which beliefs and vocation are uttered, but are set in analogy with the female genitals and transformed symbolically into a vagina. Thereby the teeth play a crucial role as they function as the only visible barrier between inner and outer body, as a symbolic "hymen", which is "deflowered" in the legend of Saint Apollonia, among others, by pulling the teeth out. Consequently in the legends of female saints, mouth and vagina, the two entrances to a woman's body, are arguably used interchangeably.

The final chapter will discuss the phenomenon of sexual and gendered hybridity among women saints. It will argue that (bodily) gender hybridity is used as a common method to indicate the transcendence of the secular, passive-feminine body, particularly among female martyrs, in order to reach a higher social acceptance within the Christian community. This transcendence is thereby achieved through the subtraction or addition of gender-signifying body parts, the saint's disguise and consequent denial of her true sex, or by employing traditionally masculine characteristics. By doing so, the female saint expands existing gender boundaries and questions the limits of the established binaries of male and female, feminine and masculine. These legends reflect the time-

[14] The text passage in the original reads, "Die jeweilige Haartracht […] ist dabei konventionell an bestimmte genderspezifische Deutungs- und Wahrnehmungskomplexe gebunden".

[15] Early versions of some ideas and arguments of chapter 3 are based on my unpublished MA thesis, "The Significance of Hair in Women's Hagiography", which was submitted to the Department of English and American Studies at the University of Paderborn in 2010.

transcending complexity of assigning a true, well-defined sex and gender in the Middle Ages and beyond. Moreover, the saints displayed permeability of sex and gender, their move into the realms of the *third*, into what Judith Butler has termed the "incoherently sexed" ("Sexual Inversions" 67), turns them into a threat for the social environment which has to be removed to restore order.

Scholarship – Research to Date on Female Sanctity and the Body

For a long time, hagiography "was [...] dismissed as too crude and too stereotypical to be truly artistic or historically informative" (20) and thus was of no or only little academic interest, as Salih writes in her introduction to *A Companion to Middle English Hagiography*. Consequently, despite the saints' overall popularity, "the genre of the saint's *Life* remains little studied" (Salih, *Companion* back cover). Fortunately, in the last thirty years, scholars have "found it necessary to rehabilitate hagiography" (2), and a "great resurgence of interest" (Schulenburg 13) in the genre, its protagonists and its cultural history has occurred in academia. As Bartlett notes, "In recent generations, however, interest in hagiography has developed to a remarkable degree, with societies and journals dedicated to it and a general recognition of its importance and value as literature, as a source for social history and as a window into medieval mentalities" (504).

Much research until now has focused on reintroducing hagiography primarily into literary and academic circles, but also making it available for a wider nonscholarly audience. This led on the one hand to the production of new editions, translations and compilations of saints' legends and on the other to more general overviews of hagiography.[16] In contrast to the renewed interest in hagiography in general, in-depth studies of female sanctity and the body, of female saints from a cultural, historical, literary and of course gendered perspective,[17] and also studies focusing on the body

[16] For encyclopaedic works see, for example, David Hugh Farmer, *Oxford Dictionary of Saints*, 5th ed. (Oxford: Oxford UP, 2004); Alban Butler, *Butler's Lives of the Saints*, rev. Michael Walsh (New York: Harper Collins, 1991); or Robert Bartlett, *Why Can the Dead Do Such Great Things? Saints and Worshippers from the Martyrs to the Reformation* (Oxford: Princeton UP, 2013). Still in use and reprinted frequently is Hippolyte Delehaye's pioneering introductory work for hagiographers, *The Legends of Saints: An Introduction to Hagiography* (1905, rpt. 2009), in which he extensively reflects on the genre's origin, development and classification and explores its complex author-text relation. Despite its ongoing popularity, recent scholarship has criticized Delehaye's strict genre classification of hagiography and has come to a more diverse assessment of the relationship between hagiography and historiography. See for example Felice Lifshitz, "Beyond Positivism and Genre: Hagiographical Texts as Historical Narrative", *Viator* 25 (1994): 95-113; see also the discussion in chapter 1.1.1. More recent introductions to the study of saints' lives start to look beyond the mere historical and narratological sphere and provide information on key themes in hagiography, such as gender, personal identity, violence or cultic activities; for example, Sarah Salih, ed., *A Companion to Middle English Hagiography* (Cambridge: Brewer, 2006).

[17] For works dealing with female saints see Jane Tibbetts Schulenburg's influential and in-depth analysis of female sanctity in relation to aspects of everyday culture, such as family, virginity or

parts analysed in this study – breast, hair(styles), mouth, teeth and tongues – are still either relatively rare or non-existent.[18] Rather than directing academic attention to analyses of body parts, recent hagiographical scholarship frequently concentrates on the exploration of the body in sensational, sensual or sexual terms, thereby analysing, for example, *The Sex Lives of Saints* (Victoria Burrus, 2004), the relationship between *Pain, Pleasure and Punishment in Medieval Culture* (Robert Mills, *Suspended Animation*, 2005)[19] or the phenomenon of female cross-dressing saints.[20]

In addition, Peter Brown's *The Body and Society: Men, Women and Sexual Renunciation in Early Christianity* (1988), James Brundage's *Law, Sex and Christian Society in Medieval Europe* (1987) and Vern Bullough and James Brundage's *Handbook of Medieval Sexuality* (2000) are among the most influential general-reference works on the body in medieval society and in regard to (early) Christianity and its urge to regulate and redefine the body. Other research to date centres on historical approaches to anatomy, sex and gender, such as Thomas Laqueur's *Making Sex: Body and Gender from the Greeks to Freud* (1992), or has tried to grant access to

motherhood: *Forgetful of Their Sex: Female Sanctity and Society, ca. 500-1100* (Chicago: U of Chicago P, 1998). For more recent book-length studies see Stavroula Constantinou, *Female Corporeal Performances: Reading the Body in Byzantine Passions and Lives of Holy Women* (Uppsala: Uppsala Universitet, 2005); Anke Bernau, Ruth Evans, and Sarah Salih, eds., *Medieval Virginities* (Cardiff: U of Wales P, 2005); and Paul E. Szarmach, ed., *Writing Women Saints in Anglo-Saxon England* (Toronto: Toronto UP, 2013).

[18] For the only monograph on the (religious) breast, see Margaret R. Miles, *A Complex Delight: The Secularization of the Breast 1350-1750* (Berkeley: U of California P, 2008). No book-length studies to my knowledge exist on the metaphors of mouth, teeth and tongues in hagiography. For the cultural and religious implications of the mouth see Gary D. Schmidt, *The Iconography of the Mouth of Hell* (London: Associated University Presses, 1995); and Sylvia Schroer, *Die Körpersymbolik der Bibel* (Darmstadt: Wissenschaftliche Buchgesellschaft, 1998). In contrast to breasts and the mouth, the cultural significance of hair has received wider academic attention. For a thorough investigation of hair in cultural history, consult Wendy Cooper, *Hair: Sex, Society, Symbolism* (New York: Stein and Day, 1971). However, up to this point research on saintly hairstyles has focused on analysing one specific hairstyle in detail rather than all three styles in comparison and in relation to each other; for example, Christine Knust, "'Allen sinen lip bedecktent die loecke': Zur Symbolik der Haare in Heiligenlegenden und Heiligendarstellungen des Mittelalters", *Haare zwischen Fiktion und Realität: Interdisziplinäre Untersuchungen zur Wahrnehmung der Haare*, ed. Birgit Haas (Berlin: LIT, 2008), pp. 115-34; or Roberta Lee Milliken, *Ambiguous Locks: An Iconology of Hair in Medieval Art and Literature* (Jefferson: McFarland, 2012).

[19] Similar topics are explored in Gabriele Sorgo, *Martyrium und Pornographie* (Düsseldorf: Patmos, 1997); Eileen Harney, "The Sexualized and Gendered Tortures of Virgin Martyrs in Medieval English Literature" (PhD dissertation, U of Toronto, 2008); and more recently in William Burgwinkle and Cary Howie, *Sanctity and Pornography in Medieval Culture: On the Verge* (Manchester: Manchester UP, 2011).

[20] For example, Thomas Honegger, *Riddles, Knights and Cross-Dressing Saints*, (Bern: Lang, 2004), in particular the article by Sandra Lowerre, "To Rise beyond Their Sex: Female Cross-Dressing Saints in Caxton's *Vitas Patrum*", pp. 55-94; or Jonathan Walker, "The Transtextuality of Transvestite Sainthood; Or, How to Make the Gendered Form Fit the Generic Function", *Exemplaria* 15 (2003): 73-110.

influential theoretical, sociological and philosophical discussions for further study, such as Mariam Fraser and Monica Greco's essay collection *The Body: A Reader* (2005).[21] Consequently, as Le Goff and Truong propose, the body itself has remained a desideratum for further research (9, 23).

The thesis at hand, with its close, intertextual reading and critical reflections on the (gendered) body and on commonly recurring body parts in women's hagiography, is located at the intersections between (art-)historical, cultural, medical, philosophical and gender-related discourses on femaleness and the body. With this interdisciplinary approach to female saints and their body-centred legends, this study attempts to fill some of the gaps in relation to medieval, religious, ideological and gender-specific representations of the female body. In addition to showing that the body not only has a history of its own but that medieval attitudes to and understandings of the body are still relevant up to the present day, this study intends to provide new starting points for further research and discussion on this particularly multilayered and promising area of medieval gender history.

[21] See also Elizabeth Alvilda Petroff, *Body and Soul: Essays on Medieval Women and Mysticism* (Oxford: Oxford UP, 1994); Peter Biller and A. J. Minnis, eds., *Medieval Theology and the Natural Body.* (York: York Medieval P, 1997); and Caroline Walker Bynum, *Fragmentation and Redemption: Essays on Gender and the Human Body in Medieval Religion* (New York: Zone, 1991). More recent book-length studies are Elmar Klinger, Stephanie Böhm, and Theodor Seidl, eds., *Der Körper und die Religion: Das Problem der Konstruktion von Geschlechterrollen* (Würzburg: Echter, 2000) and Darryll Grantley and Nina Taunton, eds., *The Body in Late Medieval and Early Modern Culture* (Aldershot: Ashgate, 2000).

1 Cultural Constructions: Femininity, the Body and the Saint

> Die Realität, in der der Mensch lebt, wird konstituiert und konstruiert.
>
> Wolfgang Lipp[1]

> Body and the senses are socially constructed, in various ways by different populations.
>
> Anthony Synnott[2]

> All saints are more or less *constructed.*
>
> Pierre Delooz[3]

Constructions of femininity, of the (female) body and of the (female) saint, are comparable to any other cultural and sociological concepts bound to and dependent on historical periods, spaces and societies. However, these concepts not only change with a steadily progressing world and the modification of its traditions and expectations, but also result in the idealization of certain behaviour or appearance. This idealization is the basis for the formation of strict categories that women of all social classes are in turn supposed to imitate, and on the basis of the degree of imitation they are judged and evaluated by society. To precisely define *the* one ideal concept of a certain time period, however, is not always as easy as first believed. In particular, the role women played throughout history has at best proven to be contradictory, ambiguous or defined as passive. Moreover, for a long time the impact women have made has been overlooked in social and political records or academic research. Whereas much research has been done with regard to the nineteenth century and its creation of the myth of the "angel in the house", scholars dealing with modern Western culture will find it rather difficult to single out *the* ideal construction of femininity, since in contrast to the nineteenth century, it appears as if currently no clear categorization and idealization of womanhood or femininity exists. Rather, there seems to be an interchangeable and indefinite number of identities a woman can construct for herself.[4]

[1] Trans.: "The reality in which humanity lives is constituted and constructed". Wolfgang Lipp, "Körper, Körpersymbolik und Gesellschaft", *Der Körper und die Religion: Das Problem der Konstruktion von Geschlechterrollen*, ed. Elmar Klinger, Stephanie Böhm, and Theodor Seidl (Würzburg: Echter, 2000), pp. 9-26, p. 9.

[2] Anthony Synnott, "Hair: Shame and Glory", *The Body Social: Symbolism, Self and Society* (London: Routledge, 1993), p. 1.

[3] Pierre Delooz, "Towards a Sociological Study of Canonized Sainthood in the Catholic Church", trans. Jane Hodgkin, *Saints and Their Cults: Studies in Religious Sociology, Folklore and History*, ed. Stephen Wilson (Cambridge: Cambridge UP, 1983), p. 195.

[4] Just recently, scholars such as Emily Matchar have come to argue that modern society is facing the rise of a New Domesticity in which young, well-educated women opt out of the economy's

The construction of femininity in medieval times was, comparable to today, far from straightforward. Even though broader categories such as *sinner* and *saint*, *wife* and *widow* existed, medieval society struggled with defining these terms, and scholars were frequently uncertain or of opposing attitudes on how a woman placed within such a category should behave in the private as well as in the public sphere. Already the term *woman* proved challenging as women were considered to be "clearly outside medieval European notions of social structure" (Bynum, *Fragmentation* 36; Duby). For a long time, women were not appreciated as human beings, but rather perceived as the right hand of the devil and as the sex responsible for the loss of Paradise. For the Latin Church Fathers such as Jerome, Augustine, Tertullian and Ambrose, women were an everyday threat to masculinity and a "permanent temptation, which had to be kept under control" (Lowerre 59). For them the presence of women was seen as destructive and distractive to the male body and mind, particularly when at prayer.[5] In order to avoid a repetition of the fatal decision Eve had made in the Garden of Eden, the Church Fathers agreed that men should be in command of women and their bodies. Misogyny was consequently widely spread among philosophers, theologians and theoreticians, which resulted in one-sided and all-male discussions about the status of women and the usefulness of their sex apart from reproduction.

This attitude was still persistent when Christianity started to spread all over Europe between the fifth and tenth centuries. Bodily purity, sexual asceticism and virginity were soon *en vogue*, and being a virgin was perceived as the new utmost goal for women to imitate. With the help of hagiographical legends and the increasing interest in and demand for (female) saints' legends and cults, this new idealized construction of femininity was supported and further propagandised (Brown, *Body* lxvi, 359; Sorgo 53; Schulenburg 128). However, that the saintly virgins often died under cruel circumstances for their virginity was perceived as a legitimate price to be paid in order to maintain a pure, untouched body.[6] After all, it was for the higher cause of sitting next to the heavenly bridegroom – a new ideal that numerous women wanted to follow in order to escape arranged marriages or the pains and burdens of matrimony and childbirth. Hagiographical legends served an important educational purpose and were created, manipulated and adapted to fit the new religious doctrines. Other significant reference works, such as the Bible, made contradictory statements about the place of the female sex in society and hence were not quite helpful in the establishment of strong categories for women and the reinforcement of patriarchal dominance. For example, whereas Genesis 1:27-28 states that men and women are basically created equal, Genesis 2:20-23 annihilates the previous statement by claiming that the woman is created second out of the male flesh and should therefore be regarded as a helpmate unto man.

insecurity to more home-centric lifestyles. Emily Matchar, *Homeward Bound: Why Women Are Embracing the New Domesticity* (New York: Simon and Schuster, 2013).

[5] An attitude also expressed in St. Paul's letter to the Corinthians.

[6] As committing suicide was and is forbidden within the Latin (Catholic) Church, martyrdom and self-mutilation were "less extreme than suicide" and "a practical methodology which would accomplish the desired end". Jane Tibbetts Schulenburg, *Forgetful of Their Sex: Female Sanctity and Society, ca. 500-1100* (Chicago: U of Chicago P, 1998), p. 173.

According to this new scale of (Christian) values, the construction of the body also became more and more bound to gendered perceptions and assumptions. Body parts have always been associated with social values or have been examined to draw conclusions on a person's health or even social status. Moreover, the human body in its entirety, but also individual parts of it, were metaphorical platforms to negotiate power and to legitimately demonstrate and explain the superiority of the male sex. The body was literally mapped into noble and ignoble parts. Upper parts, such as the head, as the place of wisdom and mind, were assigned to men; everything else – the torso, the flesh, and the reproductive system – was assigned to women. Christianity changed the perception and handling of the body further, and soon after, "virginity and celibacy had made their appearance as the dominant virtues of a Christian age", as Brown notes; "Our friend, the body, was in for a bad time" (*Body* xxxii).

The following introductory chapter intends to set the scene for the subsequent analyses of body parts in women's hagiography. The first part of the chapter will outline the historical and cultural significance of saints and the complexity of hagiography as a genre and examine the functions of saints in general and female saints in particular. The second part of this chapter will shift its attention to theoretical, cultural, metaphorical and ideological constructions of the body. It will discuss the interdependence of the *natural* and the *cultural* body in medieval times and provide the argumentative framework for the understanding of the body within this study. In addition, it will provide an insight into the cultural mapping of the body and will further illuminate the powerful role that the increasing Catholic influence had on all of the three previously mentioned constructions – femininity, the (female) body and the (female) saint.

1.1 The Significance of Sanctity

> Our sources for the years 500-1100 are incomplete, fragmentary, and rather limited. Hagiography, the most common and prolific form of writing during this early period, is frequently the only source to have survived in any substantial quantity.
>
> Jane Tibbetts Schulenburg[7]

The legends of female and male saints were, next to sermons, the most frequently read genre in medieval Europe. Saints' *vitae* became bestsellers, and their protagonists were viewed as "superheroes and [...] celebrities" (Salih, *Companion* 1) who had epiphanic visions of God and experienced a variety of miracles, but also had to fight temptations of all sorts and endure gruesome bodily tortures. During the Middle Ages the cult of the saints was at its peak and the Church successfully used these devotional lives as pedagogical tools to instruct the growing Christian community and propagandise their theological doctrines (Brown, *Cult* 1). The following chapter will provide an overview

[7] Jane Tibbetts Schulenburg, *Forgetful of Their Sex: Female Sanctity and Society, ca. 500-1100* (Chicago: U of Chicago P, 1998), p. 17.

of the specificity and complexity of hagiography as a genre, in which many of the most colourful and beloved narratives are creative constructions composed by compilers. It will portray the historical development and the manifold functions and purposes of the cult of the saints and discuss why despite their frequent fictionality, these legends are nevertheless a valuable source for the history of women as well as for the further analyses of body parts and their gendered treatment.

1.1.1 Hagiography: An Introduction

> The genre [hagiography] has two objectives: the one, devotional, to honour the saint; the other, instructive, to explain to the hearer or reader the significance for Christian truth of the saint and his life. If only one of these objectives was present the narrative would become history, or biography, or allegory, homily, or treatise, but not legend.
>
> Charlotte d'Evelyn[8]

When analysing the *passiones*, *lives* or *vitae* of male and female saints alike, the question of their historical accuracy overshadows the work of the scholar. At first sight all hagiographical narratives seem to be designed as historical biographies of extraordinary holy men and women. In fact, as Felice Lifshitz notes, "Biography, of saints or of other figures, seems to have been the most popular form of historical narrative" (97), and Bartlett adds, "the Life does indeed often start with a saint's birth or childhood and almost invariably ends with his or her death" (518). However, a closer look shows that historical authenticity, especially of the most popular and most spectacular saints' legends, is doubtful. Trying to trace a hagiographical narrative back to its roots, trying to separate fact from fiction, therefore often ends with the discovery either that it is completely fictional or that its historical accuracy is limited to the saint's name, to his or her *dies natalis* – his or her "birthday into heaven" (95) – and, if available, to some geographical data. Therefore, one of the first observations a scholar dealing with hagiographical texts will make is that between birth and death, "in between those more or less fixed markers there is considerable room for variation in structure and subject" (518). Thus, even if "the subject was indeed a real historical person" (505), the life of a saint, with all its wondrous miracles and its gruesome torture scenes, was often constructed in the creative minds of authors, compilers and editors, who not only created colourful narratives but often added their personal and ideological backgrounds to "persuade the reader that the subject was [indeed] a saint" (519).

Generally speaking, hagiographical narratives deal with idiosyncratic religious stories which ideally promoted the cult of the mentioned individual. "In order to be strictly hagiographic", Delehaye contends in his magnum opus *The Legends of the*

[8] Charlotte D'Evelyn, review of *Die englische Heiligenlegende des Mittelalters* by Theodor Wolpers (Tübingen, 1964), *Speculum* 42 (1967): 214.

Saints, "the document should be of a religious character and should aim at edification" (2). Therefore, for him, "The term may only be applied [...] to writings inspired by devotion to the saints and intended to promote it [their cults]" (2). However, as Lifshitz argues in her article "Beyond Positivism and Genre", one should not forget that there are "many writings about saints which seem never to have served for any functioning cult and many in which the dominant motives for composition are unrelated to any kind of liturgical veneration" (97). Thus, hagiographic writing is more than the listing of saints in calendars or on tomb inscriptions, such as those initiated by Pope Damasus in the fourth century. Hagiography is also more than the inclusion of a saint's *vita* in one of the popular martyrologies such as the *Martyrologium Romanum*, even if this promoted not only any form of existing cult but more significantly emphasised an individual saint as an influential source for preaching conduct and virtue to a growing Christian audience and showed the saint's global significance for the entire Catholic Church, ensuring the legend's textual and cultural survival – sometimes even to today. Hagiography is most and for all the "celebration of the saint in writing" (Bartlett 95), the "record of supernatural power" (512) and of a particular worldview (Angenendt, *Heilige und Reliquien* 142). To give an example, even though the legend of Saint Agnes has its roots in the fourth century, fragments and adaptations of her legend have survived throughout the centuries, and even nowadays she is still considered one of the most beloved virgin saints (Farmer 7-8).[9] In medieval times, legends such as that of the pure, virgin Agnes, who gave her life for Christ, proved "immensely popular" in instructing the people and in particular the young (Denomy 119), and thanks to those legends, hagiography soon became "one of the main branches of European literature" (Bartlett 504).

Fortunately for the hagiographer, the medieval audience "was not distressed by the lack of historical accuracy" (Elliot 2). As Bartlett asserts, "Medieval writers were much more thorough and shameless borrowers of other writer's words than is customary today" (520). Yet as most hagiographers, in particular of the early Middle Ages, remained indeed anonymous (313), it became relatively easy to "create a wholly fictional confection, spun from commonplaces, borrowed passages and their [the authors'] own inventions" (522) without the fear of facing any charges for historical inaccuracy. Furthermore, even if hagiographers intended to be historians or biographers, many were paid to write down the lives of specific saints or were "formally missioned to undertake their work" (514), and with only a name and maybe a date or place of origin to start with, there was much space in a creative construction of a legend that suited the ideological perceptions of the author's time and his financial sponsors. As Schulenburg notes, the hagiographers' "works were panegyrics, conscious programs of persuasion or propaganda, meant to prove the particular sanctity of their protagonists" (17), even if some "long and detailed accounts by people who knew [a] saint personally" (Bartlett 522) did exist. Due to the increasing market for saints' legends and the audience's positive response to spectacular but also cruel stories of devotion, the once rather plain tomb inscriptions and calendar insertions were altered and edited with sometimes only the basic information from the original source remaining. Saints' legends became "popular 'products': they were 'packaged,' 'promoted' or 'advertised', and then 'sold' to the faithful" (Schulenburg 59). According to

[9] For a lengthier discussion of her legend see chapter 3.

Delehaye, one result of the increasing demand for hagiographic writing was that the biographer or "the historian no longer desired to be restricted to the *rôle* of annalist or witness" (66). Rather, "he became a compiler [...] far more preoccupied with his readers' tastes than with a laborious quest after truth" (66), and hagiographers turned out to be "enterprising textual editors" (Head 44). They not only contributed stylistic changes to the individual legends, but also illuminated and developed them into colourful narratives and "flesh[ed] out portraits as well as classical and scriptural allusions" (Schulenburg 28; see also Head 20-57) to meet their readers' tastes. In the words of Pierre Delooz:

> All saints are more or less constructed in that, being necessarily saints for other people, they are remodelled in the collective representation, which is made of them. It often happens, even, that they are so remodelled that nothing of the real original is left, and, ultimately, some saints are solely constructed saints simply because nothing is known about them historically: everything, including their existence, is a product of collective representation. ("Towards" 195)

Within this process, it was not uncommon that hagiographers "pieced together evidence of a saint from earlier generations, transmitted orally or in writing, while yet others wrote about people they had known long and well" (Bartlett 522). Hence, the stories were not only altered or completely fabricated, but they were also often modified to reflect the personal, social and cultural background of the individual author.[10]

However, how much influence did the historical and personal background of Jacobus de Voragine, for example, have on his famous *Legenda Aurea*? To what extent, if at all, can personal ideology be detected in his writing? The Genoese Jacobus de Voragine entered Dominican Orders around 1244. He later became the archbishop of Genoa and died towards the end of the thirteenth century. He was beatified by Pope Pius VII in 1816 and was venerated as a saint himself by his former order (Ryan xiii).[11] His popular work, which is nowadays known as the *Golden Legend* or *Legenda Aura*, was originally published as *Legenda Sanctorum* around 1260.[12] The manuscript itself is the work of a compiler, who, in a scholarly manner, included more than 160 saints' lives, organised around the Church calendar, and who included etymological references, additional sources and often even a discussion of the legend's authenticity. The legends were "judiciously selected from over

[10] A good example for the social and cultural influences on saints' legends is the treatment of hair as presented in the legend of Mary Magdalene (see chapter 3).

[11] For more information on the historical person consult Ernest C. Richardson, *Materials for a Life of Jacopo da Varagine* (New York: H. W. Wilson, 1935). For further information on the *Legenda Aurea* consult Helmut Ripperberger and William Granger Ryan, eds., *The Golden Legend of Jacobus de Voragine* (New York: Longmans, 1941); Alain Boureau, *La légende dorée* (Paris: Edition du Cerf, 1984); Sherry L. Reames, *The Legenda Aurea: A Reexamination of Its Paradoxical History* (Madison: U of Wisconsin P, 1985); and for the development within the English-speaking world, Mary Beth Long, "Corpora and Manuscripts, Authors and Audience", ed. Sarah Salih, *A Companion to Middle English Hagiography* (Cambridge: Brewer, 2006), pp. 47-69.

[12] Manfred Görlach even proposes the year 1267, the date suggested by the earliest surviving manuscripts. Manfred Görlach, *Studies in Middle English Saints' Legends* (Heidelberg: Winter, 1998), p. 25.

one hundred sources of the common core of legendary lore, stressing the accepted mainstream tradition, but extending the coverage well into the 13th century" (Görlach 25-26) and including only those saints who had been officially recognized by the Catholic Church (Ryan xv). By the late thirteenth century the manuscript had acquired the designation *aurea* and had become the most widely distributed text of the Middle Ages. The Latin original was soon translated extensively into the vernacular, yet the *Gilte Legende*, the "first complete English-language translation of it [...] did not appear until 1438" and was based on the French edition *Légende dorée* by Jean de Vignay (Long 58). Almost fifty years later, William Caxton compiled the only surviving early English translation by using the *Gilte Legende* as well as the Latin and French sources. His effort resulted in an 880-folio *Golden Legend* that was printed several times at Westminster (Long 59; Ryan xiv). Whether intentionally or not, de Voragine had managed to create an influential "collection [which] apparently filled an encyclopaedic need and a desire to have authoritative information assembled in one volume for the complete year; and it did so much more effectively than earlier legendries had done" all over Europe (Görlach 25-26).

Jacobus de Voragine was "a man of his time and wrote for his time" (Ryan xviii). Therefore, his personal beliefs and assumptions, as well as the religious dogmas of the time, certainly influenced his writing. They are visible in his etymologies of saints' names, in which he tried to find explanations for their holiness, and in the general selection process for his compilation, as the inclusion of only those saints who were officially recognized by the Church ensured the distribution and acceptance of his work. His additional chapters on the Resurrection and the Assumption are filled with religious doctrine and instructive anecdotes, and as Ryan argues in his introduction to the *Golden Legend*, readers can also detect de Voragine's opinion about marriage as a secondary way of life and his high opinion of virginity (xviii). Consequently, even if the hagiographer was "inspired by the ideas of history current in his day" (Delehaye, *Legends* 68) and even if he tried to be as honest and authentic as possible in his work, he "unconsciously create[d] little legends" (68) by including his personal ideology, "impressions, deductions and passions" (15) in the narratives, which also turned into legends over time and which leave the presented truth "either embellished or disfigured according to circumstances" (15).

Hence, in the modern sense of the definition, "hagiography is not history" (Elliot 7), even though stigmatizing all saints' lives as "'untrue' can [...] blind us to their function as historical *writing*" (Lifshitz 95), in particular because medieval authors themselves "called such compositions *historiae*" (97) and not hagiography.[13] However, in particular the "medieval stories of virgin martyrs are not historical reports – they are fictions" (Bartlett 538), as the "supernatural support the saints receive is dramatic in the extreme" (537) even if the saints' "historical existence is almost certain" (537). Consequently, next to referring to hagiographical writing in Latin terms (*passiones*, *vitae*) or simply calling them *lives*, the term *legend* seems to be the most suitable concerning a more specific genre classification. First, in "its primitive meaning", as Delehaye explains in

[13] In fact, hagiography as a genre classification is etymologically an invention of the nineteenth century and "came into being specifically in opposition to the words 'history' and 'historian'" (Lifshitz 109). For a critical assessment of historiography versus hagiography in its cultural and political context as well as its academic discussion see Felice Lifshitz, "Beyond Positivism and Genre: Hagiographical Texts as Historical Narrative", *Viator* 25 (1994): 95-113.

his pioneering work, "the legend is the history that has to be read, *legenda*, on the feast of a saint. It is the passion of the martyr or the eulogy of the confessor without reference to its historical value" (10, see also Angenendt, *Heilige und Reliquien* 142). Second, even though the *legend* is the "outcome of an unconscious or unreflecting agent acting upon historical material" and commonly develops out of the "introduction of the subjective element into the realm of fact" (Delehaye, *Legends* 12), it nevertheless presupposes "an historical fact as basis or pretext" (9) and thus has "some historical or topographical connection" (8). The *legend* can arguably include a great variety of constructions. It can refer to "imaginary events [,] to some real personage, or it localizes romantic stories in some definite spot" (8). Therefore, finally and most importantly, in contrast to other literary genres such as the *fable*, *myth* or *romance*,[14] which throughout history have every now and then been used in relation to hagiographical writing, the *legend* is not restricted to either fictional or historical accounts. The *legend* can include both – the historical and the fictional saints – the completely real, the partly real, and those whose lives remain pure inventions except for "two or three salient facts that appear to be established with certainty" (12).

Before shifting attention to the concept of sanctity, the development of the cults of the saints, and the function of hagiographical legends, the question remains of how the fictionality and constructedness of the majority of saints' legends affects their treatment as a source – not only for modern scholars in general but for the following study in particular. Fortunately, in recent years hagiography has been reestablished as a pseudohistorical source, particularly useful for the study of medieval women. This is because until approximately the twelfth century, historical documentation of women's history is often fragmentary, limited or generally absent. Hagiography, the "most common and prolific form of writing during this early period", frequently remained "the only source to have survived in any substantial quantity" (Schulenburg 17; see also Fouracre 3). Female saints' legends, in spite of their lack of historical accuracy, nevertheless "hold a remarkable potential for historians of medieval women" (17). They not only provide an "excellent condensing lens [...] through which to view medieval perceptions of women as well as other various indices of women's opportunities, experiences, and lives", but they also allow an extensive observation of saintly behaviour and its gendered "construction and manipulation" (17). Furthermore, "hagiography is full of conventional motifs, which can be openly transferred from one saint to another" (Salih, *Companion* 14), and often it is particularly their constructedness, their repetitive patterns or their recurring usage of commonly acknowledged cultural and social motifs and metaphors that make hagiographical legends so valuable for a detailed investigation. Thus, saints' legends should be studied by embracing their fictionality as much as their historical and cultural background and by setting them in relation to each other. "Nevertheless", as Schulenburg notes,

> despite their incredible wealth, the *vitae* are complex sources to be used with caution, and we should not attempt to claim for them a greater degree of historical accuracy than is

[14] For an in-depth analysis and discussion of hagiographical writing and its genre classification, consult Hippolyte Delehaye, *The Legends of the Saints: An Introduction to Hagiography*, trans. V. M. Crawford (1905-06; Breinigsville: Kessinger, 2009), pp. 1-11.

> warranted. The *vitae* should be placed within the political and historical context in which they were read, copied, and revised. Since saints' Lives did not remain static but changed with ecclesiastical and societal perceptions and needs, scholars should study and compare, when possible, a series of subsequent Lives for the same saint. (51)

Therefore, to use hagiographical legends as a source means to be aware of their textual, cultural, social and ideological complexity and to compare and contrast them critically, as "what may appear to be the 'true', 'real' or the 'only' version of a text is often little more than a compromise between conflicting versions, rendered into contemporary language with inevitable loss of nuance" (Riches 25). The present study attempts to follow these recommendations and will, as Schulenburg and Samantha Riches suggest, reflect the individual *vitae* and their gendered usage of body parts not only in more than one accessible compilation and edition, but also in relation to other contemporary historical sources such as medical studies, canon law, the Penitentials, and iconography, as this "collective" and diversified approach to hagiography offers the most promise for a "reconstruction of the female experience" (Schulenburg 51).

1.1.2 The Cult of the Saints: Historical Development and Function

> The cults of the saints marked out time and space […] medieval travellers were aware of passing through the territories of saints.
>
> Sarah Salih[15]

> While writers of late medieval conduct books agreed that women should be gracious, humble, obedient and soft-spoken, virgin martyrs tended to be abrasive, defiant, shrewish and sharp tongued.
>
> Karen A. Winstead[16]

Throughout the centuries, the historical development and cultural significance of the concept of sanctity in the Middle Ages and beyond has been widely discussed and conceptualised. For Hippolyte Delehaye the saint was still a "hero" and a "genius". As he writes in his classic essay "Sanctus", "The saint belongs to an elite [because a] person whom the Christian places at the pinnacle of his respect and admiration is one who in the service of God lives the superior life. The saint is a hero in the moral and religious order; he is a perfect Christian" (qtd. in Schulenburg 3; "Sanctus" 235). However, as Sarah Salih notes, even though saints "were at once the superheroes and the celebrities" (*Companion* 1), they were at the same time

[15] Sarah Salih, ed., *A Companion to Middle English Hagiography* (Cambridge: Brewer, 2006), p. 7.
[16] Karen A. Winstead, *Virgin Martyrs: Legends of Sainthood in Late Medieval England* (Ithaca and London: Cornell UP, 1997), p. 98.

> locations of paradox, who could establish their sanctity by conformity to societal values or in opposition to them. They were both role models and intercessors, alien and distanced; their bodies stretched across the spaces between life and death, heaven and earth. (1)

According to John Mecklin in his work *The Passing of the Saint: A Study of a Cultural Type*, one should not forget that the saint was a culturally constructed product designed for and celebrated by the masses as a source of "spiritual power and social reform", as "the mysterious citizen of two worlds", who despite his or her spirituality was viewed as an "integral part of society" (17; qtd. in Schulenburg 3). Mecklin continues, "For the best part of the history of Christendom the 'saint' described the highest ideal – moral, spiritual, and social – of the age" – a fact to be remembered when analysing hagiographical legends "in the absence of the medieval setting which has given the term its characteristic meaning" (17; qtd. in Schulenburg 3).

Etymologically, the term *saint* has its origins in the Latin word *sanctus*, originally denoting the "sacred" and the "unbreakable".[17] Within the Christian context of the Middle Ages it was applied to those who led a religious life and were dedicated to God (C. Lewis and Short 1625; Niermeyer 937). For women, who from the early stages on played a special role within Christian communities, the additional term *sanctimonialis* existed – a term "used specifically to designate a nun", as the "majority of women saints were recruited from the cloister" (Schulenburg 2).

However, regarding the distribution of the sexes in hagiography, the most popular saints in the early centuries were men such as the Apostles Paul, Luke and John, the theologians Ambrose and Augustine and monastic founders such as Saint Benedict (Salih, *Companion* 2). The only female who was honoured at that time was the Virgin Mary, the *aula pudoris*. "Invariably", as Schulenburg notes, "it was much more difficult for women than for men to enter the ranks of the celestial hierarchy" (6). Nevertheless, the veneration of women saints progressed steadily throughout the years. Within Europe, Britain was the country with the most impressive numbers of women saints, followed by Belgium and Germany. The golden age of female sanctity occurred on the British Isles between the seventh and eighth centuries, when, according to Schulenburg, almost forty percent of the saints were female (65). Even though most of the female saints were virgins, martyrs or both, women could also be awarded with sainthood for being devoted hermits or pious queens or for their achievements as nuns or abbesses (60), as is the case with Hildegard of Bingen, whose lifelong achievements in spiritual theology, music and medicinal writings is preserved and praised even today. Unfortunately many of these cults either remained local or were unrecognized by the official Church. By the eleventh century, out of approximately three hundred popular saints, "the papacy officially designated or canonized only twenty-six; twenty-three male saints and three *mulieres sanctae* or women saints" (Schulenburg 5; see also Delooz, *Sociologie* 257). Interestingly, as Bartlett notes,

> After 1000, however, England produced no new female saints. Nevertheless, the inherited native saints, the virgin martyrs such as Catherine and Margaret, and, above all, the Virgin

[17] For an in-depth etymological analysis, consult Jane Tibbetts Schulenburg, *Forgetful of Their Sex: Female Sanctity and Society, ca. 500-1100* (Chicago: U of Chicago P, 1998), p. 2 ff.

> Mary herself provided numerous female saints for devotees, even in a society which, for some reason, was no longer producing female saints of its own. In England in the period 1000-1500 female saints were thus revered but not created. It was not that there were no female objects of veneration, but that society was not generating new ones. (147)

About two hundred years later, the cults of female saints increased immensely once again when the Franciscans and Dominicans promoted the veneration of devout persons, in particular women, who were associated with one of the two orders (Vauchez 207), and even though the Church insisted on a "policy of spiritual egalitarianism",[18] "a definite gender-based asymmetry [...] existed among the male membership of the holy dead" (Schulenburg 6).

Historically, in the New Testament the term *saint* was applied to all Christians and everyone was eligible to become a saint, as was more than once decided by local churches and local communities (Dyas 300). In contrast to today, in the early centuries no official process of canonization was involved. Miracles and martyrdom were enough of a proof for sainthood (Ryan xvii) and a person's sanctity, which was confirmed by their death, was widely celebrated. People strongly believed in the existence of saints, no matter whether formally canonized or locally appointed, and "very soon felt the desire to honour their memory and seek their intercession" (Vauchez 13). Shrines and sites of pilgrimage such as the cathedral of Saint Mary Magdalene in Vézelay were built and became, together with saints' graves, the "centre of the ecclesiastical life of the region" (Brown, *Cult* 3). The feast day to honour and commemorate the saints ideally coincided with their supposed *dies natalis* – their date of death, as it was through death that the saint had achieved what followers of Christianity longed for – a bodily apotheosis and a "joining of heaven and earth" (*Cult* 1). Consequently, saints and their cults were praised and commemorated as mediators between the sacred and the secular worlds. They were both "in heaven and ever-present; utterly and concretely present in their relics, but also, more complexly, present in their images and embodied in dramatic representation" (Salih, *Companion* 1).

The growing complexity of canonization began around the fourteenth century. Until then no distinction had been made between the officially canonized saints, who were included by the Church in such catalogues as the *Martyrologium Romanum* and the unofficial, locally appointed saints – between *sanctus* (holy) and *beatus* (blessed). From the fourteenth century onwards fewer people were awarded with sainthood right away – at least theoretically. In contrast to the modern canonization process, local churches or even individuals could still nominate people for sainthood, but the final decision, whether a person was worthy of being called *sanctus*, was now made by a council (Vauchez 64). With the introduction of organized canonization, the term *sanctus* soon denoted without a doubt those who had been canonized and venerated by the Roman Church. The designation *beatus*, however, was from then on reserved for those about whom no official declaration had been made. This more rigid distinction, which is still in use, influenced painters and sculptors as well, who began to portray canonized saints

[18] See, for example, Galatians 3:28.

with a halo and the blessed saints with rays instead (Vauchez 87).[19] Nonetheless, in spite of these changes, in practice the only major difference between the *sancti* and *beati* was that the blessed saints could not enjoy a public cult any longer – a new rule which "was interpreted in very different ways", and "in many regions it meant only that they did not possess their own office" (95). Many of those legends, which enjoyed little or no officially canonized cult, have nevertheless survived in "literary renditions" and experience ongoing popularity and interest (Salih, *Companion* 5).

No matter whether officially canonized or locally appointed, for the common people as well as for the Church the functions and purposes of saints and their lives were manifold. First, the regional cult of a certain saint could work as a geographical identifier. Saints were frequently associated with locations and regions or were even closely connected to countries, nations or cities. In this respect the life of Saint Patrick, for example, is closely related to Ireland, the legend of Saint Ætheldreda to the city of Ely, and the city of Rome is strongly influenced by the legend of Saint Paul;[20] "medieval travellers were aware of passing through the territories of saints" (Salih, *Companion* 7).

Second, saints' lives, despite their fictional components, were a common form of biography in the Middle Ages and, according to Salih, even the "dominant model for medieval secular biography" (*Companion* 19). These "biographies of saints", as Lifshitz sums up, significantly

> provided communities and institutions with written traditions; they defended the independence of communities and institutions against those who wished to subject them; they defended property rights and territorial endowments; they fuelled episcopal rivalries; they conveyed political and theological stances; they propagated an individual author's or group's notion of "the holy"; they served, in short, manifold purposes. (97 n. 7)[21]

Third, the legends were used as educational tools and were valued as ideal guidelines and daily conduct narratives, instructing the Christian community on how to become the perfect Christians through *imitatio*. The imitation of saints, who were believed to be in the highest positions of the celestial order, was, next to the *imitatio Christi*,[22] widely

[19] This change is attributed to the pictorial cycle of San Nicolò of Treviso, a Dominican church, around 1352.

[20] For further information consult William Worcestre, *Itineraries*, ed. John H. Harvey (Oxford: Clarendon, 1969), p. 15; Anneke B. Mulder-Bakker, "Saints without a Past: Sacred Places and Intercessionary Power in Saints' Lives from the Low Countries", *Invention of Saintliness*, ed. Mulder-Bakker (London: Routledge, 2002), pp. 38-57; Sarah Salih, "Introduction", *A Companion to Middle English Hagiography* (Cambridge: Brewer, 2006), pp. 1-23; and Kathleen Hughes, *Early Christian Ireland* (Ithaca: Cornell UP, 1972).

[21] See also Sarah Salih, "Introduction", *A Companion to Middle English Hagiography* (Cambridge: Brewer, 2006), pp. 1-23. For more detailed information consult Michael Goodich, "Biography 1000-1350", *Historiography in the Middle Ages*, ed. Deborah Mauskopf Delyannis (Leiden: Brill, 2003), pp. 353-58.

[22] Many scholarly manuscripts propagated the *imitatio Christi*. One example can be found in the *Epistolae ii ad virgines*, a text attributed to Ps. Clement, in which it is stated, "Doest thou wish to be Christian? Imitate Christ in everything". Ps. Clement, *Two Epistles Concerning Virginity*,

encouraged. Ideally, no matter whether male or female, the saint's behaviour was intended to be "admired, celebrated and even learned from" (Donovan 10). As Ryan writes in the introduction to the *Legenda Aurea*, throughout the Middle Ages the cults of the saints and their legends "served an important purpose: they humanized and dramatized the doctrinal point to be made. In them men and women were seen as *living* the doctrine" (xvi).

Despite of the majority of saints being male, a greater educational function was assigned to female saints, as clerics and scholars wanted to prevent another fatal incident like Eve had caused in the Garden of Eden and thus thought that the fallible sex needed more guidance than men. Consequently, the legends of pious and absolutely devoted female saints were used to instruct women on how their shameful sex could make a worthy contribution to the Christian community despite Eve's misbehaviour. Women were encouraged to imitate the behaviour of seemingly flawless saints such as Agnes by also devoting their existence to God and the Church, by renouncing any form of sexual activity and most significantly by preserving their virginity. Even though the primary audience of saints' legends was the female religious, scholars hoped that young girls in particular would identify with younger virginal saints, such as the previously mentioned Agnes, and adapt their lifestyles of bodily purity and faithfulness.[23]

In this quest for female instruction, however, it is quite astonishing that the most popular and most celebrated female saints, whose "heroic strength" was promoted by the Church as a "source of personal and public inspiration to medieval women" (Donovan 2), overtly challenge existing gender concepts and the religious doctrines of that time. In fact, whereas "writers of late medieval conduct books agreed that women should be gracious, humble, obedient and soft-spoken", the majority of "virgin martyrs tended to be abrasive, defiant, shrewish and sharp tongued" (Winstead 98) and thus were neither flawless nor displayed behaviour to be praised and imitated – at least not from the perspective of the patriarchal Church. Even though female saints were "so clearly identified with orthodoxy", their legends were nevertheless "so full of material that did not necessarily uphold the late medieval status quo" that they "provided an ideal screen for potential dangerous ideas" (Reames, "Artistry" 199). As Elizabeth Alvilda Petroff describes the role of the female saint in her work *Body and Soul: Essays on Medieval Women and Mysticism*:

> The women saints of the Middle Ages were transgressors, rule-breakers, flouters of boundaries, and yet they were also saints. Of course, in a way all saints are transgressors,

trans. B. P. Pratten, *The Ante-Nicene Fathers*, vol. 8, ed. Alexander Roberts et al. (Edinburgh: T&T Clark; Grand Rapids: Eerdmans, 1885), epistle I, ch. 6, "Divinity of Virginity"; see also *Ad virgines*, *Patrologia Graeca* 1: 350-452, 391A. See also chapter 2.2.

[23] One influential example for the influence of this form of female instruction on historical women is that of Margery Kempe (c. 1373-c. 1438), an English female mystic who is known for her extensive pilgrimages throughout Europe as well as her religiously motivated revelations and imitational practices of virgin martyrs, all of which are compiled in *The Book of Margery Kempe* – a work often considered to be the first autobiography in the English language. See Katherine J. Lewis, "Margery Kempe and Saint Making in Later Medieval England", *A Companion to "The Book of Margery Kempe"*, ed. John H. Arnold and Katherine Lewis (Cambridge: Brewer, 2004), pp. 195-216.

> in the sense that a saint lives by excess, lives in a beyond where ordinary measure does not hold; all saints, by their lives, stretch the boundaries of what we have conceived as human possibility, and their zeal in breaking through conventional limitations can be both attractive and repellent, pointlessly mad and unshakeably sane at the same time. Women saints, it seems to me, were doubly transgressors – first, by their nature as saints and, second, by their nature as women. (161)

In summary, saints and their legends were not only of local concern, but especially after their official veneration also of global significance, serving a multiplicity of meanings, purposes and even didactic functions. As Bartlett asserts, "When we consider the cult of the saints, we almost always see local or regional identity coexisting in this way with a sense of the shared collective identity of the Church as a whole" (130). Female saints, even though they were fewer in number than male saints, were empowered with special educational duties. However, as the upcoming analyses of breasts, hair and the gorge in women's hagiography will show, female saints and particularly the treatment of their bodies frequently obscured or even opposed the promoted behavioural idealism for women and instead mirrored the anxieties of the patriarchal, theological and cultural environment.

1.2 The Body as a Metaphor: Constructing the Body

> In writing this study of the body, I have become increasingly less sure of what the body is. The paradoxes illustrate this confusion. The body is a material organism, but also a metaphor; it is the trunk apart from the head and limbs, but also the person (as in "anybody" and "somebody"). The body may also be an aggregate of bodies, often with legal personality as in "corporation" or in "the mystical body of Christ".
>
> Bryan Turner[24]

In general, talking about the body in relation to women and in particular to (female) saints means to understand the historical and theoretical complexity of the human body and its cultural corporeal performance. What constitutes a *body*? Does only one *body* exist or do we need to speak of *bodies* instead? What is *the* body of the medieval time period, or is an all-encompassing concept of the body at that time nonexistent? To what extent was the body mapped and gendered and what distinguishes the saintly body from a human body? How much did the Church and its increasing urge to regulate life in all of its facets affect the perception of and attitudes towards the body? Is it as challenging as Bryan Turner indicates in his work *The Body and Society* that the more one thinks about the body, the less one is able to find an overall definition (7-8)?

Generally, as Fraser and Greco argue in their work *The Body: A Reader*, much research on the body begins by detecting and talking about its "absence" (1). Even though "the body

[24] Bryan Turner, *The Body and Society: Explorations in Social Theory* (Oxford: Blackwell, 1984), pp. 7-8.

and the organism have offered metaphors for the social world, they have not traditionally been considered relevant as subjects for [academic] analysis in their own right" (1). In fact, most of the research and interest in the body has emerged predominantly out of the various liberation movements of the 1960s and 70s, in which "the body has come to the foreground as a sociological concern" (2). Ever since then, "sociology has been led to regard the body as highly relevant to any theorisation of socially situated subjectivity, and simultaneously to problematize any notion that 'the body' can be thought of as a single and coherent conceptual entity" (2-3). Moreover, the feminist movement manifested the idea that "women's social inequality is rooted in, indeed justified by, (their) biology", leading to a still-supported "sex/gender paradigm", which limits *sex* to biological criteria and *gender* to social characteristics (8). However, this strict distinction between the *natural* and the *cultural* body, whether correct or incorrect, is doubtful for the construction of the body in medieval times. Not only was *gender*, and thus the social roles of men and women alike, much more defined than the biological understanding of the sexes (Laqueur), but also were the biological and the social bodies treated as an inseparable unit, interconnected and interdependent on each other.

Consequently, to define the body in regard to medievalism and in relation to female sainthood requires a deconstruction of body theory and a historical reevaluation of the *natural* and the *cultural* body and thus of the concepts of *sex* and *gender*. Furthermore, the following chapter will show that the *cultural* body was frequently formed according to the philosophical or religious ideas related to the *natural* body, which particularly in terms of the role of women constructed women's bodies as the "location for anti-social desire" (B. Turner, *Body* 1996: 65, see also Fraser and Greco 10). "Bodies in this perspective", as Fraser and Greco explain, "are theoretically conspicuous for their capacity to exceed, escape, defy or threaten social order" and therefore require "training or disciplining as a precondition of social life" (10). This training or disciplining of the body in general and the female body in particular will be investigated in the final subchapter, dealing with the significant influence of the Church and its unprecedented ways of controlling the body.

1.2.1 Identifying the *Natural* – Identifying the *Cultural* Body

> The human body is always treated as an image of society and […] there can be no natural way of considering the body that does not involve at the same time a social dimension.
>
> Mary Douglas[25]

Within the numerous, often contradictory attitudes on what actually constitutes the body, the ongoing body-debate has at least come to one influential conclusion so far – there is no such thing as *the* body, but *bodies* in the plural (Fraser and Greco 3). The body consists of multiple layers: "as something we have (the body as object), as something we are (the body as subject), and as something we become (the body as process

[25] Mary Douglas, "The Two Bodies", *Natural Symbols: Explorations in Cosmology* (London: Routledge, 1970, 1996), p. 78.

and performativity)" (4). This argument, however, challenges the classic feminist separations into *natural* and *cultural*, *sex* and *gender*.

Traditionally, ever since the feminist movement and the establishment of gender studies, scholars and students alike have learned to strictly differentiate between the *natural* body – male and female, the *sex* of a person – and the *cultural* body – the *gender* of a person, consisting of the social constructions of femininity and masculinity in relation to the historical time frame and space a body is analysed in. On the one hand a person has a *natural* body, which consists of limbs, intestines, fluids and their functions, and sexual organs, categorizing humans into male or female. The *natural* body is a body that is able to age, to reproduce and to decay. It is a "self-moving machine, a mechanical device, functioning according to causal laws and the laws of nature" (Grosz 48). Within this scholarly understanding, everything beyond the functional – mind, soul, consciousness – is neglected and of no importance (48). The *cultural* body, on the other hand, includes everything beyond mere function, arguing that the concept of the feminine and masculine body depends on time, space and cultural identity, on religion, upbringing or even political, moralistic ideals, turning the term *body* into a complex cultural construct whose definition and conceptualisation has employed a great variety of academic disciplines from philosophy and sociology to history and cultural studies.

However, this traditionally strict separation is challenging. Conventionally, the *natural* body is often believed to be unchangeable and static and only the *cultural* body is able to change over time (Fraser and Greco 9; Wilson 203). Yet as Mary Douglas convincingly argues, "the human body is always treated as an image of society" (78), and these images certainly change over the years. Of course, in its basic functions, the *natural* body is a static entity. Human beings still have the capacity of their ancestors to breathe and reproduce, for example, but the *natural* human body in its ideals and representations is altered by the society it is situated in. "The social body", Douglas continues, "constrains the way the physical body is perceived", and "the physical experience of the body, [is] always modified by the social categories through which it is known, sustain[ing] a particular view of society" (78). These "particular views of society" are in turn often explained with metaphors of the physical, natural body. The body, as Bryan Turner has positioned it, "is a material organism, but also a metaphor; it is the trunk apart from the head and limbs, but also the person" (7-8). Hence, the microcosmic body is often used as a reflection, as a mirror image of the existing macrocosmic outer world, resulting in metaphorical subdivisions of a socially constructed space. Therefore, in contrast to established traditions, the dualistic concepts of *sex* and *gender* can hardly be separated, and neither do they have to be. Rather, they should be treated as a symbiotic entity in which the *natural* components cannot function without the *cultural* and vice versa – because, with Douglas in mind, where does *sex* end and *gender* begin? In her influential work *Bodies That Matter: On the Discursive Limits of "Sex"*, Judith Butler's argument leads in the same direction when she asks, "If gender is the social significance that sex assumes within a given culture – then what, if anything, is left of 'sex' once it has assumed its social character as gender?" (64). Sex is not "simply what one has", but "that which qualifies a body for life within the domain of cultural intelligibility" (63).

Taking a look at the body from a historical perspective, it becomes clear that in pre-Enlightenment times and texts it was someone's *gender* that mattered rather than the biological *sex*. As Thomas Laqueur reasons in *Making Sex: Body and Gender from the*

Greeks to Freud, "*sex*, or the body, must be understood as the epiphenomenon, while *gender*, what we would take to be a cultural category, was the primary or 'real'" (8). "To be a man or a woman", he continues, "was to have a social status, a place in society, to assume a cultural role" and "not to *be* organically one or the other. Sex before the seventeenth century, in other words, was still a sociological and not an ontological category" (8). In *Rabelais and His World*, Mikhail Bakhtin argues further that the body before the nineteenth century[26] "is a body in the act of becoming. It is never finished, never completed; it is continually built, created, and builds and creates another body" (92) – an argument easily transferable as much to the medieval past as to the modern present. Even though throughout history and within Western cultures the focus seems to be set on the *cultural* body, which frequently dominates and controls the *natural* up to the point that bodily control becomes a way of social control (Douglas 78), it can be agreed that generally an indistinct space is available in which the *natural* performs a social, *cultural* role and vice versa. The body is thus not static and unchangeable as traditional scholarship proposes, but continually evolves. By performing, bodies can act as "revolutionary tools", which have a capacity of destabilising, threatening, inverting and mocking social order and social hierarchies (Fraser and Greco 10, 69; Bakhtin 92-95).[27]

Regarding the construction of the bodies' corporeal, cultural performance, the bodies of religious ascetics, saints and Christian martyrs are of special significance. The idols and role models of medieval society, monks and nuns, continually chastised their bodies to achieve enlightenment and prove their religious steadfastness. Many tried to purify the flesh and the mind by refraining from sexuality and by dedicating themselves to a lifelong vow of fasting. To discipline the mind, the pains of flagellation and the wearing of agonizing penitential belts, which were spiked with thorns and securely tied around the waist to leave throbbing wounds on the flesh, often replaced lewd thoughts. In juxtaposition to monks and nuns, for the (fe)male saints and the (fe)male martyrs in hagiographical legends the destruction of the body was usually neither voluntarily nor self-inflicted but achieved primarily via a (heathen) torturer. Moreover, in contrast to monks and nuns, the goal of the saint was not a partial chastisement or punishment of the body but death, which granted the ultimate separation of body and soul, the overcoming of the material flesh to be united with God in the divine kingdom. In fact, for the saint, death was not the end of his or her existence, but rather the renewal of the human being without the locus of the frail, seducible, unwanted body. As Bakhtin has claimed, "One body offers its death, the other its birth" (95) – and within the martyr's life, physicality was something to be overcome, to open up a new sphere of spirituality, knowledge and enlightenment outside of the flesh.

[26] Bakhtin differentiates between the *grotesque* and the *new* body. The concept of the new body begins in the eighteenth century and differs from the grotesque to the extent that it presents an "entirely finished, completed, strictly limited body, which is shown from the outside as something individual" (93).

[27] Within this study the numerous cross-dressing saints who expand and subvert social as well as sexual boundaries in order to overcome the publicly imposed role of womanhood and to reach apotheosis by "becoming male" exemplify this. For example, Saint Eugenia and Saint Euphrosyne cross-dress before entering male monastic communities in order to escape marriage. Saint Wilgefortis prays for a beard to be bodily disfigured and unattractive to her suitor.

In addition, in those hagiographical narratives, which feature colourful and horrifying torture scenarios, it is interesting to realize that the numerous, cumulative cruelties executed on the flesh miraculously cannot harm the saint. In most cases, as Constantinou has pointed out, "the female body either remains untouched during some of the tortures or is triumphantly reconstituted" (40). Even though de Voragine's Saint Cecilia is placed into boiling water for several days and her executioners try to decapitate her several times with a sword, leaving her "half dead" ("semivivam"), the torture miraculously cannot hurt her severely enough, and in the end she decides the right moment for her to die (II: 323; Graesse 777). A similar scenario is presented in Ælfric's legend of Saint Lucy, who, through prayer, manages to live as long as she wants to live even though she is wounded so thoroughly that her "entrails flowed out" (Donovan 94; "hire wand se innoð út" [Skeat I: 216]). Within hagiography, the martyr's body is not only bound to cultural and social metaphors and ideologies, but performs in God's name. The saintly body becomes the locus of power manifestations between the torturer and God – "the torturer cuts it into pieces and God puts these pieces back together, making the body whole once more" (Constantinou 40). One famous example supporting this hypothesis can be found in the legend of Saint Agatha, whose breasts are first removed with tongs, but are shortly after restored miraculously through prayer and faith (de Voragine I: 154-57; *AASS* Feb. I, 621-24; Skeat I: 195-209). Other saints, such as Saint Christina, are still able to speak clearly even after their tongues have been cut out (de Voragine I: 385-87; *AASS* Jul. V, 525-28). This is because martyrs possess what Sarah Kay and Robert Mills have come to identify as a *sublime body*. The term describes the fact that the martyrs' bodies cannot be harmed by torture and that they display an extraordinary indestructability (Kay 3-20; Mills, "Violence" 87-103). In turn, "the fact that the martyr's body transgresses its physicality and does not die despite the horrendous tortures inflicted upon it, leads to the prolongation and alteration of the tortures. The longer the body remains unharmed, the larger the tormentor's desire to harm it" (Constantinou 40). As Constantinou explains, the "indestructible or sublime bodies of the martyrs mirror their undestroyed souls; their unharmed bodies function as powerful signs of integrity and wholeness of their souls which triumph over dismemberment and death" (43). Furthermore, as she summarizes the specificity of the saintly body:

> The martyrs who possess the powerful soul and body make a distinction between body and soul. For them the body and the soul do not form a unity. They are two separate substances, a physical body and a metaphysical soul. The one – the soul – is of importance because it is eternal, whereas the body, being temporary has no meaning.[28] In fact, the martyr's renunciation of the body is what strengthens their souls and this strength of their souls, in turn, is extended to their bodies which become sublime: the martyrs do not feel pain and their bodies remain intact under torture. (44)

In conclusion, in the following study the body is understood in four ways. First, the body is a changeable entity, in which no precise boundary can be established between the *cultural* and the *natural*, as the body is a construct made up of indefinite elements

[28] The "temporary body" is without meaning only for the characters within the stories. From a cultural and literary perspective, however, this is definitely not the case.

(biological and social) which are linked, interconnected and interdependent and in which *sex* influences *gender*, the body influences the mind, and vice versa.

Second, the body is performative. Its performance is able to alter, criticize and even destabilize existing social hierarchies. In addition, on a metalevel the usage and performance of the body can be read, interpreted and analysed in order to draw conclusions about the medieval time period and its understanding of the (*natural*) body and its functions as well as of the (*cultural*) body and its representation in society.

Third, the saint's, and in particular the martyr's, body is not only *sublime* (Kay), but, as the upcoming analyses will show, it is often outside the dualistic understanding of man-woman, male-female and feminine-masculine. In particular, female saints construct themselves by questioning these binary oppositions and thus display a certain amount of unorthodoxy within a thoroughly orthodox genre. Not only do they aim at the transcendence of the body and the flesh through faith and torture, but, especially among the female saints, this (martyrical) process oftentimes is completed only through the annihilation of the constructed binaries of man-woman and male-female or by blending both together. As a result, not only can their bodies be perceived as sensational and obviously revolutionary educational tools for women and the entire community alike, but they also present an early challenge to the general acceptance of binarity.

Finally, "if gender affects sanctity, so too does sanctity affect gender" (Riches and Salih 5). "Sainthood", as Riches and Salih note, "often works by breaking with normal social values, and gendered identity may be amongst these: constructing one's gender identity differently may be a marker of holiness" (5). Consequently, by making room for the discussion of a *third* sex or gender, the saint is capable of challenging and eradicating the dualistic category not only on a natural level, but also on a cultural one. Many saints function (sub-)consciously as gender hybrids. They are portrayed as androgynes, female transvestites, or cross-dressers or they disguise themselves as eunuchs, which itself is a shadowy category of masculinity, and repeatedly combine masculine and feminine characteristics.

The following chapter will continue by providing a historical overview of biological and cultural readings of and metaphors associated with the body, which will set the basis for the subsequent analyses of breasts, hair and the gorge.

1.2.2 Hierarchical Structures: Mapping the Body

> The division of the body into higher parts ruling over lower ones became a commonplace of medieval medical and theological discourse; the head was often described as the organ containing the soul and thus the ruling body part.
>
> Martha Easton[29]

Taking a closer look at the complex construction of the (female) body and its corresponding social and cultural metaphors as well as at gender-related myths in medieval times leads to the overall conclusion that the human body constantly had to negotiate its place and value between adoration and suppression, humiliation and worship (Le Goff and Truong 14). However, as Wolfgang Lipp remarks, the hierarchical relationship between body parts is not only guided by symmetry or by a potential interior classification, but is also a mixture of asymmetry and dominance, which creates the dynamic tension between the physical body and its overlapping sociocultural counterpart (16). Consequently, mapping the body of the medieval era results in the creation of multiple maps with philosophical, social and gendered foci often influenced by ancient philosophers or early Christian scholars.

Commonly, body parts were classified depending on their location on the body. They were divided into noble parts, such as the head and heart, and ignoble parts, such as the stomach, hands and of course sexual organs. Others, such as the eyes, ears and mouth, were furthermore regarded as filters able to distinguish good from bad (Le Goff and Truong 84). Deriving from antiquity, these distinctions were a result of the metaphors surrounding the tripartite construction of head-body-limbs (*caput-venter-membra*). For the Romans, for example, the head (*caput*) was seen as the organ that contained the soul. It represented the human being as a whole, as it had the leading position in the human body and was thus the vigour of humanity (Le Goff and Truong 172-75; Schroer 93). The chest (*pectus*) was identified as the locus of thought and the heart (*cor*) as the locus of emotions. The neck and throat were believed to express pride and self-confidence, hair in its various lengths was regarded as the crown of the head, and voluminous breasts were a symbol of praise and mercy (Schroer 99, 103, 107). Interior organs such as the kidneys became the traditional loci of the sexual drive and sexual energy (Brown, *Body* 232). Symbolic associations with a certain body part were also used to strengthen the power of medieval warriors and kings (Le Goff and Truong 187). For example, the decapitation of the defeated after a battle expressed the metaphorical separation of the control centre from the rest of the body. A similar approach can be found in cutting off the hair of the defeated, as long hair during that time was a symbol of strength[30] (Schroer 93; Cooper 45). Philosophically, the body was

[29] Martha Easton, "Pain, Torture and Death in the Huntington Library *Legenda Aurea*", *Gender and Holiness*: *Men, Women and Saints in Late Medieval Europe*, ed. Samantha Riches and Sarah Salih (Abingdon: Routledge, 2002), p. 54.

[30] The Merovingians, for example, cut off the hair of their defeated.

further divided into a two-body model with the body (the flesh) on the one side and the mind (the soul) on the other. Along with the increasing influence of the Catholic Church, the expansion of consciousness, of the mind, became a significant goal for believers in Christianity. As Elizabeth Grosz explains,

> Within the Christian tradition, the separation of mind and body was correlated with the distinction between what is immortal and what is mortal. As long as the subject is alive, mind and soul form an indissoluble unity, which is perhaps best exemplified in the figure of Christ himself [...] whose soul, whose immortality, is derived from God, but whose body and mortality is human. (47)

Because of the assumed interconnection between body and mind, between the *natural* and the *cultural* body, any imbalance in a person's behaviour was believed to be mirrored in his or her health and vice versa. Diseases were the result of misbehaviour, and socially unaccepted behaviour resulted in sickness. For example, greed and lechery were believed to cause leprosy (Grosz 48). Overall, the human body "has been a potent and persistent metaphor for social and political relations throughout human history", and "different parts of the body have traditionally represented different social functions" (B. Turner, "Social Fluids"). Even today, as Bryan Turner notes, "We refer to the 'head of state' without really recognizing the metaphor",[31] just as the *Höllenschlund* or the mouth of hell has become a popular concept of hell since the Anglo-Saxon period (Le Goff and Truong 143).[32] Consequently, in the words of Douglas,

> The relation of head to feet, of brain and sexual organs, of mouth and anus are commonly treated so that they express the relevant patterns of hierarchy. Consequently I now advance the hypothesis that bodily control is an expression of social control [...]. (78)

Utilizing the metaphorisation of the body to explain specific areas of everyday life also provided arguments and explanations for the inferior role of women and the dominant role of men in society. The correspondence between body parts, masculinity and femininity resulted in the creation of *gendered cells* and supports Douglas's argument because these *gendered cells* were often socially controlled. Generally, the head as the place of rationality and understanding, as the location of wisdom, power and strength, was considered masculine and was thus assigned to men, whereas the body and its overall fallibility, the odours and body fluids coming from it, were assigned to women. This categorization has its roots in Saint Paul's first letter to the Corinthians, in which he writes, "I would have you know, that the head of every man is Christ; and the head of the woman is the man" (I Corinthians 11:3)[33] and "the man was not created for the

[31] Bryan Turner, "Social Fluids: Metaphors and Meanings of Society", online abstract, *Body & Society* 9 (2003): 1-10, *Sage Journals*, Web, 12 Sept. 2016.

[32] For a detailed description and analysis see chapter 4.

[33] "volo autem vos scire quod omnis viri caput Christus est caput autem mulieris vir [...]". All direct biblical references in English are used in accordance with the *Douay-Rheims Bible* (OT 1609/10, NT 1582). The Latin supplements throughout are taken from the *Biblia Sacra Vulgata*, 5th ed., ed. Robert Weber and Roger Gryson (Stuttgart: Bibelgesellschaft, 2007).

woman, but the woman for the man" (11:9).[34] These declarations, as well as the passage in the Epistle to the Ephesians that "women be subject to their husbands, as to the Lord: Because the husband is the head of the wife, as Christ is the head of the Church" (Ephesians 5:22-23),[35] were used as the basis for the Church Fathers to reinforce and habitually preach "a hierarchical gender doctrine designating man as 'head' and woman as 'body'" (Blamires 13). Consequently, men legitimately owned the bodies of their wives and female servants (Brown, *Body* 23; Le Goff and Truong 47), reducing women socially to objects reigned by patriarchy. Therefore, for the society of the Middle Ages, a woman's existence was primarily "body-centred". Women were thought to be "carnal or bodily beings by nature", and thus "in order to lead a spiritual life they needed to deny or renounce the sexual and reproductive aspects of their being and transcend their gender" (Schulenburg 127; see also Erickson 189-95; Salisbury). The only way for women to change their situation was to grow mentally as well as spiritually and to "become male".[36] The philosopher Philo, for example, believed that women could transcend their "material, passive, corporeal and sense-perceptive world" in order to progress and to take on the "active, rational male world of mind and thought" (qtd. in Bullough and Brundage, *Sexual Practices* 45),[37] and the easiest way to do so was "to deny their sexuality, to remain virgins" (45).

Even then, women were perceived as the inferior sex, particularly biologically. As Brown explains in his study *The Body and Society*, biologically "males were those foetuses who had realized their full potential" as they had "amassed a decisive surplus of 'heat' and fervent 'vital spirit' in the early stages of their coagulation in the womb" (9) – a fact proven by the male seed and the hot ejaculation. As Aretaeus the Cappadocian, a widely celebrated ancient Greek physician, claimed during his lifetime, "It is the semen, when possessed of vitality, which makes us men hot, well-braced in limbs, heavy well-voiced, spirited, strong to think and act" (Aretaeus 346-47;[38] qtd. in Brown, *Body* 9-10). Women, on the other hand, were considered incomplete or "failed males", whose lack of heat made them softer and more formless. The lack of heat in a woman was also a common explanation for the monthly recurring menstruation. Scholars assumed that this was the female way of burning up the surplus of passion (Brown, *Body* 9-10). Because of this biological "lack of heat", no one believed that women might need to cool down at some point. For masculinity, however, cooling down was seen as a constant, everyday threat, which, if men were not careful, would

[34] "etenim non est creatus vir propter mulierem sed mulier propter virum"

[35] "mulieres viris suis subditae sint sicut Domino / quoniam vir caput est mulieris sicut Christus caput est ecclesiae [...]". Another biblical phrase that makes this association can be found in I Timothy 2:11-13, 15.

[36] For an in-depth discussion of the concept in itself and in relation to saints' legends, consult chapter 2.

[37] Philo, *On the Creation*, ed. and trans. F. H. Colson and G. H. Whittaker (London: William Heinemann, 1963), pp. 69-70, 151, 162; and *Questions and Answers on Genesis*, ed. and trans. Ralph Marcus (London: William Heinemann, 1961), vol. I: 40. See also Richard A. Baer, Jr., *Philo's Use of the Categories Male and Female* (Leiden: E. J. Brill, 1970), pp. 46, 51.

[38] Aretaeus, "Causes and Symptoms of Chronic Diseases", *The Extant Works of Aretaeus the Cappadocian*, trans. F. Adams (London: Sydenham Society, 1856), pp. 346-47.

eventually result in the emasculation of the masculine body and behaviour. As Brown states, "No normal man might actually become a woman; but each man trembled forever on the brink of becoming 'womanish'"[39] (*Body* 11).

In general, not only were women and their sexuality regarded as inferior to men, but rather the naked, sexual body of a woman inhabited a marginal, precarious position in society (Lipp 12). This image of the female body was further intensified through "the construction of the female body in medieval science and theology alike", which

> focused on gaps, orifices and symbolic filth. Woman was positioned in the principle of disruption in the human psyche: the flesh. Her body was seen as pervious and excessive and her character both corruptible and corrupting. Consequently, the need to repair the natural accessibility of the female body became a moral and spiritual imperative in the medieval church's approach to women. Woman's natural susceptibility to sin and defilement was to be corrected through moral and physical enclosure. (Marshall 11)

Especially for ascetic Church Fathers such as Jerome or Ambrose, who in some cases were almost "fanatical celibates" (Schulenburg 129), women and their bodies were at least suspicious if not feared. The lack of medical knowledge, the complexity of female bodies and their at times unexplainable bodily functions, such as pregnancy or recurring monthly menstruation, turned the female body into a frightening and puzzling mystery of nature. The menstrual and childbirth-related bleeding of a woman was dreaded and regarded as unclean by many (Schulenburg 215), and "the vagina remained the most mysterious area of the female genitalia" (Rousselle 27). All in all, the female body was "the most alien body of all" – particularly for men and male celibates (Brown, *Body* 271).

Therefore, it is not surprising that these male anxieties and insecurities towards women and their bodies were frequently discussed in a number of scholarly texts. For early Christian Gnostics such as Valentius, "the female stood for all that was open, aimless, lacking in shape and direction [...]. It stood for all that needed to be formed by being made subject to the hard, clear outlines of the male"[40] (Brown, *Body* 105, 112). Other influential theologians formulated more radical ideas. For example, the writing of the Church Fathers focused rather on "the inherent dangers of woman's physical attractiveness for the male celibate" (Schulenburg 129). They described the female body in "abusive and disdainful terms" (129), which although "deceptively attractive [...] was to be shunned as an inherently ugly, repulsive receptacle" (Fisher 24). These ideas, deriving from antiquity, were still in use throughout the Middle Ages, and clerics such as Giovanni Della Casa formulated his ideas about women in similar terms. In his study *An uxor sit ducenda* (1537) he states that a woman is closer to an animal than to a man, because her body and mind are unbearable. For him women were dreadful creatures who as commonly believed had weak and flabby limbs, were sick incessantly, and were overall of horrendous ugliness (Bock 35).

[39] In the Roman Empire, the eunuchs, with their emasculated behaviour and feminine appearance, served as constant reminders of the "cooling down" effect and that the male body was, as Peter Brown writes, nothing else than a "fearsomely plastic thing" (*Body* 10).

[40] Plutarch, *Praecepta conjugalia*, *Plutarch's Moralia* vol. 2, trans. and ed. F. C. Babbitt, Loeb Classical Library (Cambridge: Harvard UP, 1971), pp. 339-41.

Summing up, the body in medieval times was a complex concept formed through a variety of historical, cultural and even philosophical traditions. These simultaneous, multilayered influences truly pose a challenge to finding an all-encompassing definition of the (female) body in the medieval era. Rather, one needs to be aware of these different mappings of the body in order to understand their impact on the role of women at that time. The final part of this introductory chapter will discuss another undeniable influence on the body – the rise of Christianity, whose religious doctrines and favour of celibacy redefined and controlled the body and especially the female body more than ever before.

1.2.3 Sexuality and the Church: Controlling the Body

> The Church had become a power within the state, one whose interests and aims government officials must accommodate, whether they agreed with them or not.
>
> James Brundage[41]

The early Christian communities thought it necessary to form rules for themselves, to create laws and codes as the Jews had done in order to be recognized as a new religious group and not as a pagan minority. Much thereby relied on Jewish law – for example, marital codes were adapted to the new belief with only a couple of new features, such as the abandonment of divorce or increasing prohibitions against remarriage after one spouse was deceased. In addition, around the second century the early Christian Church wanted to establish a stricter sexual discipline, which was to form the basic foundation of a behavioural code within this new community of believers (Brown, *Body* 60). The body was soon described as a "fragile reservoir", which could lose its energy by enjoying too frequent sexual activity – in particular, men were able to lose the heat their bodies apparently possessed and consequently, as mentioned previously, were threatened with the loss of their virility (18). As Brown describes, "the most virile man was the man who had kept most of his vital spirit – the one, that is, who lost little or no seed" (19). The female members of the Christian communities were also able to gain a reputation for sexual abstinence, as much as the apparently stronger males did – complete chastity was soon *en vogue*, and the restraint from sexuality, even though drastic, was an aspect which could control the disorderly world, and everybody, men, women and the uneducated, was invited to join. By the second century, Christian communities were not yet united in their teachings, which was due to the wide geographical distribution within the Roman Empire from Lyon in the west to Dura Europos, a Greek frontier town which overlooked the Euphrates, in the east. Consequently, many communities were still unknown to each other or separated by lengthy travel, a plausible reason for the different developments within the early Christian Church (Brown, *Body* 61-64).

[41] James A. Brundage, *Law, Sex and Christian Society in Medieval Europe* (Chicago: U of Chicago P, 1987), p. 78.

By the year 400, the influence of Christianity had pushed the dominance of virginity and celibacy further. Both were soon identified as the major virtues of the Christian Age, but from then on, as Brown notes, "the body was in for a bad time" (xxxii). In this respect, Tertullian was the first widely recognized and honoured scholar to ask "how a man feels in himself when he abstains from a woman. He thinks spiritual thoughts" (qtd. in Brown, *Body* 78).[42] With his response he contributed to the long-lasting doctrine in Christian communities that refraining from sexual intercourse was a successful method to achieve "clarity of the soul" (Brown, *Body* 76). Therefore, even before the historical beginning of the Middle Ages, the Church had started to "formulate norms of Christian behaviour and regulations for internal discipline" (Brundage 74). By the fifth century, as Brundage points out, "The Church had become a power within the state, one whose interests and aims government officials must accommodate, whether they agreed with them or not" (78). Only one century later the Christian worldview had turned into a systematic, highly influential theology (79). By the year 1000, the systematic control of sexuality and the body had reached its peak, and the Church's endeavour to regulate even the most intimate areas of life, such as conjugal sexuality, became more and more successful. As Brundage sums up, "Every human society attempts to control sexual behaviour, since sex represents a rich source of conflicts that can disrupt orderly social processes. Human sexuality is too powerful and explosive a force for any society to allow its members complete sexual freedom" (1). By the eleventh century, gender and related behaviours were surveilled by the Latin (Catholic) Church (Le Goff and Truong 52).

At the time, surveillance of course was not enacted through technological devices as in the modern definition of the term, but through supervision and regulation. Whereas supervision indicates a narrow space between guidance and the imposition of ideologies or rules, regulation was a more radical step (and the one which was predominantly applied), forcing humans into hierarchical categories in which behaviour outside the rules was prohibited. In a functioning society, as Brundage notes, "Some limits must be imposed, some rules agreed upon, and some enforcement mechanisms devised to implement the observances of the rules" (1).

During the European rise of Christianity, all forms of surveillance were used to control social behaviour and gender-specific actions in the growing Christian community. Surveillance was initiated through texts such as the Bible or other treatises dealing with virginity and celibacy, which in turn served as manuals for Christian behaviour and were widely spread by continual preaching within the communities in services or sermons. In this respect, these texts served on the one hand as a rather subconscious yet very powerful method of surveillance in a dominantly illiterate society and were often the foundation for laws which were created to regulate gender-specific behaviour. On the other hand, as the Church was not yet as unified concerning its teachings as it is today, numerous significant and often contradictory ideas and dual teachings coexisted – for example, on dress codes or hairstyles – challenging the Church's "doctrinal authority" (Brundage 579). This led to a continual modification and revision of guidelines and an integration of unorthodox beliefs.

[42] Tertullian, *De exhortatione castitatis*, ed. E. Kroymann, *Tertulliani Opera: Corpus Christianorum, Series Latina 2* (Turnhout: Brepols, 1954), pp. 1013-35, p. 1029.

Social behaviour and gender codes were commonly enforced via three simple words: "Thou shalt not". This arrangement of words has turned into one of the most influential beginnings of a sentence ever uttered, and even nowadays in a society which has become increasingly sceptical of religion, it has not quite lost its power. In the society of the medieval period, phrases like "thou shalt not" in combination with the threat of purgatory, the expected and descriptively supported pains of hell, and horrible stories about tortured saints were quite authoritative among primarily illiterate believers, who had neither the chance to prove what was preached to them nor the chance to counter-read the sermons.

Considering the fact that literacy was a privilege of the clergy and bearing in mind the strong belief in the dogmas of the early Church, which constantly played with essential human fears, it is easily explained why texts were powerful enough to function as a subliminal way of imposing rules on society. In addition, if people cannot read, they believe – and were often made to believe – in the knowledge and experience of those who can. The clergy not only mediated the text but was of course also able to translate, interpret and preach psalms and the Holy Scripture in relation to their own personal beliefs, political ideas or even economic interests.

For the Church, the saints' legends in particular played a significant role because they gave a voice to teachings with which the population could identify. Throughout the centuries the legends were enhanced with increasing numbers of cruel torture scenes by authors, compilers and translators to fit the individual needs of the Church. Those stories were then periodically preached and proved immensely useful as cautionary tales, as controlling didactic tools, commonly believed to be particularly beneficial for the instruction of women. The identification of the listener with the descriptive language of pain and agony helped to establish a fundamentally convenient, significantly didactic method for the Church, influential enough to regulate and code gender behaviour.

Further guidelines on gender behaviour such as sexuality were listed in the Penitentials, a new, complex "genre of Christian moral literature" (Brundage 151), famously compiled by the Archbishop of Canterbury, Theodore of Tarsus, in the seventh century. The Penitentials became increasingly influential in shaping Catholic sexual doctrine until the beginning of the eleventh century (151). As Brundage summarizes,

> By the early tenth century the Western Church's accumulated body of behavioral and doctrinal regulations had grown unmanageably large. The thousands of canons adopted by synods and councils, together with the decrees and rulings of popes and bishops, the declarations of patristic writers and other spiritual authorities, and a considerable body of royal and imperial law dealing with religious and moral matters, all comprised what was vaguely thought of as canon law. (169)

This textual influence on society was obvious in many areas of everyday life. For example, the increasing desire for regulation also led to the introduction of sumptuary laws which in Britain dictated (approximately from the reign of Edward III up to the seventeenth century) who of which rank was allowed to wear what type of clothing in which colour and fabric. Thereby the Latin Church not only redefined the cultural body, but the metaphorical body was also altered to suit Christian doctrine. Whereas the head once stood only for the locus of wisdom and knowledge, and the superiority of men over women, it now also symbolized God as the head of the Church and consequently of the Christian community (I Corinthians 11:3).

Concerning textual surveillance methods, an uneven power triangle soon emerged between text, clergy and audience. The apparently dogmatic text was often "drained" of its original intentions by the innovative clergy to suit their needs and was for a long time never directly accessed by the audience, who did not have a choice other than listening to and trusting in what they were told. Taking this a step further, the distribution of power in the medieval religious context can be compared to Michel Foucault's analysis of power distributions within prisons, as the social body was regulated by the exegesis of the text and its resulting modification as well as interpretation into personal ideologies. This turned the clergy into guards and society into inmates whose disobedience was not only punished right away, but who also lived with the constant threat of chastisement in purgatory in the afterlife. Consequently, medieval Christian society was also based on "a system of permanent registration", in which "every possible confusion" was supposed to be sorted out right away (Foucault 196-97) and in which rules and doctrines taken from texts were apparently *authorized* by God, turning him into the invisible superiority whose codex was not to be questioned.

In addition, another of the earlier influences on society was the development of a new hierarchy of (feminine) social roles, which lasted even beyond the medieval period. Virgin martyrs, virgins (*norma integritatis*), ascetics and celibates were now on top of the hierarchy, followed by nuns, abbesses and penitents because the majority of them had refrained from bodily impurity through sexual contamination and were consequently seen by society as role models of ideal behaviour for future generations. From those ranks, too, the majority of female saints emerged. Widows were valued less and could raise their status only through sexual abstinence. The lower portions of the hierarchy were reserved for the married – man and woman alike, who were of course necessary for the perseverance of the human race, but to do so they had to have sexual intercourse and consequently were valued less (Brown, *Body* lxvi, 359; Le Goff and Truong 48; Sorgo 53-55). The superiority of virginity had been stated in Saint Paul's letters to the Corinthians, and the Church Fathers used this textual basis to "firmly implant this concept in the mentality of the Latin West" (Schulenburg 128). Again, the influence of texts in the formation of the canon law[43] cannot be overestimated.

Unfortunately, even if Christianity had redefined social gender hierarchies, only a minority of women were actually able to decide for themselves to stay celibate virgins, unless their families agreed with their decision. During the Roman Empire, young women and also men were even "mobilized" for reproduction. As Brown notes, "The pressure on the young women was inexorable. […] Young girls were recruited early for their task. The median age of Roman girls at marriage may have been as low as fourteen" (*Body* 6). Statistics show that the average Roman woman had to have approximately five children in order to keep the population stable (6). Within families, fathers, brothers or male cousins decided a girl's fate. They arranged marriages that

[43] Bishop Burchard of Worms and Ivo of Chartres are responsible for the earliest canonical publications. For more information on the formation of canon law, consult James A. Brundage, *Law, Sex and Christian Society in Medieval Europe* (Chicago: U of Chicago P), 1987.

were beneficial for their own income or used to tie bonds between influential families. Virginity was nevertheless favoured, and girls were not only recruited for reproduction – virgins were also recruited explicitly by the city of Rome with the option to marry later in life (8). To save their virginity as long as possible, many girls were placed in monasteries until a suitable husband had been found and were then withdrawn by their families (261). Therefore, the legends of the virgin martyrs, who run away from their families to hide in male monastic communities (because the access to male monasteries was far more difficult than to female cloisters), are in their basic plotline not fictitious at all. Moreover, they show the difficulties a woman had to face if she dared to change her destiny as a wife and mother herself. For example, in the legends of Saint Marina/Marinus, Saint Eugenia and Saint Euphrosyne, among others, their masculine disguise leads to stirrings among the monks, and they are often judged with scenes of accused rape or homoerotic implications (see chapters 2 and 3). In the often-radical writings of the Church Fathers, however, there was no other option imaginable than for a woman to be enclosed and out of sight of male Christian believers in order to avoid the seduction of the "pure" male. Many even proposed the destruction or at least negation of a woman's outer appearance to remove her disturbing attractiveness (Schulenburg 129). Nevertheless, next to these misogynist attitudes,

> In practice, the monastic institutions of the early Middle Ages met the needs of many religious women concerned with espousing a life of virginity and accruing future heavenly rewards: and for a select few, monasteries provided the all-important career ladder to sainthood. Monasticism also afforded, for the first time, an honourable alternative to forced marriages and provided an effective escape from the very real fears and dangers of childbirth. (139)

If a girl managed to remain in the cloister as a consecrated virgin, she was from then on no longer considered a woman; she turned into a *human ex voto*, a "bride of Christ" (Eusebius, qtd. in Brown, *Body* 260[44]), and as a "sexless, gender-neutral being […] these virgins were viewed as spiritual equals" of Christ (Schulenburg 128).

For Western society, the secluded nuns, those "brides of Christ" who followed Mary, the *aula pudoris*, soon became the stereotypical representatives of idealized virginity and not the Desert Fathers who lived ascetic, eremite lives in the desert. In the mind of the Christian believer, the virgin state was a closed state in which the womb withdrew completely from sexual activity and the continual potential for childbirth (and its dangers) and consequently remained pure, not only by its bodily intactness, but also by a purity of the mind – the side effect which was supposed to be achieved. By the "closedness of her body, the mind, the heart, and the hands of the virgin woman had come to open wide – to the Scriptures, to Christ, and to the poor" (Ambrose, *De institutione virginis*, qtd. in Brown, *Body* 363[45]). The virgin's intact, closed body, which was opened only for the visions of Christ, became the most precious flesh imaginable within the Christian society, even if her steadfastness and loyalty to the saviour was

[44] Eusebius of Emesa, *Homily 6.18*, *Eusèbe d'Émèse: Discours conservés en latin*, ed. E. M. Buytaert, Spicilegium Sacrum Lovaniense 26 (Louvain: Spicilegium Sacrum, 1953), I: p. 162.
[45] Ambrose, *De institutione virginis*, *PL* 16: 319-347; 9: 58, 62, 335C, 336A.

often threatened, as the legends of the virgin martyrs will show in the following chapters (Brown, *Body* 271[46]). Nevertheless, as Schulenburg has stated, this "life of sexless perfection was of paramount importance", and "the status of *virgo intacta* was nearly a prerequisite for sainthood"; and it was often through the defence of this pure, intact, unwounded state that virginal women were awarded the status of sainthood (127, 128).

The development of Christianity thus strongly influenced peoples' attitudes towards sexuality and gender with new rules and taboos. Texts influenced the clergy, who consequently formed doctrines, canon laws and the Penitentials out of them to survey and control the behaviour of the growing Christian community with great success. Religious women and men alike tried to find their place in these newly established gender hierarchies at whatever price necessary, and the legends of the virgin martyrs proved immensely helpful in understanding and constructing not only the female body and its perception, reception and treatment within society, but also femininity in general.

[46] Eusebius of Emesa, *Homily 6.18*, *Eusèbe d'Émèse: Discours conservés en latin*, ed. E. M. Buytaert, Spicilegium Sacrum Lovaniense 26 (Louvain: Spicilegium Sacrum, 1953), pp. 162-79. See also Kirsten Hastrup, "The Semantics of Biology: Virginity", *Defining Females: The Nature of Women in Society*, ed. Shirley Ardener (New York: Wiley, 1978), pp. 49-65.

2 Female Breasts – Female Weakness?

> The breast is a marker of the female, the beard of the male.
>
> Allen Frantzen[1]

> Are you not ashamed to cut off from a woman that which your mother suckled you with?
>
> Saint Agatha[2]

> Ist eine Frau ohne Brüste noch eine Frau? Im patriarchalen Denken und Fühlen ebenso wenig wie ein kastrierter Mann noch als richtiger Mann gilt.
>
> Heinz Herrmann[3]

Culturally, the female breast has been a phenomenon, a body part whose pure existence was and still is fascinating for female and male fantasies alike. From its complex biological function as a nurturing, lactating resource to secure the growth and strength of newborn babies to the healing abilities of a mother's milk to erotic fantasies – breasts were and still are the most significant indicator of womanhood and the most obvious and visible display of femininity. Even today, Frantzen's claim that "The breast is a marker of the female, the beard of the male" has validity for archetypal impressions and definitions of this body part (76).

Within hagiographical narratives, however, the breast as a distinctive marker of femininity is challenged and threatened. Often, just the fact of possessing breasts causes dangers of various degrees for the individual saint's life. Conversely, within this theological text corpus, the breast functions primarily as a locus for negotiation – either of the expected roles of women in society or of theological statements. Moreover, it also changes into a place for executing sadistic, pornographic desire, turning the historically "gratifying" breast into a "hostile" object (Miles, *Complex Delight* 2). In the cause of action, this most recognizable and evident indicator of femininity is either removed violently through mastectomy, a gender-driven torture method known throughout the Middle Ages, or hidden by the female saint herself, thereby indicating that either her femininity is seen as a threat to the patriarchy or that the explicit denial and hiding of

[1] Allen J. Frantzen, *Before the Closet: Same Sex Love from Beowulf to Angels in America* (Chicago: U of Chicago P, 1998), p. 76.

[2] Jacobus de Voragine, *The Golden Legend: Readings on the Saints*, 2 vols., ed. and trans. William Granger Ryan (Princeton: Princeton UP, 1995), I: 155. "non es confusus amputare in femina, quod ipse in matre suxisti?" (Graesse 171).

[3] Horst Herrmann, *Sex und Folter in der Kirche: 2000 Jahre Folter im Namen Gottes* (München: Bassermann, 2011), p. 92. Trans.: "Is a woman without breasts still a woman? In patriarchal thinking as little as a castrated man counts as man".

her womanhood can make her "male" and consequently an established member of society.

Gruesome torture narratives in which hot tongs are used to cut off the virgin martyr's breast, and legends in which the categorical hiding of the breast ends in accusations of rape, raise the question of whether the breast in the medieval time period, and especially in hagiographical legends, is meant to signify that this most obvious female body part is a symbol of female weakness, of the female body being subordinate to the male. As Margaret Miles proposes in her work on the iconographic development of breasts through 1750, the breast is culturally a "complex delight" to be explored – a theory which will be addressed in the first part of this chapter, investigating this body part's representation and function in everyday life, theology and iconography. Afterwards, the chapter will consider these female signifiers in the legends of several female saints, from Saint Agatha and Saint Christina to Saint Eugenia, arguing that within the narratives only two major treatments are applicable: torture and the resulting amputation of the breast or its hiding to deny and overcome the limitations and restrictions of womanhood.

In regard to torture, the first subchapter concentrates on the question of whether the cutting off of breasts is a form of male sexual aggressiveness or rather a form of *imitatio*, using the legends of Saint Agatha and Saint Christina as a basis for investigation. In addition, the subchapter will explore the significance of body fluids, such as milk, blood and sperm, as the inflicted wounds in several cases leak milk instead of blood and therefore stylistically remind one of the iconographic *Virgo Lactans* – the lactating Virgin, hinting at cultural and narratological phenomena surrounding these holy women.

Subsequently, the chapter will progress to an analysis of the concealment of womanhood among the so-called transvestite saints, who will also play a crucial role in the third chapter with regard to hairstyles. Within those narratives the breast is "cut off" in a more metaphorical, sublime way. It is hidden behind clothes, or it is tied firmly to the woman's body, so that she is able to access male monastic communities, in which her fair, emasculated appearance stirs up the male inhabitants. Thereby homoerotic (lesbian and gay) tensions between the "male" saint and either the monks or the female believer she cares for are implied, making the exposure of the breast in public the only possibility for Saint Eugenia, for example, to escape death.

2.1 "A Complex Delight": Illuminating the Symbolism of Breasts

> There is no pretense about a true mother; the breasts she displays are full for the taking […] pressing the milk.
>
> Bernard of Clairvaux[4]

The female breast and its various functions are a "complex delight" for scholars of numerous disciplines, as Margaret Miles proposes in her work on the secularization of the breast in iconography (*Complex Delight*). Whereas Miles focuses on the later Middle Ages and primarily takes an art-historical approach, other scholars, such as Robert Mills (2005), Sarah Salih (1999) and Thomas Heffernan (1988), have talked about the breast primarily in regard to torture or as a threat to femininity. Still others, such as Caroline Walker Bynum (1991), have confined their research predominantly to the biological function of the breast – lactation – and what this means in regard to theology, sanctity and femininity. The breast as a "complex delight", then, has so far not been given the attention it deserves. Apart from the scholars just mentioned and some medical treatises on breasts, no larger volume on this body part so far has been published which deals with it from all angles possible. This subchapter is consequently dedicated to the breast itself, providing an overview of the most significant attachments – culturally, historically and theologically within the medieval context. In this respect, it will establish the breast as an essential symbol for religious purposes, which will set the scene for the upcoming analysis of a principally negative treatment of this body part in women's hagiography.

From a biological perspective, the main function of a woman's breast is nourishment. Even in our modern Western society, midwives and gynaecologists agree that there is nothing healthier for the growth and the immune system of the neonate than the milk it receives from its mother. Yet whereas in Western societies breastfeeding can nowadays be easily replaced with the help of nutritious supplements and industrially produced milk for infants, in developing countries nursing is often still the key to the survival of the infant – a situation also found in the medieval time period. "Woman was food", Bynum states straightforwardly in her work *Holy Feast and Holy Fast*, and the milk from a mother's breast was the first sort of nourishment human beings encountered (269).

Already in societies predating the medieval era, the (large) size of a woman's breast was regarded as a merciful blessing.[5] In Israel, for example, women with full breasts were cherished as icons of wealth and salvation (Schroer 82, 99). For the people of the medieval and early modern period, the breast, with its nutritious function and even its

[4] Sermons 9 and 10 in *On the Song of Songs*, trans. Kilian Walsh, vol. 1 of *The Works of Bernard of Clairvaux*, 2 vols. (Kalamazoo, MI: Cistercian, 1976), pp. 57-58, pp. 62-63; qtd. in Caroline Walker Bynum, "'…And Woman His Humanity': Female Imagery in the Religious Writing of the Later Middle Ages", *Fragmentation and Redemption*: *Essays on Gender and the Human Body in Medieval Religion* (New York: Zone, 1991), pp. 151-79, p. 160.

[5] This was represented, for example, in Palestinian figures of goddesses.

exposure in public, was thus a part of daily life – and therefore far from being an abstract or undefined image. In addition, in a society without the ability to either preserve food over a long time or transport it over a long distance, access to milk often decided the life or death of an infant (Miles, *Complex Delight* 37). Thus the newborn's survival and development "depended on [...] milk of good quality" (McLaughlin 115). Milk deriving from cows or goats, from animals in general, was considered damaging, "since infants were thought to acquire the physical appearance, intelligence, and personality of their milk source"[6] (Miles, *Complex Delight* 37). As Miles sums up, "In societies that lacked refrigeration and in which animal milk was thought to foster stupidity in the infant who imbibed it, almost all people experienced their first nourishment and pleasure at a woman's breast" (8). Despite the existing lack of medical documents, the importance of the breast in medieval society cannot be underestimated – "It was women's bodies, [...] that fed with fluid from the breast", and "medieval people clearly found this fact symbolically useful" (Bynum, *Fragmentation* 106).

This symbolic "usefulness" was particularly convenient within the growing Christian communities. For the Church, the breast was undoubtedly no sign of female weakness, but rather a useful "tool" which allowed the transition of a well-known everyday image into theological realms. It was used to indicate "God's provision for the Christian, ever in need of God's grace" (Miles, *Complex Delight* ix) and signified God as the lifesaver, nourishing his community with his "blood" (milk).[7] The breast as a religious symbol was particularly visible in medieval iconography, in which the *Virgo Lactans* – the lactating Virgin Mary – was one of the most frequently painted iconographic themes in the Christian artistic world of the later Middle Ages (Bynum, *Fragmentation* 102-03).[8] Geographically, scholars assume that the *Virgo Lactans* has its origins in the Byzantine regions and spread to Western Europe in the thirteenth century through Venice and Sicily (Miles, *Complex Delight* 33).[9] Paintings and statues of the time[10] show the Virgin Mary, with the infant Jesus in her arms or on her lap, exposing or revealing one breast to the viewer at which the neonate is either sucking or is ready to suck. It shows the significance of breastfeeding not only for infants in general, but for Jesus's survival, whose life depended on the goodwill of his mother to nurse him. Going

[6] Whether saint Theodora/Theodore consequently wants to foster stupidity in the infant she raises or whether she feeds it goat milk out of pure necessity is a question that this study will leave open for future scholars to discuss. For the complete story see Jacobus de Voragine, *The Golden Legend: Readings on the Saints*, 2 vols., ed. and trans. William Granger Ryan (Princeton: Princeton UP, 1995), I: 365-68.

[7] The relationship between the two body fluids will be discussed in chapter 2.3.

[8] The breast as a religious symbol changed over time. Margaret Miles argues that the breast was still a religious symbol in 1350, yet within four hundred years of development – at least iconographically – the breast had been eroticized and medicalized and was consequently no longer *en vogue* as a religious metaphor.

[9] See also Millard Meiss, *Painting in Florence and Siena after the Black De*ath (New York: Harper, 1964), pp. 133ff – proposing a Tuscan origin; and Victor Lasareff, "Studies in the Iconography of the Virgin", *Art Bulletin* 20.1 (1938): 26-65.

[10] For example, Giovanni Pisano (1248-c. 1314), *Nursing Madonna*, before 1314, Museo Nazionale di San Matteo, Pisa; or Anonymous, *The Divine Mother* (Galaktotrophousa), ca. 1600, collection of Dr. Amberg-Herzog, Kölliken, Switzerland.

a step further, Mary's benevolence arguably ensures not only Christ's existence, but also the survival of the entire Christian community. The inclusion of the community is furthermore detectable in other images of the Virgin and the baby in which the breast is either not directed at the neonate but at the viewer or in which the baby "invites" the viewer to drink – offering a share of this blessed substance and thus inviting the viewer/the Christian community to be "fed" with this holy milk. Artistically, the baby is placed aside, suggesting that the viewer is able to "share the baby's need for sustenance and that Mary offers to use the blessed food" (Bynum, *Fragmentation* 103). As time went by, the breast, as Miles alludes, "lost its hegemony as a religious symbol as Christian churches lost authority in the sixteenth century, largely due to the emergence of Protestant alternatives to the 'one true Church'" (*Complex Delight* 4). As a result the breast's symbolism was altered as well. More and more frequently, "the deliberate exposure of a single breast was replaced by depictions of both breasts", hence changing the religious symbol in the early modern period into images which "depended for interpretation on the immediate location and context of representation" (10).

Within theological circles in the Middle Ages, however, the virgin's bare breast became a useful symbol of "God's loving provision of life, the nourishment and care that sustain life, and the salvation that promises eternal life" (Miles, "God's Love" 22). The image of the "nourishing breast" was so powerful that it was transferred to other religious subjects, such as paintings of the crucifixion scene. Here Jesus is portrayed with a bleeding stigmatic wound positioned at the same height as the female breasts, implying that the Christian "nourishment" derived correspondingly from "God's breasts" (22). For the medieval audience, no matter whether male or female, the body on the cross, which "in dying fed the world", was in "some sense female" (Bynum, *Holy Feast* 270). As Bynum reminds us, "since Christ's body was a body that nursed the hungry, both men and women naturally assimilated the ordinary female body to it" (272-73).[11]

Next to its biological and theological use, the breast is, at least in modern Western societies, also connected to pleasure and eroticism (Miles 22). For the medieval audience, the connection between the revealed breast of the Virgin and sexual excitement was less important than its connection to nourishment, at least in iconography (Bynum, *Fragmentation* 86). However, it remains difficult to draw a clear boundary between an erotic display and one with only a religious intention – the boundaries are blurred, a fact especially obvious in hagiographical texts. Even though the sexual component is, at least artistically, not the focus of the artist and viewer, this combination of nourishment and pleasure, of "woman's sexuality and maternity" (Heffernan 243), leads to more negative treatments of the female breast.

Within female saints' legends the breast is often treated negatively. It is frequently threatened, humiliated and turned into the "focus of torture" (243), into a "target" (Bartlett 536) for sexual assault of all kinds. Historically, the torment of breasts was a culturally established practice, which adds a bitter taste to otherwise positive

[11] To refer to Christ as female seems contradictory at this point, not only to the general assumption of the superiority of the male sex, but also to the general ideology imposed on women to "become male" if they wanted to achieve the Christian ideal. A female Christ figure resembles the legend of the bearded and crucified Saint Wilgefortis, as discussed in chapter 3, and touches on the aspect of gender hybridity conceptualized in chapter 5.

associations, making one yearn for a redefinition of "pleasure". With torment in mind, positive erotic pleasure is turned into sadistic, painful pleasure – the pleasure exclusively enjoyed by the male tormentor when he cuts off the symbolically significant body part within this theological context. The treatment of the breast then shows, as Miles reasons, "two […] fundamental theological lessons, namely God's love and human perversity" (*Complex Delight* 1).[12] Comparable to psychoanalytical readings[13] of the infant's relation to the breast, the breast in the hagiographical context is divided into a "gratifying" and a "hostile" breast, into a "powerful symbol of provision and source of the earliest frustration", as the infants' life depends upon the goodwill of its mother (2). In female saints' lives, the passive infant is reborn into the active heathen, who can act out his anxiety to remove this unreceptive object, which the virgin martyr withholds from him. This turns the breast into a target for executing and reenacting power and control over the now supposedly weak female. As Miles summarizes, "After several decades of detailed analysis of gender arrangements in many societies, it was possible to suggest that the infant's experience at the breast informs men's concerted efforts to control – to design and administer – gendered social arrangements that maximize male pleasure and minimize frustration" (*Complex Delight* 3).

The specific torture is, as Salih has proposed in "Performing Virginity: Sex and Violence in the Katherine Group", an attack on femaleness (104), showing once more that the body does not belong to the woman herself – but is dominated by patriarchy. "Women […] did not own the breast", Miles proclaims, but fathers and husbands who "dispensed the breast and its provisions" (*Complex Delight* 3). She continues, "As bearers – not owners – of the breast, women experienced the most evident damage from men's mechanisms for coping with the anxiety of the ambiguous breast" (4) – a statement to be explored in the following chapter.

[12] It has to be noted that Miles relates her writings to the beginning of Augustine's *Confessions*, in which he recites his personal childhood experiences with the breast and not in relation to hagiographical narratives. However, the statement seems to be perfectly transferable to this context. For Augustine's writing consult Augustine, *Confessions* I.6/I.7, trans. Rex Warner (New York: Mentor, 1963).

[13] For a detailed psychoanalytical reading of infancy and the breast as an emotional object consult Melanie Klein, "The Psycho-Analytic Play Technique" and "A Study of Envy and Gratitude", *The Selected Melanie Klein*, ed. Juliette Mitchell (New York: Free Press, 1987), pp. 35-56, pp. 211-29. For a discussion of Klein's theories in the religious context, see Margaret R. Miles, *A Complex Delight: The Secularization of the Breast 1350-1750* (Berkeley: U of California P, 2008), pp. 1-6.

2.2 The Torture of the Breast: On Imitatio Christi, Gendered Torture and Body Fluids

> The idea of "mortification of the flesh" has been a soteriological aspect of Christianity since the crucifixion.
>
> Robert Mullen[14]

> Women deform their faces with glass, with acid, with their own fingers; they bind their limbs, carve up their bodies, pierce, bruise, cut and torture themselves. The most highly praised mystical writings speak of Christ's love in terms of rape. [These women] abase and abuse themselves. They do it for love of Jesus and the church applauds them.
>
> Sara Maitland[15]

To amputate breasts was a common form of gender-related punishment for female sinners of the medieval period. Tongs belonged to the basic equipment of the European torture chambers, used in particular with noses, fingers, toes and nipples. Flat-nosed pliers were utilized to tear apart or burn off penises (Herrmann, *Sex und Folter* 272-73). Specially made tongs nipped off breasts "with pleasure"; brutally designed *Brustkrallen*[16] slowly tore apart the breasts of uncountable numbers of women who were accused of adultery, abortion or other acts involving a violation against morality (282).

Twisted, crushed, torn off, cut off, burned off – the vocabulary describing the treatment of the saintly martyr's breast is comparable to historical documents not at all inviting for closer examination for the scholar and reader. And yet, as this chapter argues, the torture itself is arguably a coded spectacle, particularly in religious narratives. As Constantinou states in regard to female martyrdom, "Female roles of sanctity are basically formed according to how a heroine treats her body, or allows it to be treated. The martyr wins the crown of holiness by defending the Christian faith in a pagan world with her virginal body and her blood" (15). Consequently, "in contrast to their male counterparts, holy women achieve sanctity almost exclusively through their bodies" (16).

However, before looking at specific legends for a closer analysis of how the protagonist "allows" her body to be treated, some preliminary questions have to be answered. What is the difference between torture and self-mutilation? Where do both overlap historically and fictionally? And what is the role of the reader of these scenes?

The reader, and in the Middle Ages the listener, intentionally or unintentionally becomes the witness, the secret attendant, the voyeur of these horrifying and sickening

[14] Robert Mullen, "Holy Stigmata, Anorexia and Self-Mutilation: Parallels in Pain and Imagining", *Journal for the Study of Religions and Ideologies* 9.25 (Spring 2010): 91-110, p. 95.

[15] Quoted in Darryll Grantley and Nina Taunton, *The Body in Late Medieval and Early Modern Culture* (Aldershot: Ashgate, 2000), p. 13.

[16] The term *Brustkrallen* is a German compound out of *Brust* (breast) and *Krallen* (claws).

spectacles and is fascinated and repulsed at the same time.[17] This voyeurism is a central point in the establishment and survival of literature in general and hagiography in particular.[18] There is, however, a difference between fictional and nonfictional literature. The intensity of voyeurism increases with the level of reality involved in the narratives. In the case of autobiographies, fictional autobiographies and hagiographical legends, the reader experiences a special closeness to the protagonists. Every hagiographical legend, be it fiction or scientifically proven fact, serves as a voyeuristic arena for the reader and listener, who attempts to believe in the conveyed "reality". It is the curiosity and fascination of the audience to be part of the scenes, to study, reread and readapt the content of the narrative. The audience turns into secret observers, the secret invaders of the scenes, who cannot intervene in the horrible happenings. In addition,

> The audience was gathered as a group in order to make the martyrdom's public form possible. The fear which the tortures of the punished were supposed to provoke, aimed at influencing each individual member of the audience, pagans as well as Christian. The fear caused by tortures was expected, on the one hand, to prevent pagans from converting to Christianity, and, on the other, to convince Christians to renounce their faith. (Constantinou 21)

The intention of hagiographical legends is thereby not too far from that of erotic literature. Arguably, both genres can have the desired effect of emotional reaction only if the reader, the secret intruder of the scenery, is emotionally responding to the textual, visual or auditory material. As Jean Marie Goulemot describes in relation to erotic narratives:

> Everything turns on the gaze: the reader must be made to see, for the book can give rise to the desire for pleasure, only by describing those bodies offered up to stimulate desire or by depicting the gestures and postures of the moment. Therein lies the origin of its own tension, its strange and undeniable power. (43)

The same formula is applicable to hagiographical narratives, as the overall success of the legends also depended on the use of picturesque language and colourful descriptions. The crueller or more fantastic the legend, the wider it was spread among the population. Hagiography thereby gives "rise to the desire for pleasure", the "pleasure" of being united with God, the "pleasure" of the torturer and the "pleasure"/desire to imitate the powerful, incorruptible virgin in her quest to maintain her chastity.

In addition, comparable to erotic literature, within hagiographical legends the body is a focus, and the body and the creation of certain imagery are key elements for a successful narrative. Everything is centred on the body, its performance and the

[17] Some of the following ideas concerning the function of the reader and a possible relationship between hagiography and pornography were recently published in Sarah Schäfer-Althaus, "Painful Pleasure: Saintly Torture on the Verge of Pornography", *Mirabilia Journal* 18 (2014): pp. 151-59, p. 155, Web, 17 Sept. 2016; see also chapter 4.

[18] Other forms in which voyeurism is of central significance are of course pornographic and erotic texts, whose aim is to involve the reader in the happenings in order to arouse sexual desire.

hidden codes its penetration transmits. In fact, as William Burgwinkle and Cary Howie note, the body is produced "as a spectacle" to such an extent that the "viewer believes that s/he can feel what the other is feeling or that the other is in him even more than himself" (8). Thus, the spectacular (mal-)treatment of the body attracts not only the reader's attention, but, particularly in hagiography, the recurring, cumulative tortures of specific body parts explicitly sensitises the reader to them. Consequently, in the legend of Saint Agatha the reader is sensitised to the breast, in the legend of Saint Apollonia to the martyr's teeth and in the martyrdom of Saint Christina to her glossectomy (see chapter 4).

According to Goulemot, the body is offered to the eye from a distance, a necessary distance in the creation of imagery, because the reader should "take up the proper distance in order to see, to admire and to examine" (47). "The more the body speaks and the more it is tortured and effectively restored, the longer the text becomes", Constantinou claims (58). This text-body interrelation works both ways: "The less functional, the shorter the text" (58). As Constantinou summarizes, "This analogy between text and body suggests that the one stands for the other; the body 'writes' the text and the text 'writes' the body" (58).

Within the pedagogical range of hagiography, this fascination with certain plot constructions is especially visible in a number of saints' lives, which either follow specific patterns – such as the legends of the transvestite saints – or let the body "speak" at length about its treatment and thus relate specific pictures of religious value to images from everyday life, including torture methods which were well known to the audience. Hence, the reader-listener experiences closeness – not to the torturer or the surrounding gazing crowd sometimes described within the stories, but to the protagonist, the tortured.

As Gabriele Sorgo points out in her work *Martyrium und Pornographie*, the stories deal with an *imitatio*, "ein Sich-Einfühlen in den Leidenden"[19] (175). This *imitatio* works in two ways – from the perspective of the reader, who feels sickened by the gruesome details some legends have to offer, and from the historical knowledge of martyrical behaviour, as martyrs were commonly described as "enjoying" these often sexually connoted torture methods because they recalled the painful death of Christ. With this knowledge in mind, it is less puzzling that Saint Agatha, for example, calls the torture "her delight" (de Voragine I: 155; "poenis ita delector" [Graesse 171]). Psychologically, as Robert Mullen claims, torture as well as self-mutilation or the occurrence of holy stigmata "often exhibit either depersonalization or disassociation or both" (92). It is rather the "intense emotional quest for transcendence – the modification of one self to another" (92).

Is this not exactly what the saintly martyr wants? Does the torturer not even do him or her a favour when mutilating the body, as the highest goal of a martyr was to *depersonalize* his or her body, to *transcend* it into *another*, immaterial being – without body, made only of purity and soul? There is, however, a difference between *imitatio/torture* and *imitatio/self-mutilation* – as even though both go in the same direction and often overlap, both actions have different motivations and intentions. Whereas the self-mutilator voluntarily decides for himself or herself to torment the body, torture is involuntary. It is forced upon somebody, and in the course of action it is

[19] Trans.: "to express empathy with the suffering".

the torturer who decides which part or parts will be destroyed, as well as how and with what results (in hagiography this is usually death). In contrast, as Janice McLane argues, "Self-mutilation reinstates the boundary between existence and non-existence of self" (112) – and in the course of history, the *existence* of the self, and moreover the maintenance of virginity, often depended on sacrificial self-mutilation.

As Schulenburg notes, "The Church provided the ideological context for these desperate acts of virginal defence" and "the methodology of self-deformity or facial disfigurement [...] which these early female religious utilized in their heroics of virginity was part and parcel [...] of this time" (148). Historical documents, such as the story of Saint Ebba and her nuns of Coldingham (ca. 870) or the documents involving Saint Eusebia (ca. 738),[20] give accounts of several female religious who, in fear of losing their virginity, cut off their noses and lips or lacerated their faces to disfigure their bodies for the approaching male enemy threatening this most precious bodily symbol.

However, self-mutilation was not always practiced out of fear and desperation. During the Middle Ages it was *en vogue* to imitate Christ and his suffering. The *imitatio Christi* had no real possibility to become Christ or to become equal to him because, as Sorgo notes, "Christians always remain God's children".[21] However, those who tried to imitate Christ, to see him as the ideal being, would be granted access to the holy community, the celestial family (104). With this *imitatio sanctorum*, Sorgo continues, a deathly logic developed – those who give their lives as blood witnesses are especially holy and serve the community best (274).

In particular, women thought this to be a virtuous idea while seeking religious inclusion and yearning for spiritual perfection. It was common that women "starved and beat themselves to enter into a relationship with Christ in which the erotic and spiritual come together in ecstatic visions in which the women frequently speak of God as lover; of tasting him, of kissing him and becoming soaked in his blood" (Marshall 13). And many did so based on hagiographical narratives, as "it is commonplace that one function of hagiography was to function as a model for imitatio" (Salih, *Companion* 18). Consequently, the gruesome *imitatio/torture* scenarios described in the legends were often used as the basis for *imitatio/self-mutilation*, as many of these real-life female religious believed in the healing capacities after the torture, that if they cut off their noses they would heal through faith, as, for example, with Saint Agatha's breasts.

No matter to what extent self-deformation was applied – whether one merely stopped eating, cut one's hair or went into extremes and ripped off noses or cut off lips

[20] For the story of saints Cyr and Eusebia see Simon Verne, *Sainte Eusebie, abbesse, et ses quarante compagnes martyres à Marseille* (Marseille: Imprimerie Marseillaise 1891), and for Saint Ebba consult Roger of Wendover, *Flowers of History: Comprising the History of England from the Descent of the Saxons to A.D. 1235*, trans. J. A. Giles (London, 1849), vol. I, p. 191. For excerpts of the stories plus background information and analysis see Jane Tibbetts Schulenburg, *Forgetful of Their Sex: Female Sanctity and Society, ca. 500-1100* (Chicago: U of Chicago P, 1998), chapter 3, "At What Cost Virginity?" plus notes.

[21] The text passage in the original reads, "Desgleichen bot die Imitatio Christi nicht die Möglichkeit, so wie Christus zu werden, denn die Christen würden immer Kinder Gottes bleiben. Aber wer ihm als Ideal nacheiferte, wurde in diese überirdische Familie, in die himmlische Gemeinschaft sicher aufgenommen, wo das göttliche Familienoberhaupt persönlich die Seele entgegennahm. Selbst Jesus sitzt nur zur Rechten des Vaters, aber nicht auf dessen Platz" (Sorgo 104).

– it is the body and its wound(s), no matter whether visible wounds or psychological or symbolic inflictions, which become the "critical element in the formation of identity of sense of self" (Glucklich, "Self and Sacrifice" 502).[22] The wound mirrors the *imitatio*, mirrors Christ's suffering, and is the outer, visible transformation which reflects the interior effort to become a new spiritual being who has overcome the material body.

At this point the transition can be made to the tortured body, as within the hagiographical narratives wounds are also of specific significance. The explicit description of Saint Agatha's wound after her breasts have been torn apart, which in the course of the narrative heal again, and the recurring motif of the milk-leaking wound are included for a reason. The illustrated wounds of the tortured are symbols of religious doctrine; they are places where the heathen fights with God over legitimate ownership, where power is executed, where one destroys and the other heals or sets an example. "The martyr's body is the means through which both the torturer and God alike manifest their power: the torturer cuts it into pieces and God puts these pieces back together, making the body whole once more" (Constantinou 40). With regard to torture and the resulting wounds, the female body is thereby particularly "characterised by a constant change" of "form and appearance" (40).

Whereas the self-mutilator has a choice, the female martyr in the legends does not. In order to maintain her chastity she has to undergo torture, and readers as well as the protagonist know from the beginning that the outcome of the story will be death – a mortification of the flesh. However, even though historically the torture of some body parts, such as the genitals, noses, or breasts, was gender-driven, within the religious context of stories the analysis will have to go further, because where do *imitatio* and self-mutilation end and torture and mutilation of a person begin? What is the role of the male torturer? What is the code behind the amputation of breasts? Does the mastectomy within the saintly context provoke sexual male aggressiveness? Can the mastectomy be a symbol of a male anxiety to remove something so visible and so necessary for the survival of humanity and, figuratively, for the survival of Christianity? And, on a meta-level, is the removal of this source of nourishment for the neonate an attempt to cut off nourishment for the Christian community or the Church itself?

The following subchapter will consider the treatment of the breast within the torture narratives. First, a detailed analysis of the legend of Saint Agatha will be given in which the torture of the breast is most precisely narrated in various sources throughout the centuries. Her legend allows for a two-tiered reading of the torture, which on the one hand relates to the elimination of "nourishment" and on the other includes the transcendent aspect of castration. Afterwards, the subchapter will deal with the legend of Saint Christina, who bleeds milk from her severed breasts – a reappearing topos in female saints' legends, calling for a closer analysis.

[22] See also Ariel Glucklich, "Sacred Pain and the Phenomenal Self", *The Harvard Theological Review* 91.4 (1998): 389-412.

2.2.1 Saint Agatha: Serving Breasts on a Silver Plate

> Impious, cruel, brutal tyrant, are you not ashamed to cut off from a woman that which your mother suckled you with? In my soul I have breasts untouched and unharmed, with which I nourish all my senses, having consecrated them to the Lord from infancy.
>
> Saint Agatha[23]

Around the years 250 to 253, approximately during the reign of the Roman emperor Dacian,[24] a young girl was slapped in the face, stretched on the rack and eventually had her breast twisted and violently removed from her body. The legend of her martyrdom became extremely popular from the early Christian time period through the Middle Ages; Saint Agatha was publicly venerated, as the earliest documents reveal, since the end of the fifth century. Poems and letters mention her from the sixth century on – the century in which the first complete Latin version of her story was composed as well (Donovan 37).[25] As Donovan notes in her study *Women Saints' Lives in Old English Prose*, "In medieval Europe, the legend of Agatha was one of the most popular women saints' lives [...]. At least forty texts containing versions of one recension of Agatha's Latin life survive in continental manuscripts dated before 1100" (37). Her cult spread far into the Anglo-Saxon world; for example, Aldhelm mentions her in both his *Carmen de Virginitate* and *De Virginitate* (late seventh century), and Bede includes her in his famous *Martyrologium* (c. 725-731 AD) in praise of her virginity as well as in his hymn to Æthelthryth in his *Historia ecclesiastica* (731 AD).[26] Today, the martyrdom of Saint Agatha has its permanent

[23] Jacobus de Voragine, *The Golden Legend: Readings on the Saints*, 2 vols., ed. and trans. William Granger Ryan (Princeton: Princeton UP, 1995), I: 155; "Cui Agatha : impie crudelis et dire tyranne, non es confusus amputare in femina, quod ipse in matre suxisti? Ego habeo mamillas integras in anima mea, ex quibus nutrio omnes sensus meos, quas ab infantia domino consecravi" (Graesse 171).

[24] Other sources have used variations of the emperor's name, such as Decius or Decian. Regarding the time frame the *Acta S. Agathæ* as well as the *Legenda Aurea* attest that she was martyred during Emperor Dacian's reign (249-251 AD). However, the *Legenda Aurea* explicitly states the year 253 (I: 156), which is too late for Dacian. Bede in contrast places her under the reign of Emperor Diocletian (284-305 AD); see *The Complete Works of Venerable Bede in the Original Latin*, ed. J. A. Giles, vol. IV (London: Whitaker, 1843), p. 33.

[25] *Acta S. Agathæ, AASS* Feb. I, 621-24; *Acta Martyrum et Sanctorum*, ed. Paul Bedjan (Paris: Otto Harrassowitz, 1890-97), Feb. I, p. 595; and *Bibliotheca Hagiographica Latina Manuscripta*, ed. Société des Bollandistes, (Université Catholique de Louvain), pp. 133-36.

[26] *Aldhelm: The Poetic Works*, trans. James L. Rosier and Michael Lapdige (Cambridge: Brewer, 1985) and *Aldhelm: The Prose Works*, trans. Michael Lapidge and Michael Herren (Cambridge: Brewer, 1979); Bede, *Martyrologium. Édition pratique des Martyrologies de Bédé, de l'Anonyme Lyonnais et de Florus*, ed. Jacques Dubois and Geneviève Renaud (Paris: CNRS, 1976); and *The Complete Works of Venerable Bede in the Original Latin*, ed. J. A. Giles, vol. IV (London: Whitaker, 1843), p. 33. See also Bede, *The History of the English Church and People*, trans. Leo Sherley-Price, rev. R. E. Latham (New York: Penguin, 1968), bk. IV, ch. 20. Ælfric's *Lives of*

place in the martyrologies. Of all the tortures she has to endure, of all the wonders her narrative includes, and of all her functions as a patron saint – she is the patron of bell-founders and is prayed to when fires break out (Farmer 6-7) – it is the torture of her breasts that has made her famous. In this matter, the reception of her legend sets the focus unmistakably on the breast – a fact predominantly visible in iconography. Within the sacred arts it is through her breasts that she is identifiable in every well-equipped classic art gallery even today. The reference to her legend is painted mostly in two forms – either the paintings display the moment before the torture, in which Saint Agatha is portrayed naked and in agony, the torturers having placed their tongs at the breasts, ready to twist them at any moment, or she is shown fully clothed and holding a platter on which her cut-off breasts are placed, making it look as if she is "serving" them, offering them to the viewer.[27] This association with "serving" is furthermore connected to her additional patronal functions for the Christian community, as "St. Agatha, appropriately enough, became the patron saint of wet nurses and nursing mothers, as well as those who suffered from abscesses or cancer of the breast" (Schulenburg 239).

The subsequent traditions that surround this martyrdom allow some preliminary conclusions. First, of all tortures she has to bear, it is the violation and restoration of her breasts that is singled out. Second, taking the iconographic portraits as starting points, which portray the state either before or after the mastectomy, the breasts arguably experience several phases, or even transformations, of which the torture itself and the miraculous healing afterwards are of special significance. With the destruction of the breasts, not only is Agatha's body transformed and altered, but her interior attitude towards her body and mind is also transformed, bringing her one step closer to the divine death.

In addition, within the narratives a third phase can be identified, which takes place right after the removal of the breast, as readers of the legends encounter Agatha's verbal reaction to the mutilation. The reader is consequently present at the moment of destruction, encounters her reaction (and here it is significant to look at several stylistic versions of this account), and is present at the intimate moment in the prison when her breasts are healed through her vision of the apostle Peter. Furthermore, recalling the constructedness of hagiographical writing, the torture of the breast and the establishment of three phases have a significant narrative function and are placed within the legend for a reason, as they are connected to the inner transformation of Agatha into a virgin martyr. Therefore, as the following analysis argues, the breast is used metaphorically, and arguably each phase (destruction, reaction, restoration) builds up a gendered or religious metaphor.

The incidents leading to the crucial events in question should thereby not be left unnoticed. Agatha, like many other virgin martyrs, is of noble birth, a stunning beauty

Saints also includes the story of Saint Agatha. See Ælfric's *Lives of Saints*, ed. Walter W. Skeat, Early English Text Society Original Series (London: Oxford UP, 1881-1900).

[27] One popular example of Agatha holding her breasts on a plate is the painting *St. Agatha* by Francisco de Zurbaran (1630-33). Sebastiano del Piombo, by contrast, finished a vivid image of Agatha's pretorture moment in 1520 called *The Martyrdom of Saint Agatha* (Palazzo Pitti, Florence, Italy).

and a believing Christian. With the first two attributes she attracts Quintianus, the consular official of Sicily, a man known for being greedy, “libidinous” and of heathen status (de Voragine I: 154; “libidinosus” [Graesse 170]).[28] As Agatha is unwilling to sacrifice to his gods and to join him in marriage, he hands her over to the custody of a procuress, who “tortures” her metaphorically with the exposure to human sexuality – and presumably, any contemporary who heard the legend had ideas about the sexual activity going on in a medieval brothel. Until that point, and the worst is still to come, the legend has already exhibited several transgressive features indicating violations of the existing gender norm, which are nonetheless necessary to create Agatha’s uniqueness. Agatha does not subordinate herself to masculinity and does not become what Quintianus wants her to become – a “passive female” (Frantzen 87). She is not willing to change her mind, and even the heathen governor “quickly perceive[s] the firmness of her resolution” (de Voragine I: 154; “ejus immobile propositum cognovisset” [Graesse 170]), a determination which helps her overcome the thirty-day exposure to sexuality – the first step of her martyrdom. Sexual harassment and even attempted rape was seen as a preceding stage, “the critical test point to represent women’s strength and courage as well as their virtue”, as Schulenburg points out (136-37). She continues, “the maintenance of chastity was also a major type of martyrdom”, as a woman “was both virgin and martyr because virginity was not possible without martyrdom” (148) – and sexual assault, this “fate worse than death” (172), represented a threat to the ultimate goal of dying untouched for the higher cause. Within the first couple of sentences, Agatha has already taken the primary steps on her way towards death. The progress of transforming the resolute virgin into a virgin martyr has now begun, and the protagonist is aware of that fact as she “prayed and wept day after day, thirsting to attain the palm of martyrdom” (de Voragine I: 154; “flebat quotidie et orabat sitiens ad martirii palmam pervenire” [Graesse 170]). Eventually, she is summoned again before Quintianus, who requestions her steadfastness and her obedient behaviour – towards Christ, not towards him – and as “what she said was making him look foolish in the public eye” (I: 155; “quia voce eum publice confundebat” [Graesse 171]), Agatha is slapped in the face and is forced to spend the night in prison.

At this point, two strands of narration are active. On the one hand, the beating is the first *physical* punishment she has to suffer, and on the other hand, her behaviour at this moment reminds one of the *imitatio*, as it demonstrates her willingness to suffer and to die. Whereas during her days at the brothel, where she weeps and prays for it to be over soon, to jail “she went happy and triumphant, as if invited to a banquet, and commended her trial to the Lord” (de Voragine I: 155; “ad quem laetissime et glorianter ibat et quasi ad epulas invitata agonem suum domino commendabat” [Graesse 171]). Her transformation from a virgin girl into a virgin martyr is in progress. The second physical

[28] Note that the opponents are usually heathen men who are character-wise exactly the opposite of the virgin martyr. The legends thereby often deal with binary oppositions. In de Voragine’s version of Saint Agatha she is contrasted with Quintianus: “The virgin Agatha was highborn and a great beauty, […] she worshipped God at all times and in all holiness. Quintianus […] was baseborn, libidinous, greedy, and a worshiper of idols” (I: 154); “Agatha virgo ingenua et corpore pulcherrima […] Deum semper in omni sanctitate colebat, Quintianus […] cum esset ignobilis, libidinosus, avarus et ydolis deditus” (Graesse 170).

torment she has to endure increases in severity – she is stretched on the rack, which according to Alban Butler is a "torment generally accompanied by stripes, the tearing of the sides with iron hooks, and […] burning with blazing torches" (I: 256). To these gruesome happenings, however, Agatha replies,

> These pains are my delight! It's as if I were hearing some good news […]. The wheat cannot be stored in the barn unless it has been thoroughly threshed and separated from the chaff; so my soul cannot enter paradise unless you make the headsmen give my body harsh treatment. (de Voragine I: 155)[29]

This utterance, indicating Agatha's wish to transcend into an immaterial being, leads the angry Quintianus to order that her breasts be cut off. What is noticeable is that Agatha herself views her body as "chaff", as leftover material which has to be separated harshly from the "wheat", from the useful core, in order to enter the "barn", the house of God. She calls for harsh treatment, which recalls the idea that martyrdom is not possible without torture. As suicide is a sin, according to Christian belief, and consequently self-mutilation is disapproved of as well, the mutilation of the self via the heathen tormentors is essential for the *imitatio Christi*.

Even though, except for some minor differences, all of the medieval narratives of Saint Agatha consulted for this study are correspondent in their structure, significant changes are apparent regarding the number of breasts which are detached in the course of her martyrdom. Whereas the *Legenda Aurea* and others talk of just one breast being removed ("to twist her *breast* for a long time and then cut *it* off" [de Voragine I: 155]; "ejus mamillam torqueri et tortam diutissime jussit abscidi" [Graesse 171][30]), in other near-contemporary versions of her legend, for example in Bede's martyrology, both of her breasts are explicitly amputated.[31] The cruelty of the narrative is not dependent on the number of breasts tortured and removed, and yet the removal of just one breast recalls the images of the *Virgo Lactans*. The iconographic symbol of virginity, the mother of Christ who exposes one breast from which all of Christianity is fed, may have been the prototype on which Agatha's breast torment is based, demonstrated in particular by her exclamation after her breast(s) have been removed: "Are you not ashamed to cut off from a woman that which your mother suckled you with? In my soul I have breasts untouched and unharmed, with which I nourish all my senses, having

[29] "ego in his poenis ita delector, sicut qui bonum nuntium audit aut qui videt […]. Non enim potest triticum in horreum poni, nisi theca fuerit fortiter conculcata et in paleis redacta. Sic anima mea non potest intrare in paradisum cum palma martirii, nisi diligenter feceris corpus meum a carnificibus attrectari" (Graesse 171).

[30] Emphasis added. See also "mamillia" (breast) in the *Acta S. Agathæ*, *AASS* Feb. I: 622; or "breoste" (breast) in Ælfric's *Natale Sancte Agathe* (Skeat I: 202).

[31] "post eculeum et tortiones, post mamillarum abscissionem", *The Complete Works of Venerable Bede in the Original Latin*, ed. J. A. Giles, p. 33. See also Aldhelm's *Carmen de Virginitate*: "Pectora virgineis fraudantur pulchra papillis"; "Beautiful breasts are robbed of virgin nipples", l: 1750. For other medieval texts which highlight the removal of both breasts in the legend of Saint Agatha, consult Osbern Bokenham, *Legendys of Hooly Wummen,* ed. Mary S. Serjeantson (London: Oxford UP, 1938); or *The South English Legendary*, eds. Charlotte D'Evelyn and Anna J. Mill (London: Oxford UP, 1956).

consecrated them to the Lord from infancy" (de Voragine I: 155; "non es confusus amputare in femina, quod ipse in matre suxisti? Ego habeo mamillas integras in anima mea, ex quibus nutrio omnes sensus meos, quas ab infantia domino consecravi" [Graesse 171]).[32] In this statement the focus is set on the breast as a nourishing body part, related to infancy and sucking. As Allison Gulley notes, "Agatha draws attention to her breast as baby's nourishment and becomes a maternal figure" (115). Directly after the torture itself, the gendered body part is stylistically connected to maternal basic instincts. On a meta-level, this symbolic mastectomy is an attempt to destabilize the Church. Agatha, as a "tool" of God who encompasses all ideals of early Christianity, is deformed. For the heathen the subtraction of her breast cuts off the metaphorical connection between herself, the ideal Christian woman, and her possible imitators, whom she symbolically nourishes with her behaviour. For Quintianus the case is won at this point – as he believes to have satisfyingly disconnected her from God, from her community and from transferring her selfless behaviour to others. Agatha's body has at this moment changed into a place to negotiate power between the heathen and God. It is no longer a body in the biological sense, but a "sublime body", which cannot be harmed by torture and in which the soul is of more importance than the carcass which contains it. As Frantzen summarizes, "The governor disfigures her womanhood but leaves her spiritual identity untouched, for the true nature of her faith does not reside in her outer breast but rather in her inner breast, the soul" (76).

Subsequently, Agatha, battered and wounded, returns to the prison, where she prays and receives a vision of Saint Paul, who heals her wounds and restores her breasts. As Gulley remarks, "Agatha prays in thanksgiving and, looking at her breast, discovers it has been restored, which symbolically represents her successful rebirth into Christ after having shed blood in his name" (116). The restoration of her bodily disfigurement underlines the superiority of the Christian God to heathen gods and implies that no torture executed on the saintly body can harm it or its function within the theological realm. The rebirth into Christ is then the end of Agatha's earthly, bodily transformation. Now she is no longer a human being but has given up her material body, has managed the separation of body and soul, and is ready to die as a martyr to complete her transformation. Constantinou confirms this argument, stating,

> The state of one's soul is reflected in the condition of one's body; the quality of one's soul determines that of one's body and state of one's body in turn, is the indicator of the essence of one's soul. The martyr's bodily tortures elevate the body's physicality into a means of access to the divine. The indestructible or sublime bodies of the martyrs mirror their undestroyed souls; their unharmed bodies function as powerful signs of the integrity and wholeness of their souls which triumph over dismemberment and death. (43)

Whereas most literary traditions of Agatha maintain the focus on her breast and include maternal implications, Agatha's speech about her spiritual breast in Ælfric's *Natale Sancte Agathe*, by contrast, starts slightly differently, declaring, "ne sceamode þe to ceorfanne þœt þœt ðu sylf suce" (Skeat I: 202; "Are you not ashamed to cut off that which you yourself wanted to suck"), an alteration which adds a stronger sexual

[32] Agatha makes an almost identical speech in *AASS* Feb. I, 622 E-F.

component to the legend. The maternal implications are set aside and the torture itself is turned into a form of male sexual aggressiveness towards women and consequently into sexually motivated penetration.[33] This reading is not too far-fetched as the amputation of breasts, as stated earlier, was evidently a sexually driven form of torture. As Gulley notes, the torture itself has an "association of failed sexual corruption with Agatha's breast [which] encourages the audience during the later torture scene to view the cut off breast as a sign of successful sexual penetration, particularly when compar[ing] the torn flesh with the clearly intact flesh" (113-14).[34] At this moment, recalling Miles's argument, the breast then shows its full ambiguity. The heathen destroys the female delight, the body part that has ensured the survival of humanity from the beginning of time. If he cannot have this symbol of female perfection, this "gratifying" object he himself longs to possess, then no one shall have it. For him, the breast's role is suddenly reversed; it has become a "hostile" object onto which he projects all his anxieties and his envy. His "breast-envy" results in his allegorical defloration of the saint. This practice of cutting off breasts is thus, as John Anson suggests, a "euphemism for the pre-execution defloration of virgins practiced to meet the Roman law that forbade the execution of virgins" (26). Yet the defloration remains unsuccessful, as Agatha herself states that this outer destruction will not alter her inner completion. In this reading the mastectomy refers to a strong masculine anxiety to eliminate this life-giving body part. The heathen's effort to obtain the breast can be seen as the "informing moment for Western social arrangements", in which "patriarchal societies are extensions of the infant's devises of splitting and projection" (Miles, *Complex Delight* 135). "The masculinist cultural project is to manage women in such a way that men retain access to the delight, limiting or eliminating the frustration" (135). This elimination of the breast is implemented in the case of Saint Agatha, but only from the outside, as her inner breasts have remained intact. Whereas her "outer breast" (her body) is now destroyed, her "inner breasts" (her soul) can still nourish the "hungry" community and distribute salvation among the believers.

The analysis of the life of Saint Agatha has yielded the following insights into the treatment of breasts within female saints' legends. Torture and *imitatio* are strongly connected, and no clear boundary can be established between the two. In the legend of Saint Agatha the breast undergoes a metamorphosis linked to the transformation of the protagonist herself from the ordinary to the spectacular. Whereas on the outside Agatha's body is altered from a human body to a saintly sublime body – indicated in the three phases the breast has to endure – on the inside Agatha's attitude towards torture and consequential death is also altered. The amputation of her breasts, then, outlines her martyrdom. Concerning the symbolism of "breasts" themselves, two ways of interpreting the narrative have been established. On the one hand, the breast is connected to nourishment and motherhood; on the other, from a psychoanalytical perspective the amputation of the breast is a form of male sexual aggressiveness towards a "nonmale" body part about which the torturer experiences sexual frustration and envy related to the

[33] For further connections between pain and sexual pleasure in relation to Saint Agatha see Sarah Schäfer-Althaus, "Painful Pleasure: Saintly Torture on the Verge of Pornography", *Mirabilia Journal* 18 (2014): pp. 151-59, p. 152, Web, 17 Sept. 2016.

[34] The "intact flesh" is the hymen.

breasts' significance for the survival of humanity. On a meta-level the breast therefore develops, at least in the legend of Saint Agatha, into a place where the battle for power between God and the heathen is exemplified. The mastectomy then becomes an (unsuccessful) attempt to destabilize the Church, which is metaphorically nursed by the Virgin's breast. Nursing is also a focus among legends in which the elimination of the breast results in milk-leaking wounds. The following chapter will move from the detailed analysis of a particular legend to the investigation of an entire group of narratives' concentration on the connection between milk and blood as well as milk-leaking wounds and the breast.

2.2.2 Holy Women and Milk-Leaking Wounds

> Julianus had Christina's breasts cut off, and milk flowed from them instead of blood.
>
> Saint Christina[35]

> All ancient biologists thought that the mother's blood fed the child in the womb and then […] transmuted into breast milk.
>
> Caroline Walker Bynum[36]

Among the female martyrs, a couple of legends are especially notable because they incorporate the topic of bodily fluids. Saint Catherine of Alexandria, for example, is said to have had milk pour out of her throat after being beheaded (de Voragine II: 339).[37] A similar pattern can be found in the legend of Saint Sophie and her three daughters (Faith, Hope and Charity). The *Legenda Aurea* notes about one of them, "Faith was punished, first, by being beaten by thirty-six soldiers, secondly, by having her breasts torn off, and all saw milk flowing from the wounds and blood from the severed breasts" (de Voragine I: 185; "Fides primo a XXXVI militibus caeditur, secundo mamillae praecisae coram cunctis evelluntur, lac de vulneribus, sed de mamillis sanguis profluit" [Graesse 203]). And the gruesome martyrdom of Saint Christina states in relation to breasts, "Julianus had Christina's breasts cut off, and milk flowed from them instead of blood" (de Voragine I: 387; "Tunc Julianus mammillas ejus praecidi mandavit, de quibus lac pro sanguine fluxit" [Graesse 421]). Somehow, then, the frequency of the

[35] Jacobus de Voragine, *The Golden Legend: Readings on the Saints*, 2 vols., ed. and trans. William Granger Ryan (Princeton: Princeton UP, 1995), I: 387; "Tunc Julianus mammillas ejus praecidi mandavit, de quibus lac pro sanguine fluxit" (Graesse 421).

[36] Caroline Walker Bynum, *Fragmentation and Redemption: Essays on Gender and the Human Body in Medieval Literature* (New York: Zone, 1992), p. 100.

[37] "When the saint had been beheaded, milk flowed from her body instead of blood […]" (de Voragine II: 339); "Deinde cum decollata fuisset, de ejus corpore pro sanguine lac emanavit […]" (Graesse 794). For the legend of Saint Catherine of Alexandria see also *Seinte Katerine: Re-Edited from MS Bodley 34 and the Other Manuscripts*, ed. S. R. T. O. d'Ardenne and E. J. Dobson. (London: Oxford UP, 1981), pp. 2-130.

milk-blood metaphor implies that “this motif of milk flowing from wounds is a hagiographical topos” (Harney 241). In this respect the question arises, where and when did this coexistence between milk and blood develop? To what extent is the relationship between these body fluids of specific importance in regard to the historical circumstances in which the saints’ lives were compiled and, more particularly, in regard to the subtraction of breasts?

Throughout history, blood has hardly been regarded and evaluated as what it biologically is: “a gender neutral fluid, which provides life to both genders, men as well as women” (Herrmann, *Sex und Folter* 182). Culturally, blood was connected to a great number of issues. It was believed to form the basis of the social hierarchy, for example, separating not only the clergy from laymen, but also laymen from the aristocracy (Le Goff and Truong 44). Furthermore, as Le Goff and Truong explain, blood played a crucial role in terms of sexuality. In this respect blood had been regarded as taboo since the twelfth century, and sexuality was consequently considered the lowest degree of bodily shame (45). Therefore, in the construction of gender, blood, and especially female blood, was generally thought to be unclean. In particular, menstrual blood or the blood associated with the pains of childbirth, as Schulenburg notes, caused a “fear of pollution” by these natural happenings within the female body (215). Brown notes, “Continence had been actively encouraged for women as well as for men. Less merit was attached to motherhood. The sense of pollution by blood, which had tended to exclude women as a source of menstrual impurity, was not entirely abandoned in Christian circles” (*Body* 146).

Yet even though female blood was regarded as a degrading bodily substance (Herrmann, *Sex und Folter* 183), it was still considered the basis of humanity. Thereby, the closeness between blood and milk dates back to antiquity. Even then, scholars such as Aristotle had made the connection between women’s blood and milk, as it was believed that blood changed into milk after giving birth (Rousselle 30; Peck[38]). In the Middle Ages this thinking was still widespread. According to Bynum, “medieval physiological theory saw all bodily fluids as reducible to blood and saw bleeding basically as purging” (*Fragmentation* 87). In addition,

> All ancient biologists thought that the mother’s blood fed the child in the womb and then, transmuted into breast milk, fed the baby outside the womb as well. Thus, blood was the basic bodily fluid and female blood was the fundamental support of human life. Ancient theory also held that the shedding of blood purged or cleansed those who shed it. [...] Thus medical theory not only associated female bodies with flesh and blood, it also saw bleeding as feeding and as the purging away of excess. (100)

Is the bleeding of milk from an open wound consequently a metaphor for nourishment? Obviously, milk equals blood and is generally used as a stylistic device within female saints’ legends, as in relation to the female body, milk has slightly less negative implications than “impure” female blood. Yet with this observation one merely scratches the surface.

[38] Peck’s translation of Aristotle’s *Generations of Animals* is listed under Aristotle in the bibliography.

Within the theological realms of the early Christian church, blood was of particular significance. In common Christian belief it was blood and sperm that hindered the human being from entering heaven, and consequently a strict separation between the pure blood of Christ and unclean human blood was made (Le Goff and Truong 45, 47). However, in early Christian belief the spilling of blood by martyrs was of particular importance. As Rousselle notes, "Everyone was insistent on the necessity of spilling blood, as it was the price to be paid for the survival of the community and for the salvation of each individual" (128). And clearly most of the blood was spilled in the course of martyrdom. The bloody death of the martyrs was often regarded as a second sort of baptism in which the *imitatio Christi*–related self-sacrifice was believed to result in the forgiveness of postbaptismal sins (Lensing 17; Angenendt, "Sühne" 457-58). The spilled blood of the innocent was said to have the power to heal, and with the *Blutstaufe*[39] direct access to heaven was granted for martyrs (Lensing 17). The blood squirted at martyrical decapitations onto the group of witnesses of the trial often marked the conversion and baptism of those who were stained by it (Sorgo 183). Presupposing that the blood shed by the martyr is valuable for the salvation of each individual and that people actually "bathed" in the substance – after a decapitation, for example, by trying to be blotched with blood – what connection can then be drawn between blood and milk pouring out of the wounds, in particular the breast wounds, of Christina, Faith, Catherine of Alexandria and other holy women? Where is the connection between milk and blood?

First of all, "the bodies of holy women were frequently seen by medieval people as excuding miraculous fluids, substances, or odors" (Bynum, *Holy Feast* 211). The ambiguous interrelation between milk and blood, the perception of holy women among the medieval population, and the ancient and medieval scholarly and religious assumptions about the interconnections between body fluids lead to the following interpretation: the milk-leaking wounds are a reference to nursing (and the breast-milk-leaking wound is thereby of specific significance), to suffering, and to the salvation of the group present at the martyrical spectacle as well as of the individual herself.

Concerning nourishment, the hint at maternity and breastfeeding seems obvious. Similar to the legend of Saint Agatha, Saint Christina and Saint Faith are able to nurse the community, the "infant" believers, through their ideal behaviour even though they are virgins and consequently far away from biological motherhood. Within these scenarios, the loss of blood at birth, which was considered unclean, is substituted with the loss of milk, which in contrast to blood was regarded as pure. Thus metaphorically speaking the milk-leaking breast wound resembles a sort of "breastfeeding", turning the virgin martyr into a symbolic, spiritual mother. As Bernard of Clairvaux remarks, "There is no pretense about a true mother; the breasts she displays are full for the taking [...] pressing the milk".[40] Thus, in female saints' legends, even though the outer breast

[39] The term *Blutstaufe* is a German compound out of *Blut* (blood) and *Taufe* (baptism).

[40] Sermons 9 and 10 in *On the Song of Songs*, trans. Kilian Walsh, vol. 1 of *The Works of Bernard of Clairvaux*, 2 vols. (Kalamazoo, MI: Cistercian, 1976), pp. 57-58, pp. 62-63; qtd. in Caroline Walker Bynum, "'...And Woman His Humanity': Female Imagery in the Religious Writing of the

is destroyed, the "inner breast" is still able to nourish; the milk-leaking breast wounds are still "full for the taking […] pressing the milk". The "inner breast" can hence be regarded as the intact soul or spirit of the saint, her true dedication to Christ, which she is able to share even after her body has been torn apart.

Furthermore, several real-life holy women such as Catherine of Siena and Mechtild of Magdeburg are also said to have claimed a connection between milk and blood. Bynum writes in regard to both saints' *vitae*:

> Mechtild of Magdeburg, for example, not only drew a parallel between blood and milk, she also spoke of blood as superior food and saw her own prayer and suffering for other souls as nursing them with blood. When Catherine of Siena spoke of drinking blood from the breast of mother Jesus, she explicitly glossed blood as suffering – both Jesus' suffering and her own. (*Holy Feast* 271)

In addition, it becomes clear that another common denominator between milk and blood is the aspect of suffering. As previously stated, for the majority of the Christian world the dying and crucified Christ was seen as in some sense female (see chapter 2.1). The iconographic relationship between the wounds of Christ and the female breast of the *Virgo Lactans* are thus related to each other as suffering and nursing, or Christ's blood and women's milk. The milk-wound of the breast is turned into an *imitatio* of Christ's blood-wounds located (iconographically) in the same position. This becomes obvious in regard to Catherine of Siena, as she explicitly uses "the metaphor of the nursing mother to describe [her] own suffering for others, sometimes clearly implying that [her] spilling of blood-milk was *imitatio* of Christ's nurturing and inebriating wounds-breasts" (Bynum, *Holy Feast* 272-73). As bleeding was commonly believed to cleanse the body and compensate for earlier sins (Bynum, *Fragmentation* 87), stigmatic wounds that exude a different liquid than biologically expected also represent a cleansing of the body, which, while purging the soon-to-be-left bodily carcass of the saint, nourishes the community and allows for its salvation. Bynum asserts that in women saints' lives this process is a reference to the "literal becoming of the crucified body" (*Holy Feast* 273) in which "woman's wounds-breasts recapitulated the wounds-breasts of Christ" (274). Consequently, she adds, "one suspects that stigmata appeared most frequently on women's bodies because stigmata […] were not merely wounds but also breasts" (273).

Thus, the symbolic attachment of the breast and its secretions works in a circular fashion. The biological breast is in the course of action associated with the theological subject, then glides into a grey zone in which symbolism and biological functions or associations are blurred, overlap or even change places before being linked to Christ's suffering. In the next step, then, the breast is transformed into a "literal becoming of the crucified body" (Bynum, *Holy Feast* 273) and indicates Christ's ability to "feed" his followers through his suffering and thus reconnecting it to the biological.

Before coming to a conclusion on this phenomenon, another radical interpretative approach should be taken into consideration. Blood, as a basic body fluid, is responsible

Later Middle Ages", *Fragmentation and Redemption: Essays on Gender and the Human Body in Medieval Religion* (New York: Zone, 1991), p. 160.

not only for the production of milk in a woman's body, but also for the creation of male sperm. Both Aristotle and Galen proposed a connection between blood and sperm in general (Rousselle 30, 123). Aristotle also claimed that a correlation between women's blood and male sperm existed, as "a woman is, as it were, an infertile male" (Peck 103) and "the female is as it were a castrated male; the menses are a type of impure sperm" (qtd. in Rousselle 30; see also Peck). If, in ancient and medieval conviction, blood turns into milk and sperm is also made out of blood, is milk then related or even equal to sperm? And if this is the case, are milk-leaking wounds, metaphorically speaking, also sperm-leaking wounds and consequently similar to an ejaculation? The thought may seem absurd at first; however, Sorgo writes of the death trials of martyrs, "Das Heldentum wird vergeistigt, statt Samen spritzt, ähnlich einer Ejakulation, das Blut aus den Hälsen der Enthaupteten"[41] (67). The idea that sperm is made out of blood, and the claim of the Church Fathers that the blood of the deceased (and here one can add the milk of the deceased as well) is the "semen of Christianity", supports the equation of blood and milk-spilling wounds with ejaculation (Sorgo 183; Laqueur 39-68). Even in iconography, as Bynum remarks, there are pictures "in which the artist calls attention both to Christ's penis and to his mother's breast" and others "in which the blood flows from Christ's own breast into his crotch" (*Fragmentation* 84). To speak allegorically, then, the milk-wounds are also a metaphor for "sowing the seed", as the Parable of the Sower suggests, for a connection between the death of the individual and the salvation and conversion of the group – an image recalling once more the death of Christ on the cross. The interchangeability within female saints' lives of blood, milk and sperm is of course a stylistic device that the authors and compilers employed to make these virginal women even more exceptional than they are in the first place.

Consequently, within female saints' legends, milk-leaking wounds yield the following conclusions: the mixture and interchangeable usage of blood, milk and sperm is a result of the ancient and medieval assumptions about body fluids and their relationships with each other. If milk is employed instead of blood, a connection can be established with nourishment and breastfeeding, and consequently, with the spreading of Christian belief and the ideal yet martyrical behaviour of the saints. In addition, the breast-wounds are set side by side with the wound of the crucified Christ, who in contrast to the female martyrs redeems the unfaithful through the spilling of his blood. On the whole, no matter from which point of view one tackles this phenomenon, the message is "sowing the seed", spreading the word of God, working on the salvation of the group and the individual. The third reading of the milk-leaking wounds, connecting them with male semen, supports this. The body of the saint is thus employed to establish a connecting path between God and the human through the usage of body fluids (Le Goff and Truong 80).

[41] Trans.: "Heroism is spiritualized; similar to an ejaculation, instead of semen, blood squirts out of the throats of the decapitated".

2.3 Denying Nature: Transvestite Saints and the Concealment of Womanhood

> As long as woman is for birth and children, she is different from men as body is from soul. But if she wishes to serve Christ more than the world, she will cease to be a woman and shall be called man.
>
> Jerome[42]

> Others change their garb and assume the mien of men, being ashamed of what they were born to be – women.
>
> Jerome[43]

The breast so far has been the locus of torture, of a total, violent eradication of femininity from saints' bodies. In spite of torture being the prevalent method employed within female saints' legends to deal with the female breast, another set of narratives exists in which the concealment of womanhood is undertaken voluntarily by the saint herself. Within the *vitae* of the transvestite saints (the legend of Saint Eugenia will be used as an example here) the breast is metaphorically "cut off" as it is hidden behind clothes, which marks a first step in the transformational process of "becoming male"[44] – an idea of ancient and medieval scholars to be investigated in this chapter. By cross-dressing, as the analysis will show, the saint is able to access male monastic communities and to live an ideal outside the social gender hierarchy. However, the saint's fair, emasculated appearance, her existence between both genders, results in homoerotic temptations until the only way to escape death is the exposure of the breast in public.

The idea of "becoming male" derives predominantly from the writings of the Church Fathers. Comparable to his contemporaries as well as to other ancient and medieval scholars, the Church Father Jerome (ca. 347-420) thought it of the utmost significance to deal with the female sex, to come to terms with a form of human being which seemed, in the eyes of many, in particular in the eyes of male ascetic writers, so full of physical and spiritual flaws and imperfections. In spite of the large time span between Jerome's writings and the historical end of the medieval time period, women still were not included in the European ideas of social structure (Duby 89, 95, 131-33, 145, 209). Nevertheless, scholars asked themselves what a woman was expected to be and was allowed to do if she were not included in the social order. Several came to the conclusion that the female sex could adopt masculine traits if she were willing to deny her femininity and renounce any kind of sexual activity – a notion prevailing at least

[42] Quoted in Joyce E. Salisbury, *Church Fathers, Independent Virgins* (London: Verso, 1991), p. 26.

[43] Jerome, "Letter XXII: To Eustochium", *Nicene and Post-Nicene Fathers*, 2nd ser., vol. VI, ed. Philip Schaff and Henry Wace (Edinburgh: T&T Clark; Grand Rapids: Eerdmans, 1892), *Christian Classics Ethereal Library*, Calvin College, Web, 17 Sept. 2016.

[44] The second step in the denial of femininity is achieved by receiving the holy tonsure, which marks the ultimate transformation of the saint in "becoming male". For the analyses of hairstyles in general consult chapter 3; for the significance of the haircut see chapter 3.3.

until the twelfth century, as Jonathan Walker notes (83). Whereas at first sight it seems that male scholars supported cross-dressing, the writings of Jerome denote a contrasting picture. According to Jerome in his letter to the virgin Eustochium, a woman cross-dresses and hides her gender in masculine garb only because women are simply ashamed of their own gender (Letter XXII). The possibility that women existed who wanted sexual freedom, who wanted to pursue an education of some sort and consequently saw cross-dressing as the only possibility to escape their predetermined social fate, is apparently not thought of. The following chapter will investigate the controversy surrounding the idea of "becoming male" and show how the problem is depicted in the legends of transvestite saints. In this respect it will deal with the attempt to "queer the Church", provide an explanation for the importance and consequences of transvestite sainthood and analyse the usage of the denied breast within the legend of Saint Eugenia.

2.3.1 Queering the Church

> The ideal scenario – from the point of view of the regulators – was one in which a person's social station, social role, gender and other indicators of identity in the world could be read, without ambiguity or uncertainty.
>
> Marjorie Garber[45]

Even though their breasts are removed, the virgin martyrs, such as Agatha, Christina, Faith and others, can still undoubtedly be identified as female; and even though they are mastectomized, phenomena such as the milk-leaking wounds lead to an association with femininity and womanhood. With the so-called *transvestite saints*, only the viewer/reader, the protagonist herself, and some of her close companions are aware of her true femininity. A popular representative of the medieval transvestite saints, whose legend has been turned into numerous books and even movies and who has perhaps "caused the greatest anguish to Catholic historians" (Bullough and Brundage, *Sexual Practices* 50), is Pope Joan, who apparently ruled as pope under the name John Anglicus and whose gender-crossing was detected only upon her giving birth during a procession.[46] Other saints belonging to the group, such as Saint Eugenia and Saint

[45] Marjorie Garber, *Vested Interests: Cross-Dressing and Cultural Anxiety* (New York: Routledge, 1997), p. 26.

[46] There are uncountable works on Pope Joan, which can generally be placed in three categories: pro-Joan, anti-Joan and scholarly writings. A summary of her legend can be found in *The New Catholic Encyclopaedia*, 15 vols. (New York: McGraw-Hill, 1967). Pro-Joan writings include Alexander Cooke, *Pope Joan* (London: Blunt and Baring, 1610), and Clement Wood, *The Woman Who Was Pope* (New York: Faro, 1931). A useful recent and more critical overview of the perception and reception of this most prominent Christian myth is Alain Boureau's *The Myth of Pope Joan*, trans. Lydia G. Cochrane (Chicago: U of Chicago P, 2001).

Euphrosyne, challenge the socially constructed yet accepted reality of what the feminine gender is expected to be by wearing masculine or unisex attire and by removing their long hair. Comparable to the virgin martyrs, whose breasts are identified as a place for executing power, the bodies of the cross-dressing saints, with their unfixed gender identity, are also used as a contested site – this time, however, in order to come to terms with the conflicting ideas of "becoming male" or "staying female". In this respect, the disguise of the breast plays a crucial role. Recalling Marjorie Garber, their identity cannot be "read" without doubt or insecurity, which leads to recurring accusations of rape and homoerotic temptations in their holy biographies.

Many of the ambiguously gendered and sexed saints analysed in this study are generally dismissed as hagiographic fiction, and again, it is apparently not quite clear whether these women are mythical or semimythical. Yet as Terence Weldon notes in his blog *Queering the Church*,[47] "Whatever the full historic truth, it seems [...] these are useful stories to hold on to as reminders of the important place of the transgendered, and differently gendered, in our midst"[48] – and the aspect of the gender hybridity or gender fluidity of saints has yet to be theorized in the course of this study (see chapter 5). As queer studies is still a relatively new field of research, Weldon's statement reflects the ongoing interest in transvestite historical figures – which are of course even more fascinating within a conservative, frequently homophobic environment such as the Catholic Church. However, is this fascination a modern reaction to these colourful "historical" figures? How would a person of the Middle Ages have reacted upon the discovery of a cross-dresser amongst his or her midst? Before analysing the problematic cross-dressing of Saint Eugenia, this chapter will have to show what the controversies about cross-dressing and the issue of "becoming male" actually are. Furthermore, it has to be clarified whether there is a difference between cross-dressing and transvestism. Where does the terminology come from and when was it introduced? What did medieval society think about cross-dressing in general and female cross-dressing in particular?

From an etymological perspective the terms *cross-dressing* and *transvestism* can be used interchangeably. The term *transvestism* obviously has a Latin origin. It is a compound of *trans* (about, beyond) and *vestire* (clothed) and the Latin is commonly translated as cross-dressing. The German sexologist Magnus Hirschfeld coined the term *transvestism* in his study *Die Transvestiten* (1910), a study uncovering the different attitudes towards gender among androgynes and transvestites[49] (Hirschfeld; Garber 131-

[47] The title of this chapter is owed to Terence Weldon's quite informative blog. Weldon claims that his mission is to open up strict Catholic Church doctrines towards a "reality-based theology". Among other subjects, he also investigates and depicts homosexuality and cross-dressing within Church history and names a large number of gay, lesbian and transvestite figures related to the Church or the Bible, such as Popes Leo X and Sixtus IV, who were accused of having male lovers, or the homoerotic implications in the biblical and quite emotional relationship between Ruth and Naomi (Old Testament, Book of Ruth).

[48] Terence Weldon, "Nov 9th: Matrona/Babylas of Perge", *Queering the Church*, 9 Nov. 2010, Web, 12 Sept. 2016.

[49] Hirschfeld found out that androgynes were concerned primarily with physical gender attributes (beard, breasts, genitals), whereas transvestites occupied themselves more frequently with psychological gender signifiers, such as names or dress codes.

32). Even though the actual translation of cross-dressing and transvestism is identical, the cultural and social connotations indicate minor differences between the two terms. Bullough and Bullough convincingly define cross-dressing in the following words:

> Cross-dressing is a simple term for a complex set of phenomena. It ranges from simply wearing one or two items of clothing to a full-scale burlesque, from a comic impersonation to a serious attempt to pass as the opposite gender, from an occasional desire to experiment with gender identity to attempting to live most of one's life as a member of the opposite sex. (vii)

Thus, cross-dressing focuses exclusively on the exchange of gender-related clothing. To exemplify this, wearing a skirt is traditionally associated with femininity, pants with masculinity. Since the female liberation of the 1960s, almost every woman has become a cross-dresser in this sense. On the other hand, a skirt-wearing man could be considered a cross-dresser in most contexts, but what about the Scottish kilt, which is worn exclusively by men? In both cases, however, cross-dressers usually do not deny their biological identity and still regard themselves as male or female. In contrast to cross-dressing, any degree of "adopting masculine identity" can, according to Susan Crane, be regarded as female transvestism (73). Therefore, female saints who not only wear men's clothing but also cut their hair and behave like men are more than just simple cross-dressers and should therefore be considered transvestites. Whereas nowadays, the occurrence of medieval holy transvestites renews interest in hagiographical writing, "most medieval writers and readers of hagiography", as Walker reminds us,

> show[ed] little interest in parenthesising or accounting for these cross-dressed saints, suggesting either that transvestites posed little threat to conventional notions of bodily and social gender or that the medium in which transvestite saints were embodied and socially distributed possessed an interpretive framework that deflected any gender transgression [...]. (75)

Hence, even though transvestism "represents a symbolic incursion into territory that crosses gender boundaries" (Bullough and Bullough viii), it was not seen as a sign of homosexuality in the Middle Ages, no matter in which direction (male to female or female to male), and it was regarded as relatively harmless until the eighteenth century, when "it became associated with effeminate homosexuality" (Bullough and Bullough x). Thus it has to be kept in mind that medieval society refused to link transvestism primarily to sexuality, as happens today, but considered it to be a more or less legitimate way to escape one's gender – at least for women. However, this "legitimacy" was problematic in narratives, especially in pious narratives, which were meant for instruction and used as educational tools. Consequently, the numerous transvestite saints' legends were a subject of interest within scholarly debates. Frequent discussions revolved around them, which "took as the main investigative concern the problem [of] how to explain the occurrence [of transvestism] in a pious biography [...] explicitly forbidden by Scripture" (Walker 76). In scripture, the Old Testament strictly prohibits wearing the clothes of the opposite sex. It states that "a woman shall not be clothed with man's apparel, neither shall a man use woman's apparel: for he that doeth these things is abominable before God" (Deuteronomy 22:5)[50] – a prohibition which was highly influential on Christian attitudes (Bullough, "Cross Dressing" 224-25). Do women who disguise their sex with the intention of entering a monastic community to pursue a religious education seriously offend God and his creation? If this is the generally prevailing assumption, why did scholars such as Jerome argue that women should become "manlier"? Is there a possibility of "becoming manly" without dressing in men's clothes?

Many Church Fathers as well as ancient philosophers claimed repeatedly that the only way for a woman to overcome her inferior status and to improve was by "becoming male". The ancient Jewish philosopher Philo (20 BC-50 AD), for example, stated that "progress is indeed nothing else than the giving up of the female gender by changing into the male, since the female gender is material, passive, corporeal and sense-perceptible, while the male is active, rational, incorporeal and more akin to mind and thought"[51] (qtd. in Baer 46). A similar argument persisted and is introduced by Saint Ambrose a few hundred years later (ca. 337-397):

> She who does not believe is a woman and should be designated by the name of her sex, […] [for] she who believes progresses to perfect manhood […]. She then dispenses with the name of her sex, the seductiveness of youth, the garrulousness of old age.[52] (Qtd. in and trans. Bullough, "Cross Dressing" 227; see also Walker 83)

What both scholars agree on is that the crossing of gender boundaries is a form of progress for a woman and thus a sign of evolution. As Bullough states, "The female who wore male clothing or who somehow effectively impersonated a man was not only gaining status but making herself more rational" ("Cross Dressing" 227). As a matter of fact, "Women were frequently described as manly, if they showed some virtue greater than expected of them: courage, equanimity, or sexual modesty" (Kuefler, *Manly* 30) – thus, the idea of "becoming male" goes way beyond the act of cross-dressing. To some extent, the ancient scholars agreed that "virgin women were men", as according to Jerome "the word *virgo* (virgin) was derived from *vir* (man)" (*Manly* 231).[53] By the twelfth century the all-male monasteries were "overflowing with women who wanted to

[50] "non induetur mulier veste virili nec vir utetur veste feminea abominabilis enim apud Deum est qui facit haec".

[51] Philo, "Quæstiones on Exodus I: 8", *Philo's Use of the Categories of Male and Female*, Richard A. Baer (Leiden: Brill, 1970), p. 46. See also Bullough, "Cross Dressing", p. 227.

[52] Ambrose, *Expositionis in Evangelium secundum Lucum libri X*, *Patrologiae Cursus Completus: Series Latina*, ed. Jacques-Paul Migne (Paris: Garnieri Fratres, 1887). "Quae non credit, mulier est, et adhuc corporei sexus appellatione signatur; nam quae credit, occurrit in virum perfectum, in mensuram aetatis plenitudinis Christi, carens jam nomine saeculi, corporis sexu, lubrico juventutis, multiloquio senectutis" (*PL* 15: 1844).

[53] See also Jerome, Epistula 49: 2, in Jerome, *Epistulae*, 8 vols., ed. and trans. Jerôme Labout (Paris: Belles Lettres, 1949-63) and "Letter XLVIII [XLIX]: To Pammachius", *Nicene and Post-Nicene Fathers*, 2nd ser., vol. VI, ed. Philipp Schaff and Henry Wace (Edinburgh: T&T Clark; Grand Rapids: Eerdmans, 1892), *Christian Classics Ethereal Library*, Calvin College, Web, 17 Sept. 2016.

join the orders" (Lowerre 61-62), a development which lasted well into the postmedieval era (Bullough, "Cross Dressing" 232). Real-life women were indirectly encouraged by the transvestite saint narratives to cross-dress, since society assumed that they wanted to become more like the male population and, as Bullough and Bullough state, were "striving to better themselves" (46). "A female who might try to pass as a man was not considered abnormal. That a female might desire to be a male, in fact, seemed to be a healthy desire, a 'normal' longing" (67). To pass as male and to enter the all-male monastic communities, a woman thus had to change her garb and to hide everything that represented her femininity – breasts and hair. "Nonetheless", as Kuefler reminds us, "the orthodox fathers also clarified that women became men only in a metaphorical sense and that Roman women who were Christian should not try to imitate the holy transvestites and attempt to pass as actual men" (*Manly* 232). Transvestite saints' legends therefore posed a threat to existing social gender normativity because "they gave sanction to cross dressing for women" – not for men – in real life (Bullough, "Cross Dressing" 229), providing women with (fictional) female idols who were courageous enough to escape the expected gender norms of the time by adopting masculine attire – even if they were in most cases able to maintain their new (masculine) social role with all of its advantages and responsibilities for only a short period of time (232). According to Donovan, approximately twenty-three stories of female transvestite saints circulated on the European continent before 1050 (67). Cross-dressing and transvestism are recurring themes in iconic legends of female saints, even though they are controversial and problematic as the acceptability of the act was liminal. Even if "the transvestite female saints of the Middle Ages were legion as well as legend, despite the Deuteronomic prohibition" (Garber 213), the idea to "become male" was only theoretically acceptable and should under no circumstances have been turned into practice. If this is the case, how do religious narratives deal with the prohibited act of transvestism, and what role does the breast play in this respect?

2.3.2 Saint Eugenia: Denying and Exposing

> Rightly do you call yourself a man, because you act like a man though you are a woman.
>
> Saint Protus and Hyacinthus[54]

The legend of Saint Eugenia is "a tale of a woman, who in order to pursue a better education, dressed as a monk and was accused of a crime she could not commit" (A. Butler IV: 612). In the course of action she not only denies her femininity by hiding her breasts in male attire, she also has to expose her breasts to her own family later on to avoid death. The situation presented in the narrative is by far less brutal than that of

[54] Jacobus de Voragine, *The Golden Legend: Readings on the Saints*, 2 vols., ed. and trans. William Granger Ryan (Princeton: Princeton UP, 1995), II: 165; "recte vir diceris, quia, cum sis femina, viriliter agis" (Graesse 603).

Saint Christina or Saint Agatha, yet it adds a new twist to the dominating question of whether the female breast is a sign of female weakness after all.

The historical authenticity of Eugenia, like that of many transvestite saints, remains uncertain. The *Legenda Aurea* claims that Eugenia suffered under the emperors Valerian and Gallus around 256 AD and a saint with the same name was apparently martyred in the third century in Rome and buried in the cemetery of Apronian on the Via Latina (de Voragine II: 167; A. Butler IV: 612). By the late fifth century, her cult was already widespread in Western Europe and the Near East, and not only is her legend mentioned in early martyrologies such as Bede's *Martyrologium*,[55] comparable to Saint Agatha, but she is also the only transvestite saint included at length in Ælfric's *Lives of Saints*.[56] The commonly taught legend is based on the Latin translation[57] of a Greek text[58] deriving from the fifth century. By 1100, approximately twenty-five manuscripts had been copied into Latin, which included the legend of Saint Eugenia, who is today considered one of the most popular transvestite saints (Donovan 67-68). In the *Legenda Aurea*, Saint Eugenia does not have a separate entry but appears in the legend of her two male confidants, Saint Protus and Saint Hyacinthus/Jacinctus, who were the personal eunuch slaves to Eugenia as well as her companions in the study of philosophy (de Voragine II: 165-67; Graesse 602-05).

The *Legenda Aurea* states that when Eugenia, daughter of the pagan Roman prefect Philippus, was fifteen years old, the son of the consul proposed to her, which she vehemently refused. At the same time or as a result – this is not made clear – Eugenia, already well educated in Greek philosophy and Latin, obtained the teachings of Saint Paul and "gradually became Christian at heart" (de Voragine II: 165; "coepit animo fieri christiana" [Graesse 602]). She secretly converts to Christianity – a problematic situation as her father had previously expelled all Christians to the outskirts of Alexandria. Frightened about her father's reaction and eager to continue her education, Eugenia resolves that the only way out was to leave her family, and hence she asks her two companions to cut off her hair and disguise her womanhood with the help of men's clothing ("hyre fæx forcurfon on wæpmonna wysan and mid wædum gehiwodon swylce heo cniht wære", *Natale Sancte Eugenie*, Skeat I: 28).[59] This deliberate choice to negate

[55] See *SS. Proti et Hyacinthi: qui errant eunuchi S. Eugeniæ*, in *The Complete Works of Venerable Bede in the Original Latin*, ed. J. A. Giles, vol. IV (London: Whitaker, 1843), p. 122; see also Aldhelm's *Carmen de Virginitate*, *Aldhelm: The Poetic Works*, trans. James L. Rosier and Michael Lapdige (Cambridge: Brewer, 1985).

[56] For Ælfric see *Natale Sancte Eugenie*, Ælfric's *Lives of Saints*, ed. Walter W. Skeat, Early English Text Society Original Series (London: Oxford UP, 1881-1900), I: 25-50. According to Donovan, the legend of Saint Eugenia and Saint Euphrosyne are the only surviving legends of transvestite saints in the Old English tradition (67).

[57] *Patrologiae Cursus Completus: Series Latina*, ed. Jacques-Paul Migne (Paris: Garnieri Fratres, 1844-91), *PL* 21: 1105-22; *Bibliotheca Hagiographica Latina,* 3 vols. 1889-1901 (Brussels: Société des Bollandistes, 1949), p. 2666.

[58] *Bibliotheca Hagiographica Graeca*, ed. François Halkin (Brussels: Société des Bollandistes, 1957), pp. 607-08.

[59] In the *Legenda Aurea* the shortening of her hair is not explicitly mentioned: "Eugenia put on men's clothing" (de Voragine II: 165); "assumto habitu viri" (Graesse 603). For an in-depth discussion of the aspect of hair see chapter 3.

her femininity, to hide her breasts and to generally adopt and prefer a masculine identity to a feminine one, is obviously linked to the marriage proposal. The gender negation results from Eugenia's female "awakening" at the moment of her personal crisis between childhood, sexual maturity and adulthood, indicated by the marriage proposal and her resultant – so it seems – conversion (Garber 214; Elliot 95). As Alison Goddard Elliot comments, this motif of a "secret flight" to escape marriage and protect one's bodily purity is quite common in women's hagiography and particularly in transvestite saints' legends (92):

> A wedding represents not just the union of a man and a woman, it is in many ways the best symbol of man's civilized state, for man alone, in opposition to the beasts, undergoes (or is supposed to undergo) the ritual sanction of the marriage ceremony before coupling sexually to produce legitimate offspring. It is the ultimate *rite de passage* between childhood and adulthood; the married individual is considered to be fully assimilated into the society and, it is assumed, is thereby pledged to perpetuate its values as well as the race. (95)

If Eugenia consents to the marriage proposal, she would have to give up her studies, in which she has acquired knowledge about the significance of virginity for the Christian community. The proposal marks the starting point of a socially coerced assimilation process, which Eugenia is not willing to undergo.

According to Victor Turner, a *rite de passage* is a ritualized change in status or identity and involves a negation of existing features towards an affirmation of another order and another hierarchy (157-58, 196).[60] The denial of Eugenia's femininity through cross-dressing, among other aspects,[61] can be considered her *rite de passage*, marking her transition into a new status, subverting prevailing gender binaries. At the moment in which Eugenia refuses her biological sex, her soul is awakened and she becomes an "active" person. Comparable to Saint Agatha, as Frantzen notes, "Were Eugenia to follow her father's wishes, she would retain her status as a passive female" (87). With her new masculine disguise and her resulting new social role, she successfully enters the monastery and receives the monastic habit from Bishop Helenus. According to the *Legenda Aurea* and to Ælfric's *Natale Sancte Eugenie*, Helenus claims that he was aware already of her womanhood through his belief (de Voragine II: 165; Skeat I: 28). "Rightly do you call yourself a man, because you act like a man though you are a woman", Helenus exclaims (de Voragine II: 165; "recte vir diceris, quia, cum sis femina, viriliter agis" [Graesse 603]). Ælfric's version adds that Helenus even took Eugenia aside and told her, "hwæt heo man ne wǽs and hwylcere mægþe and þœt heo þurh mægð hád mycclum gelicode þam heofon-lican cyninge þe heo gecoren hæfde" (Skeat I: 28, 30; "that she was not truly a man, but was a maiden, whose virginity greatly pleased the Heavenly King she had chosen" [Donovan 70]). Helenus's statements thus support not only the teachings of Philo, Jerome, Ambrose and others that a woman has to become male in order to act rationally and deliberately, but also

[60] See also Alison Goddard Elliot, *Roads to Paradise: Reading the Lives of Early Saints* (Hanover, NH: UP of New England, 1987), p. 170.
[61] See chapter 3.

praise the high and pleasing status of virginity among Christianity, therefore also supporting Eugenia in her decision.

Coming back to Elliot's statement once more, the question arises of whether her argument does not contradict the teachings of the ancient scholars. Of course not all women were able to maintain their virginity; otherwise the human race would have been drastically reduced in Christian societies. But if marriage was considered to be *the* assimilation process for a woman (and a man) in order to be an accepted member of society, what does that mean for the female transvestite saint? What processes of assimilation does Eugenia have to go through? First of all, she negates her true sex and somehow blends awkwardly into the opposite one. In addition, even though the saint withdraws from public life and her expected role in it, she nevertheless enters a different kind of society where she has to assimilate again to avoid detection. Arguably, she moves from an open space to an enclosed space, to a community within a community with different rules and a different social order, values and guidelines. Access to this community is possible only with this *rite de passage*, which started with her deliberate hiding of her breasts (femininity).

In the beginning, the careful negation of her true sex has only positive results for Eugenia, who is called Eugene/Eugenius soon after she has entered the monastery (de Voragine II: 166; Graesse 603). She can protect her virginity and consequently escapes the social reality for a medieval woman, namely marriage, defloration and the resulting childbearing. In addition, she can continue her education with the Holy Scripture and is of such piety, devoutness and intelligence that within the monastery she is chosen to be an abbot. At this point of no return, as one might say, Eugenia, who never states that she is unwilling to stay in her feminine gender and whose true identity was even revealed to the bishop right from the start, has to remain in her masculine disguise (de Voragine II: 166; Skeat I: 32-33).

The motif of disguise is common in women's hagiography, particularly in the stories of women who, clothed as men, flee from home. Elliot states this has mostly practical reasons, as it "made pursuit more difficult and also protected the heroine from unwelcome sexual advances. In some cases the woman abandons the disguise after she reached safety, but others continue as men until their deaths" (119). Eugenia, then, seems to be the prototype, the perfect example of a woman who combines the lectures of the philosophers and the Church Fathers. Not only has she "ceased to be a woman" (Jerome), she has also accepted the idea that a woman has to give up her sex to achieve "perfect manhood" and progress to the perfect gender role (Philo, Ambrose). As a man she can act according to her belief, can be educated further in the Scripture and can protect the purity of her body. As Frantzen asserts, "Being a woman is not enough: a man's appearance is essential to her mission" (73). In addition, "The woman cannot be too manly" (73). Due to her extraordinary religious steadfastness, Eugenia has achieved the status of a leader within the monastery – a fact which, in the Old English tradition, the maiden grew "mycclum hoh-ful hú heo æfre wæras wissian sceolde" (*Natale Sancte Eugenie*, Skeat I: 32; "extremely anxious about, how she was ever to direct men").[62] A woman ruling over men is an issue that has to be dealt with by the reestablishment of the gender hierarchy.

[62] Eugenia's anxieties are omitted in the *Legenda Aurea*, in which only the election of Eugenia as abbot is mentioned (de Voragine II: 166).

Assuming male roles is different from actually performing them, and even though female cross-dressing was unofficially accepted, the coin always has two sides. "Neither the trouser role nor the cross-dressed saint is allowed to approach the status of a fully functioning, fully sexualized male – that is, a man with a wife, mistress, lover or children", Frantzen reminds us (73), and "becoming male" was, as mentioned earlier, meant only metaphorically. Eugenia, who in her new role fulfils community service within the city of Alexandria, is believed to be a "young man [...] elegantly youthful and personally attractive" (de Voragine II: 166; "hominem esse [...] elegantiam juventutis et pulchritudinem corporis" [Graesse 603]) by Melantia, a widow and noblewoman, who then tries unsuccessfully to seduce her – a disastrous encounter for Eugenia's later life (de Voragine II: 166; Skeat I: 32). The atmosphere of the so far positive and encouraging narrative is subverted at this point by the introduction of a sexual undertone, indicating homoerotic temptations. Despite the fact that Eugenia must presumably have been quite an unmanly figure, the widow woos the young woman. Eugenia, with her fair appearance, was probably mistaken either for a young, prepubescent monk or for a eunuch, a common figure among the clergy. For many married women in particular, sexual intercourse with eunuchs was desired, as it had no consequences because of the eunuch's castration. Although Eugenia vehemently refuses, the widow, feeling hurt, accuses the disguised monk of raping her.

The accusation of rape marks another *rite de passage* within Eugenia's legend, as it results in the end of her disguise. Eugenia is indirectly punished for the denial of her feminine identity. She is imprisoned and has to defend herself in front of her father, who as emperor acts as the judge, and her two brothers. At the trial Eugenia, in order to escape death, can no longer hide her femininity and thus "opened her robe from top to the waist, and was seen to be a woman" (de Voragine II: 167; "tunicam a capite usque deorsum sive usque ad cingulum scidit et femina apparuit" [Graesse 604]). Walker's claim that "the process of cross-dressing and revelation, then, is a structural topos by which a saintly woman first achieves a higher spiritual existence under the guise of maleness, and finally receives recognition for her sanctity once the disguise has been removed" (102) is questionable here, as Eugenia does not receive any appreciation for her male disguise. "Religious communities are segregated by sex", Frantzen reminds us, and "once she is no longer cross-dressed, Eugenia obviously loses her right to preach to males, who are better proselytized to other men" (84). Without her disguise and back in her feminine identity, and even though she is able to convert her entire family through her act, she is vulnerable to another pagan's attack on her virginity at a later point in the narrative, finally leading to her assassination as a virgin martyr.

Even more, the revelation of her breasts to her father and her brothers as the only way out seems awkward, in particular because her father seems to identify her only because of her naked breasts and not because of her facial expressions or gestures, which would be more understandable. However, the situation does recall Margaret Miles's statement in chapter 2.1: "Women [...] did not own the breast", but rather fathers and husbands who "dispensed the breast and its provisions" (*Complex Delight* 3). The recognition of their daughter and sister through the exposure of her breasts is then obvious – the breasts as an object belonged to the patriarchal divisions of the family.

Because Eugenia's life ends tragically, the question remains of whether the legend of Saint Eugenia can be evaluated positively or negatively. Is her life, even though lived piously and devotedly, a subject of *imitatio* for other women? Is the negative turning point in her story a result of scholarly attempts to explain the prohibited act of cross-dressing and to prevent other women from this imitation? Evidently, the metaphorical "cutting off" of the breasts changes her life tremendously. One can agree that at first sight it does make her life easier, but she constantly has to fear the discovery of her true sex until she has reached the point of no return, when she is so completely immersed in her new masculine community that the revelation of her true identity is no longer possible. Her continuing disguise is thus problematic for several groups: first for the common people and the social hierarchy of man above woman, and for the Church and its teachings about "becoming male" mentally, but never "physically". In addition, her disguise is against the prohibition of cross-dressing in Deuteronomy. Finally, the sex change is challenging for the compiler and translator of her story, who has to take all of these previously mentioned aspects into consideration, yet still wants a fascinating, publishable tale. The addition of a twist is consequently needed for the rehabilitation of the story and general satisfaction among the readership. Eugenia's disguise draws her into a vicious circle of outrageous circumstances, at the end of which she has to restore her natural body and lift the veil of gender indistinctness to escape damage.

Even though the story of Eugenia does not end on a positive note, cross-dressing, as well as the revelation of her breasts, does have a positive undertone. Her eunuch-like disguise as a monk allows her to live a virtuous, chaste life in Christianity and to be educated, and thereby she is able to fulfil the idea of Jerome and other ancient scholars that a woman can transcend her femininity and "become manly" – rational and wise. Even though the inclusion of Melantia, the woman leading to Eugenia's downfall, is of course tragic for the protagonist, her addition to the story serves a significant didactic and comparative function, as she embodies everything a "common woman" was expected to be: she is lewd, seductive, sexually driven, selfish and body-centred. Eugenia, on the other hand, is described as selfless, mind-centred, noble and pure – characteristics attributed most prominently to men. In addition, with the revelation of her breasts, the only visible and hardly changeable fact of her womanhood, her innocence in regard to the accusations of rape as well as her sexual bodily purity are maintained.

Overall, Eugenia's life exemplifies perfectly that medieval society was not much concerned with biological female characteristics. Instead, gender is "an achieved status [...] based on tasks performed" (Bullough and Bullough 5), and with her tasks performed, Eugenia was highly regarded within her community. Yet the breast remained the "crucial and concealed marker of her womanly identity" (Frantzen 77) and her weak point.

2.4 Concluding Remarks

I am a wall and my breasts like towers.
Jerome[63]

In this first analytical chapter, the question was raised of whether a woman's breast is a sign of her weak sex within a patriarchally dominated community, an assumption which accompanies reading the legends of female saints who are battered and tortured and whose breasts are violently removed. A first glance at the legends of cross-dressing saints, who carefully hide their most visible signs of femininity to escape socially imposed gender norms, does not alter the assumption. Even though these saints face lesser tortures, their disguise grants them access to a complex new system in which their cross-dressing usually ends drastically in order to restore social and clerical attitudes about femininity.

In the words of Miles, the breast is truly a "complex delight" to be analysed, a body part with numerous physical, ideological, theological, symbolical and of course gendered facets which make it difficult to answer the question straightforwardly. A first look at the representation and function of the breast in everyday life and in theology and iconography shows that within the biological and even cultural understanding, the breast is not weak at all. Rather it is a significant body part for the survival of humanity, thought to be important enough to be transferred into the realms of theology and to be used as a strong and often powerful symbol for the early Christian communities.

Within hagiographical narratives, in which the breast is treated in misogynistic, painful and cruel ways, in which women have to hide their femininity to opt out of social structures, a detailed look implies that a positive or negative answer depends on each *vita*. Generally, what can be agreed on is that the breast in all legends experiences a metamorphosis of meaning linked to the saint's inner change in attitude towards her martyrdom. The breast changes throughout the story symbolically and physically and significantly outlines hagiographies such as the martyrdom of Saint Agatha.

Of the three primary legends analysed within this chapter, only the legend of Saint Eugenia slightly indicates the breast as the saints' weak point. It is the breast and thus her true sex that she has to hide in order to overcome a woman's fate. Even though her breasts save her life at the trial, the exposure of her breasts nevertheless leads to her persecution as a virgin saint and eventually to her death. The hardly changeable fact of her womanhood thus certainly turns her into a tragic figure. While it undoubtedly does not make her a weak person, as she is able to fulfil a powerful, leading, masculine role within her narrative, it is this unchangeable attribute of her body which on a meta-level is the reason for her disguise and the cause of her death later on, and thus certainly her weak point.

[63] Jerome, "Letter CVII: To Laeta" in Jerome, *Letters*, *PL* 22: pp. 325-1197, p. 874, sec. 7; trans. in *Nicene and Post-Nicene Fathers*, 2nd ser., vol. VI, ed. Philip Schaff and Henry Wace (Edinburgh: T&T Clark; Grand Rapids: Eerdmans, 1892), *Christian Classics Ethereal Library*, Calvin College, Web, 17 Sept. 2016. See also Song of Solomon (Canticle of Canticles) 8:10.

The situation presented among the tortured saints' legends, however, leads to a different conclusion. In the legend of Saint Agatha, the heathen torturer experiences sexual frustration for not possessing a body part which is depicted as a strong symbol of motherhood and nourishment for the entire Christian community, a body part so powerful that the expressed male anxiety can be abolished only through the breast's destruction. However, Agatha's breast wounds heal, and thus the breast is presented as a significant place where the power struggle between God and the heathen is exemplified and in which the mastectomy becomes an (unsuccessful) attempt to destabilize the Church, which is metaphorically nursed by the virgin's breast. In addition, the affirming milk-leaking wounds in the legend of Saint Christina indicate a connection between nourishment, breastfeeding, and the spreading of Christian belief through the ideal, martyrical behaviour of the saints. Therefore, even though battered and mastectomized, the symbolism attached to the breast is powerful and overall quite affirming, making it difficult to generalize the breast as a form of female weakness. It is only the physical outside, the flesh, that is fragile and destructible; yet on the inside the saints remain strong, or to say it in the words of Jerome, "I am a wall and my breasts like towers".[64]

[64] Jerome, "Letter CVII: To Laeta" in Jerome, *Letters*, *PL* 22: pp. 325-1197, p. 874, sec. 7; trans. in *Nicene and Post-Nicene Fathers*, 2nd ser., vol. VI, ed. Philip Schaff and Henry Wace (Edinburgh: T&T Clark; Grand Rapids: Eerdmans, 1892), *Christian Classics Ethereal Library*, Calvin College, Web, 17 Sept. 2016.

3 Details that Matter: The Implications of Hair(Styles)

The female head is a particularly rich and important site in the symbolization of gender.

Howard Eilberg-Schwartz[1]

Considering only the biological facts, hair is nothing but protein cells growing out of the epidermis. However, taking cultural and literary history into consideration as well, then hair – its length, colour and style – is far more than just cells. The portrayal of hair and its various styles in paintings and old photographs as well as in literature allows conclusions in regard to time periods and social contexts. Furthermore, hair is attributed with uncountable adjectives and can be perceived as sinful, virtuous, revolting, transforming or even disguising. It can enable a distinction between social classes, historical periods and gender and it plays, as the following chapter will show, a meaningful role within the theological and hagiographical context.[2]

While numerous studies on hair exist, dealing with its general symbolic development, its biological or scientific formation, or its perception in specific cultural surroundings, studies on hair in women's hagiography are rare.[3] Could a reason for an absence of scholarly debate be that hair is far less subject to torture than the breast, for example, and is thus overlooked as a minor and rather insignificant feature? Even though the forced cutting of hair was a common torture practice for women (Herrmann, *Sex und Folter* 94), an aspect visible in several legends,[4] it is not so much the torture

[1] Howard Eilberg-Schwartz, "The Spectacle of the Female Head", introduction, *Off with Her Head: The Denial of Women's Identity in Myth, Religion, and Culture*, ed. Eilberg-Schwartz and Wendy Doniger (Berkeley: U of California P, 1995), p. 1.

[2] As stated in the general introduction, early versions of some ideas and arguments in this chapter are based on my unpublished MA thesis, "The Significance of Hair in Women's Hagiography", which was submitted to the Department of English and American Studies at the University of Paderborn in 2010.

[3] To this point, scholars who discuss hairstyles in women's hagiography often either mention hair as a side issue to support more popular theories, such as cross-dressing in medieval society, or focus on one hairstyle in particular. For a discussion of longhaired saints such as Saint Agnes or Mary Magdalene as well as the bearded Saint Wilgefortis, see Christine Knust, "'Allen sinen lip bedecktent die loecke': Zur Symbolik der Haare in Heiligenlegenden und Heiligendarstellungen des Mittelalters", *Haare zwischen Fiktion und Realität. Interdisziplinäre Untersuchungen zur Wahrnehmung der Haare*, ed. Birgit Haas (Berlin: LIT, 2008), pp. 115-34. For an analysis of the transvestite saints in the *Vitas Patrum* see Sandra Lowerre, "To Rise beyond Their Sex: Female Cross-Dressing Saints in Caxton's *Vitas Patrum*", *Riddles, Knights and Cross-Dressing Saints*, ed. Thomas Honegger (Bern: Lang, 2004), pp. 55-94.

[4] For example, Saint Julia's hair is torn out in the course of her martyrdom (*De Sancta Julia*, *AASS* May V, 168-72), and the multitortured Saint Christina (see chapters 2 and 4) also has her head shaved as a form of suffering (de Voragine I: 386-87).

within these *vitae* which attracts attention but rather the variety of hairstyles and their metaphorical usage. For example, within hagiography it is interesting to register that only three types of hairstyles are emphasized and connected to multiple, often contradictory cultural assumptions: long hair, short hair and the female beard. Even without torture, the aspect of hair, its described sudden growth or its cutting as a form of disguise, or even one female saint's prayer for the growth of a beard, therefore provides rich material worth investigating in detail. The following chapter will concentrate on how these *gendered cells* challenge the naturalization of the medieval concept of femininity. It will argue that hair, in all of the hagiographic legends analysed, is the final performative action to transform a sinner into a saint or a woman symbolically into a "man", and frequently it is even the final step in the saint's attempt to achieve the apotheosis. To depict hair's cultural and historical significance, the chapter will first identify hair as a social and symbolic phenomenon before analysing the aspect of hair in several female saints' legends. The analysis will thereby move from the most feminine hairstyle (*long hair*) to the most radical violation of what medieval society claimed to be feminine (*female beard*), showing that hair frequently blurs the line between perception and deception of medieval gender roles.

3.1 Gendered Cells: Hair as a Social Phenomenon

> It is about hair really, hair and what it signifies for women – who must grow it long and cut it off, who must keep it beautiful and keep it covered, who must strive to be both princess and saint; and who must always and forever, put up with evil husbands.
>
> Sara Maitland and Wendy Mulford[5]

What does hair signify for women? Socially, a significant interest in female hair existed in the Middle Ages and still exists today, where women spend hours and lots of money at hairdressers to turn these biologically dead cells into cells full of life and meaning. Culturally, hair is much more than *dead cells*. It can be the expression of a way of life or a *rite de passage*, and its various lengths and colours are surrounded by myths which invite interpretation – not only for women. The statement made by Sarah Maitland and Wendy Mulford hence needs to be expanded: what does a woman's hair signify for herself and for those looking at her and subconsciously interpreting her? How far can historical and theoretical approaches to hair and medieval biological knowledge about women be connected to the social construction of a woman's gender and the aspect of hair as a social phenomenon?

For centuries, scholars have tried to make the female sex and feminine gender accessible and interpretable. The focus is often either on the cultural circumstances –

[5] Sarah Maitland and Wendy Mulford, *Virtuous Magic: Women Saints and their Meanings* (London: Mowbray, 1998), p. 128.

when and why women were dominated, suppressed and finally liberated – or on the female body and its sexual and reproductive body parts. However, in addition to interpreting a woman's sexual and reproductive organs, as discussed in the first chapter, it is in particular the (female) head and particularly (facial) hair which can function as a significant symbol of gender concepts (Eilberg-Schwartz 1).

Without the head, human beings may still be classified as male or female, but it is the head with which human beings are individualized and separated from each other. Hair is thus a symbol of individuality, which, as Svetlana Balabanova explains, affects the impression one has of someone's personality (7). Hair beautifies or deforms a human being and furthermore allows for conclusions on the individual's health and wellbeing (7). In this respect, the individual and his or her hair are always interpreted as an entity (Haas 10).[6] Moreover, the head not only provides humans with a location for identity, it is also responsible for the mind and the voice, which in respect to femininity often threatens "the classic gender distinctions that have linked men to speech, power identity and the mind" (Eilberg-Schwartz 1).[7] Thus, the head and everything belonging to it fulfils a performative function for the body. It is a screen on which social expectations about social reality and gender are projected. Moreover, facial hair especially is able to carry such symbolic meaning because it is a "body part which is easily subject to change: it can be dyed, shaped, worn loose, bound or be removed" (Coates 8).

In its biological origin, the growth of hair on a human's body was intended to function as a protective instrument for the body. Its job was to serve the body as a garment, protecting it primarily from the influence of temperature – cold and heat – but also from natural impacts such as insects or impurities of any sort (Balabanova 7). Men were hairier than women, in particular on their faces and on their chests, whereas throughout millennia of evolution the bodily hairiness of women has been reduced to certain areas, such as the pubic region and the armpits.

The cultural history of humanity, however, demonstrates that hair has always been considered much more than its original evolutionary purpose. From the beginning of written history, hair had symbolic meaning attached to it and was among the first body parts to be described in detail (Balabanova 12). It was pronounced the "mirror of the soul", where wisdom, knowledge, power, thoughts and vitality were located, which reflects the assumption of men being the "head" and women the "body" (Balabanova 11; Knust 131). The connectivity between head and hair was developed further, Sylvia Schroer claims, as hair soon communicated political issues as well (107). Hair was presented as an indication of power and reputation, and medieval society distinguished different social classes according to one's hairstyle (Balabanova 66). Hairstyles became a visible characteristic, indicating who was free and who was not. For example, in the twelfth and thirteenth centuries, the kings of the Stauffer and Carolingians connected long hair to personal liberty and sovereignty and associated short hair with submission

[6] As Haas continues, this idea of the unity of hair and the individual existed well into the second half of the twentieth century. At that point a new hypothesis emerged, namely that hair and its styles are rather to be interpreted in relation to society than to the individual. Birgit Haas, ed., *Haare zwischen Fiktion und Realität: Interdisziplinäre Untersuchungen zur Wahrnehmung der Haare* (Berlin: LIT, 2008).

[7] For a detailed analysis of linguistic eloquence, speech and hagiography see chapter 4.

and submissiveness (Haas 18-19). Whereas long hair identified the sovereign and fertile, short hair was shameful for every man of high rank, as cut-off hair and, even worse, baldness were associated with monks and slaves, whose hair was deliberately sheared as a symbolic form of castration or as an indicator of submission (Berg 21).

In addition to political statements, as the connection to fertility and castration indicates, hair was also assumed to have strong sexual functions (Leach 82). Particularly in regard to women, hair has frequently been considered the main characteristic of their sex appeal. As Wendy Cooper asserts, "Its colour, its texture, its softness, its scent are potent weapons in her sexual armoury" (65). The powerful perception of hair in relation to sexuality is, according to Cooper, a result of its distribution and its extensive growth in certain areas related to puberty (7). In *The Unconscious Significance of Hair*, the psychiatrist Charles Berg adds that from a psychoanalytic perspective, facial hair – then and now – is seen as analogous to pubic hair (21). Cooper's argument leads in the same direction when she notes,

> The human female has become so denuded of hair on face and body that, by contrast, her remaining largest area of hair has gained in desirability, and secondly that, by "displacement", a woman's head hair is to the male a symbol of her pubic hair and hence of her very womanhood. (65)

Arguably, then, next to the secondary sexual characteristics, hair is the most essential, visible sexual symbol (Schroer 108). Women's hair, so it seems, is perceived in sexual terms even more than that of men. In his first letter to the Corinthians the apostle Paul writes that a woman's hair is her glory and pride, but "her hair is given to her for a covering" (I Corinthians 11:15),[8] a statement underlining that the analogy between pubic hair and facial hair existed even in time periods predating the Middle Ages. Hence, not only does hair honour women, underlining their beauty and attractiveness, but it can also be dangerous for the carrier, as the sexual perception of female hair was for a long time regarded as a threat to the stable social order and particularly for men (Walter 313-15). For surely practical reasons, the coverage of a woman's head and hair followed quite idealistic motives often connected to sexuality, sexual dominance and the threat of exploitation. Therefore, hair is strongly bound to gender-specific perceptions as it "surrounds the most expressive part of the body, the face, [and] any changes made to it are inherently visible and noticeable" (Coates 8).

In women's hagiography, hair has an ambiguous role. Generally speaking, as the following analyses will show, hair is a minor detail in the course of the narratives, yet one with a great effect, a detail that matters. On the one hand, the exuberant hairstyles of the saints, as Hedwig von Beit proposes, are a sign of their selected status by God and demonstrate their religious steadfastness, thereby setting them apart from the normal human being and indicating God's power (131). On the other hand, the cultural symbolism revolving around hair and hairstyles frequently contradicts not only the theological doctrines of that time but also the naturalised medieval concept of femininity, posing a textual challenge to editors and compilers. Female saints' legends were designed for other women to admire and imitate. Yet the legends of Mary

[8] "[…] quoniam capilli pro velamine ei dati sunt".

Magdalene and Mary of Egypt, for example, who are both described as having long, sensual locks, are both connected to prostitution. In the legends of Euphrosyne and Eugenia, both saints obtain the tonsure, which hides their female identity and grants them access to all-male monasteries. The most radical challenge to the Church's doctrines and medieval gender reality, however, appears in the form of the bearded female saint, who is presented as the ultimate violation to medieval normativity.

The following discussion of each hairstyle will analyse how the challenges of social, gendered and religious ideals are dealt with in the texts and how this has led to new adaptations in the case of the two Marys. It will show how the blurring of sexual and gendered roles is punished in the texts with accusations of rape and homoerotic temptation and how the bearded woman is a taboo even today.

3.2 Saint or Sinner? The Ambiguity of Long Hair

> Hair, free-flowing, would be the sign of the virgin and, covered, that of a married woman. The exception would be the prostitute.
>
> Robin Bryer[9]

> Loose, uncut hair is seen both as a symbol of virginity and as a symbol of promiscuity.
>
> Wendy Cooper[10]

Throughout history, nothing has been considered more feminine, sensual and erotic than long, unkempt hair. However, in the lives of certain female saints, the unveiled exposure of long hair is controversial and ambiguous because it can be both: on the one hand a symbol of desire, physicality, an indication of sexual provocation, but on the other also a representation of virginity, protecting the virgin's (nude) body from the public gaze.

When it comes to long hair in particular, the Middle Ages were a divided period in Europe. "The early part was a frankly sexual age", Cooper states (108). She continues that "men mostly wore their hair long and many wore beards" and "the hair of young girls was usually long and loose, and plaited or braided in older women", and nudity was not considered obscene or something to be ashamed of (108). From time immemorial, long, flowing hair represented strength, virility and, in regard to femininity, fertility. It was a God-given symbol representing the power of life, but it was also a demonic sign, strongly linked with the erotic, unrestrained sexuality and the irrepressible and unmanageable woman (Eilberg-Schwartz 4; Schroer 109). This eroticization of the female head turns it into a "sexually provocative organ", which as a result makes it figuratively "part of the woman's genitalia" (Eilberg-Schwartz 1).

[9] Robin Bryer, *The History of Hair: Fashion and Fantasy down the Ages* (London: Robert Wilson, 2000), p. 29.
[10] Wendy Cooper, *Hair: Sex, Society, Symbolism* (New York: Stein and Day, 1971), p. 67.

Consequently, it is not surprising that the provocative treatments of long hair caused disturbances within the Church. In the later part of the Middle Ages, parallel to the increasing influence of Christianity, people soon started to be more serious about and ashamed of their bodies. As Cooper claims, "The Church grafted its moral codes, its sexual taboos, its dogma of celibacy, and its disapproval of long hair […] onto this medieval sexuality" (108). This disapproval of uncovered long hair was also expressed by Saint Paul, who claimed in the New Testament that

> the head of every man is Christ; and the head of a woman is the man; and the head of Christ is God. Every man praying or prophesying with his head covered, disgraceth his head. But every woman praying or prophesying with her head not covered, disgraceth her head: for it is all one as if she were shaven. […] The man indeed ought not to cover his head, because he is the image and glory of God; but the woman is the glory of the man. […] Doth not even nature itself teach you, that for a man indeed, if he nourish his hair, it is a shame unto him? But if a woman nourish her hair, it is a glory to her; for her hair is given to her for a covering. (I Corinthians 11:3-15)[11]

Therefore, even though a woman's hair is her glory and she should never cut it, it was also perceived as a disturbance to masculinity. Saint Paul vehemently disapproved of women wearing their hair down, in particular when at prayer, as according to his belief it would be distracting for men (I Corinthians 11:3-15). As a result, the Church argued that, unless a virgin, long female hair "must be hidden" (Cooper 108; see also Bryer 28). Thus, in order to be considered a chaste and virtuous woman, female members of society were expected to cover their hair to avoid any deliberate or inadvertent arousal of sexual feelings in the opposite sex. For this purpose the wimple and other coverings were designed, which were supposed to give the female head an innocent and virtuous appearance (Cooper 108). The exception to all of this was the prostitute. In medieval society, prostitutes or harlots were, comparable to virgins and wives, easily identifiable by their hair and its style. In addition, analogous to virgins, prostitutes did not cover up their hair as chaste and married women did. Loose, uncut and unveiled hair was consequently a symbol of promiscuity (67), and prostitutes were quite aware of that fact, displaying their *gendered cells* on purpose to attract more customers.

These controversial interpretations regarding long hair are also reflected in the lives of several *mulieres sanctae*. The following chapter will take a closer look at the legends of Saint Mary Magdalene and Saint Mary of Egypt, also known as Maria Aegyptiaca. Both are strong representatives of repentant prostitutes, whose hair before their conversion is foremost associated with sexuality. With their repentance and complete withdrawal from the social and material world, however, the sexual symbolism of their hair is transformed as well from sinful to virtuous, purifying both women and giving them a virginlike status. In contrast to these two holy harlots, the legend of Saint Agnes depicts one of the most famous virgin saints, who during her early martyrdom converts

[11] "volo autem vos scire quod omnis viri caput Christus est caput autem mulieris vir caput vero Christi Deus / omnis vir orans aut prophetans velato capite deturpat caput suum / omnis autem mulier orans aut prophetans non velato capite deturpat caput suum unum est enim atque si decalvetur […] nec ipsa natura docet vos quod vir quidem si comam nutriat ignominia est illi / mulier vero si comam nutria gloria est illi quoniam capilli pro velamine ei dati sunt […]".

an entire brothel into a house of prayer after she is sent naked through the town, miraculously covered only in her hair. Whereas, as the analyses will show, hair in all three *vitae* protects the women in some way or the other and helps them to progress spiritually, Agnes's hair and its sudden growth also functions as a significant demonstration of God's power.

3.2.1 Harlot Saints and Hairy Repentants

> The attention paid to saint's hair helps to underscore the bodily or sinful past.
>
> Roberta Milliken[12]

> Mary is called Magdalene, which is understood to mean 'remaining guilty,' […] armed, or unconquered, or magnificent. These meanings point to the sort of woman she was before, at the time of, and after her conversion.
>
> Jacobus de Voragine [13]

Historically, the legend of Mary Magdalene, who supposedly lived in the first century, is the oldest of those analysed in the scope of this study and is probably one of the most well known female figures of premedieval as well as medieval times. In particular, in the Middle Ages an active Magdalene cult existed, which was patronized by Pope Leo IX (Brundage 211-12) and which derived partly from modifications of the manifold legends surrounding her person and their inclusion of an innovative topic at that time – the possibility of the repentance and rehabilitation of prostitutes. Even though the Bible does not explicitly state that Mary of Magdala – or, as she was known later, Mary Magdalene – was a prostitute, the western Church discredited her reputation and associated her with the unspecified "sinner" (prostitute) mentioned in Luke 7:36-50,[14] who washes Jesus's feet and anoints them with her long

[12] Roberta Lee Milliken, "Neither 'Clere Laude' nor 'Sklaundre': Chaucer's Translation of Criseyde and Sensual and Holy Locks: A Study of Hair in Women's Hagiography", Diss. (U of Toledo, 1995), p. v.

[13] Jacobus de Voragine, *The Golden Legend: Readings on the Saints*, 2 vols., ed. and trans. William Granger Ryan (Princeton: Princeton UP, 1995), I: 374ff. "Magdalena dicitur, quasi manens rea, vel Magdalena interpretatur munita vel invicta vel mangifica, per quae insinuatur, qualis fuit ante conversionem, qualis in conversione et qualis post conversionem" (Graesse 407).

[14] "And behold a woman that was in the city, a sinner, when she knew that he sat at meat in the Pharisee's house, brought an alabaster box of ointment. And standing behind at his feet, she began to wash his feet, with tears, and wiped them with the hairs of her head, and kissed his feet, and anointed them with the ointment"; "[E]t ecce mulier quae erat in civitate peccatrix ut cognovit quod accubuit in domo Pharisaei adtulit alabastrum unguenti / et stans retro secus pedes eius lacrimis coepit rigare pedes eius et capillis capitis sui tergebat et osculabatur pedes eius et unguento ungebat" (Luke 7: 37-38).

and apparently unveiled hair. If Mary Magdalene truly is the unnamed sinner written about by the apostle, it is understandable why she has been denunciated by the Church ever since. A woman who was not only not a virgin but, even worse, a prostitute, conflicted vehemently with the early Christians' fundamental belief in virtue, chastity and virginity. Furthermore, Mary Magdalene belonged to the closest friends of Jesus Christ and even witnessed his resurrection, and their companionship, which is often considered to have been rather a love affair than just friendship, could have been just too much for the early Christian Church. How should the Church deal with a person who was a woman and a prostitute and one of the saviour's best friends? How were clerics supposed to instruct their followers that Jesus led an ascetic, nonsexual life if there were a woman who was considered to be his lover? It seems as if it was Mary Magdalene's fate to be turned into a sinner, whether she was one or not. Otherwise, sooner or later, her person would have threatened to destabilize the power and credibility of the institutional Church.

For many Christians, the biblical Mary Magdalene and her hair were primarily linked to sexual desire and her "unrestrained sexuality" attained through her presumed career as a prostitute. The attention paid to her hair in the texts highlights her femininity, physicality, desirability and attraction for men (Milliken, "Neither" 41). The biblical scenario of Mary Magdalene wiping tears from Jesus's feet with the hair of her head has added to her sensual character description and is often interpreted not just as simple caress, but rather as a physical and almost erotic situation. According to Roberta Milliken, the "image of the beautiful woman using her long flowing hair in such a tender way was apparently quite stirring and hard to forget" (25). The association of Mary Magdalene as the sensual lover and sometimes wife of Christ has constantly renewed and modified interest in her. Scholars, artists, modern authors of fiction such as Dan Brown, and even the film industry show an ongoing fascination with the ambiguous, mysterious figure of the Magdalene and the sexual tension her legend implies, which is the primary reason for her enduring resonance in the medieval and postmedieval world.

Whereas in popular belief the *dies natalis* of Mary Magdalene, the 22nd of July, was seen as the best day of the year for young girls to take care of their hair in order to grow the strong, healthy and beautiful locks of the Magdalene (Knust 115), the connection of her hair and its colour with the idea of her sensuality, beauty and "unrestrained sexuality" was manifested further in paintings. In visual culture, from the fourteenth century onwards the Magdalene is portrayed as a beauty with long, flowing hair (Knust 115; Keller 411-15). In paintings of crucifixion scenes she is identifiable by her uncovered head, whereas the hair of the other women around Jesus is neatly pulled back and modestly veiled.[15] This portrayal of "loose hair" in iconography, as Maitland and Mulford argue, originally derives from the idea of the "loose woman", or in modern terms, the prostitute (97). In addition, many painters, particularly from the sixteenth century onwards,[16] feature Mary Magdalene with

[15] See for example Jakob Wüger's *Kreuzigung* (1868).

[16] See for example Titian and his work *Penitent Mary Magdalene* (sixteenth century), Guido Reni's *The Penitent Magdalene* (1635) or Peter Paul Rubens's painting of the crucifixion scene entitled *Jesus und die reuigen Sünder* (seventeenth century).

blonde or golden hair, which was historically regarded as the symbol of erotic attraction (Haas 9) as throughout history "blondes [had] a reputation for being natural deceivers" (Cooper 77). According to scholars and etymological references,[17] it is not known for sure where the word *blonde* comes from. It might derive from the Latin term *blandus* (charming) or the Old German *blund* (yellow) (Warner 362-63). Within Christian belief, however, blondness symbolized light (366). Parallel to the development of the English language, it soon became a synonym for *fairness*, but also *beauty* and *pleasure* (363). The colour associations support the ambiguity of long and unveiled hair as virtuous and pure but at the same time immoral and erotic. As Marina Warner states, "Although blondeness's most enduring associations are with beauty, with love and nubility, with erotic attraction, with value and fertility, its luminosity made it also the traditional colour of the virgins' hair" (367). Thus Mary Magdalene's golden hair deepens this long-lasting dispute, the vagueness and the myths surrounding her person calling into question who she really was: a sinner, a lover of Christ or just an ordinary follower of Jesus.

Whereas in the visual arts Mary and her hair remain an ongoing symbol of sensuality, in postbiblical legends the symbolic codes of her hair are radically different. Where these legends originate remains for the most part uncertain and is still discussed amongst scholars. However, if the story of the Magdalene does not end with the resurrection of Jesus Christ, someone apparently wanted to change Mary Magdalene's negative reputation as a notorious sinner and rehabilitate her person to suit the agenda of the Church. According to the legend, she converts to Christianity after Jesus has ascended to heaven, and she decides to lead a solitary life as a hermit. The *Legenda Aurea* describes the situation as follows: "Mary Magdalene, wishing to devote herself to heavenly contemplation, retired to an empty wilderness, and lived unknown for thirty years in a place made ready by the hands of angels" (de Voragine I: 380; "Interea beata Maria Magdalena supernae contemplationis avida asperrimum eremum petiit et in loco angelicis manibus praeparato per XXX annos incognita mansit" [Graesse 413]).[18] Her withdrawal from society and her departure into the hardships of the desert also mark her renunciation of the material and sexual world. Even though the *Legenda Aurea* does not explicitly mention the growth of Mary's beautiful long hair, "it became very common to include the notion that since she was rejecting the world by pursuing a hermetical existence, she also rejected clothing" (Milliken, *Ambiguous Locks* 198). However, de Voragine notes towards the end of his entry that another version of the legend of Mary Magdalene, compiled by Hegesippus (or Josephus) exists. This *vita*, which "agrees in the main with the story just told" (I: 381; "satis cum praedicta historia concordat" [Graesse 415]), has however "added that the priest who went to her found her closed up in a cell. At her request he reached out a garment to her, and when she had put it on, she

[17] See for example "Blonde", *Online Etymology Dictionary*, n.d., Web, 13 Aug. 2012.

[18] Next to the *Legenda Aurea*, the legend of Mary Magdalene also appears in the *South English Legendary* (*SEL*), ranging in date from about 1300 to 1500. A reprint of the *Life of Mary Magdalen*, taken from the *Bodleian Library MS Laud Misc*. 108, fols. 190r-197r can be found in Sherry L. Reames, ed., *Middle English Legends of Women Saints* (Kalamazoo: Western Michigan UP, 2003), pp. 51-110. The *SEL* also specifically mentions her golden/yellow hair colour ("yelouwe heres"), p. 62.

went with him to the church" (de Voragine I: 381; "Addidit tamen, quod sacerdos, dum ad eam venisset, reperit eam in cella clausam: qui ad ejus petitionem vestem sibi porrexit, quam induens in ecclesiam secum ivit" [Graesse 415]). As Milliken sums up, "Whether it was due to these details of the legend that imply Mary's nakedness or simply the length of the time she spent in the wilderness combined with the imagination of the artists, Mary Magdalene is often described and depicted during this par of her life as being 'clad in only her golden hair which entirely covers her'" (Haskins, qtd. in Milliken, *Ambiguous Locks* 198), and as such her hair was for a long time the only protection of her body from the impacts of nature and from the public gaze.

A similar plot structure can be found in the *vita* of Saint Mary of Egypt, or Saint Maria Aegyptiaca. Whether the obvious parallels between the legends of Mary of Egypt and Mary Magdalene are only a coincidence or whether they are textually one and the same person remains unknown. What is certain, however, is that even though both legends may be penned by the same person or may share the same background, throughout the centuries Mary of Egypt has developed a cult of her own. According to Jacobus de Voragine, a person named Mary of Egypt lived around AD 270, at the time of the emperor Claudius (I: 227). The account of her life probably originates in Greece and is a combination of two oral traditions written down in Cyril of Scythopolis's *Vita Cyriaci* and in the *Pratum Spirituale* by Johannes Moschus (A. Butler II: 14; Kunze 9-11). Her cult and popularity increased when around AD 614 numerous Christians fled from Palestine to Italy, in particular to Rome, apparently taking the legend of Mary of Egypt with them. Even though these Greek exile communities already honoured her as a saint in the seventh century, another two hundred years went by before her legend was translated into Latin (Kunze 26; see also *Vita Sanctæ Mariæ Ægyptiacæ* in *PL* 73: 671-90[19]) and was consequently made available for a larger audience and geographical distribution.[20]

Similar to Mary Magdalene, the legend of Mary of Egypt also plays with the common hagiographical image of the repentant prostitute.[21] The legend states that before her conversion to Christianity, Mary of Egypt led a life of prostitution, enjoying her carnal desires. As Mary "herself"[22] is cited in the *Legenda Aurea*, "I plied my trade as a public woman and never refused my body to anyone" (de Voragine I: 227; "publice libidini me subjeci et nulli ullatenus me negavi" [Graesse 248]). In this respect, it is certainly no coincidence that her story is located in Egypt, which was traditionally regarded as the land of the prostitutes (Kunze 23). The legend continues that Mary wants to join a group of pilgrims on their way to the Holy Land, Jerusalem. As she has no money to pay the fare, she prostitutes herself repeatedly during the journey (de

[19] The entry in the *Patrologia Latina* from the ninth century became, according to Donovan, "an extremely popular exemplar of repentance and redemption for medieval Christians" (98).

[20] For the text's distributional history in English and England, see Leslie A. Donovan, *Women Saints' Lives in Old English Prose* (Cambridge: Brewer, 1999), pp. 97-99; and Alice-Mary Talbot, ed., *Holy Women of Byzantium: Ten Saints' Lives in English Translation*, Byzantine Saints' Lives in Translation (Washington, DC: Dumbarton Oaks Centre Studies, 1996).

[21] Next to the two Marys, the legends of Saint Thais and Saint Maria Meretrix are also structured around the motif of the repentant prostitute.

[22] Her life is told retrospectively from her point of view upon the encounter with Zosimus.

Voragine I: 227). Upon her arrival in Jerusalem she tries to access a church, but because of the sins she has committed she is not allowed to enter:

> I arrived at Jerusalem and went to the church with the others to worship the holy cross, but suddenly, by an invisible force, I was pushed back from the door and not allowed to enter. Again and again I got to the threshold of the entrance and suffered the pain of being repulsed, while the others went in freely and encountered no obstacle. (de Voragine I: 227)[23]

Ashamed of herself and realizing "that this was happening to [her] because of [her] dreadful crimes" (227; "quod hoc mihi ob scelerum meorum immanitatem accideret" [Graesse 248]), she prays to the Virgin Mary and converts to Christianity. Analogous to Mary Magdalene, Mary of Egypt chooses to live a solitary life in the desert after her repentance and successfully hides from the world for almost fifty years (de Voragine I: 227-29; *AASS* Apr. I, 68-90; *PL* 73: 671-90). At one point in her solitary existence a monk named Zosimus accidentally comes across her on his journey through the desert, where he is supposed to meditate and experience the ascetic lifestyle as a hermit for a lengthy period. He finds Mary completely naked except for long white hair covering her otherwise "black" body ("corpore nigerimo, præ solis ardore denigrata, et capillos capitis habens ut lana albos, modicos et ipsos, non amplius quam usque ad cervicem descendentes" *Vita Sanctæ Mariæ Ægyptiacæ* in *PL* 73: 677A; see also Keller 410; de Voragine I: 227).[24]

Taking the possibility into consideration that both Marys are the same person or at least share some similarities in their biographies, it is also plausible that their hairstyles have been linked throughout the years and that the long sensual locks of Mary Magdalene and the white hair of Mary of Egypt convey identical or at least related symbolism. As Knust reminds us,

> wenn sich die Legendenschnipsel der Maria Ägyptiaca auf Maria Magdalena übertragen können, so ist dies zumindest in diesem Punkt auch umgekehrt möglich. Maria Magdalenas langes Haar, mit dem die beliebte Heilige immer wieder verbunden wird, bedeckt dann eben auch den Körper der alten, nicht ganz so bekannten Büßerin. (117)[25]

[23] "Cum autem Hierosolimam pervenissem et pro adoranda cruce usque ad fores ecclesiae cum aliis devenissem, subito et invisibiliter repulsam patior nec intus intrare permittor. Iterum autem atque iterum perveni usque ad limen januae et subito injuriam patiebar repulsae. Cum tamen omnes liberum haberent aditum nec aliquod invenirent impedimentum [...]" (Graesse 248).

[24] That hair explicitly started to grow to cover her body is omitted in the *Legenda Aurea*. De Voragine's version solely includes the image of the black body.

[25] Trans.: "if one can transfer pieces of the legend of Mary of Egypt to Mary Magdalene, then the opposite is also possible. Mary Magdalene's long hair, with which the popular saint is connected, can thus also cover the body of this old, not so well known repentant". Christine Knust, "'Allen sinen lip bedecktent die loecke': Zur Symbolik der Haare in Heiligenlegenden und Heiligendarstellungen des Mittelalters", *Haare zwischen Fiktion und Realität. Interdisziplinäre Untersuchungen zur Wahrnehmung der Haare*, ed. Birgit Haas (Berlin: LIT, 2008), pp. 115-34, p. 117.

In addition to the image of the repentant prostitute, both legends portray their protagonists as hairy hermits, which was a frequent motif in male and female hagiographical narratives alike (Elliot 98-99). As Elliot clarifies, the

> goals of the ascetic life were alienation and separation – total estrangement from the values of the classical and urban past, and the animal-like hermit attained it to a superlative degree. He (or she) looked like an animal and lived its life. Like the beasts, hair was his [or her] only bodily covering. (170)

Thus, with their inner and outer transformation from sinner to saint, the symbolism of their hair is altered as well. It no longer functions as an erotic symbol and provokes an arousal of sexual desires in the opposite sex, but instead is attributed with garmentlike characteristics, as both literally "wear" their hair as a form of bodily protection. Through this rejection of the social dress code with which humans distinguish themselves from animals, the saints have "allied [themselves] with the beasts, and with men before the Fall, who did not need artificial coverings for [their bodies]" (Elliot 99). Parallel to the conversion, their long hair is refitted into its original main function, namely to be a protective organ of the body from "heat, cold and mechanical influences" (Balabanova 7) and thus is desymbolized. The bodies of the two Marys arguably not only retire from the secular and sexual world, but their hair, through which particularly Mary Magdalene was (and still is) identified, is cleansed in the texts of every previously attached metaphorical and social conventions. Their long, unveiled hair is no longer considered sinful, immoral, or even obscene. It no longer "underscores the 'bodily' or sinful past of the saint" (Milliken, "Neither" v), but with the devotion to Christianity it "returns" to its biologically intended purpose and protects the female body from contamination and in this case from social impurity. According to Elliot, sinners already represented the margins of society, but within both female saints' legends this marginality is doubled as these saints are both "prostitutes and women" (174). Consequently, before the conversion their long hair conceptualises social and female marginality and ostracises both as outcasts of society (Firth 262). After repenting, however, their long hair, which now covers their entire bodies, suddenly signifies the ultimate separation from the hermits' past and former lifestyle. In the case of Mary of Egypt, the transition from secularity to spirituality and the drastic separation from the past that accompanies this process are underlined by the legend's contrast of her black body with her white hair. At first sight, her black body is surely an indication of her fifty years of extensive exposure to the sun, and her white hair indicates her advanced age, since she must be well into her seventies when Zosimus meets her. Symbolically, however, the contrast supports her sinner-to-saint transformation. Whereas the colour black is in Western societies connected to darkness, (symbolic) filth, decay and death, white is linked to purity, innocence and truth. In physics, white is the sum of all colours and has no negative connotations – it is regarded as *the* perfect colour, the *ideal*, and marks a new beginning.[26] Arguably, then, in relation to the biblical statement that "the spirit is indeed willing, but the flesh weak" (Matthew 26:41),[27] Mary's

[26] Andreas Heck, "Farbpsychologie und Symbolik", *Farbcodes*, Filmakademie Baden-Württemberg, 2002, Web, 1 May 2010.
[27] "[...] spiritus quidem promptus est caro autem infirma"

black body serves as a reminder of her sinful life as a prostitute, and the contrasting white hair underlines her new spiritually pure and cleansed mind.

Finally, comparable to the torture of the breast in the legend of Saint Agatha, in which the culmination of tortures reflects Agatha's inner transformation to sainthood, the inner transformation of the two Marys is not complete without the significant external alteration of their hair. Whereas the breast becomes a place to execute God's power, long hair serves as a connection between good and bad, sinner and saint, God and humanity. With the transition and repentance, both saints leave their former lives behind, and in Mary Magdalene's case even her earlier, negative biblical identity. They are rehabilitated to the social and religious ideal of the pious and chaste woman. In particular, Mary Magdalene is thereby refitted into the doctrines of the institutional Church, which clearly did not want a prostitute to be the closest and dearest follower of their Messiah. This modification and expansion of her legend suddenly provided the Church with a perfect example of how a female sinner of the worst kind repents and converts, showcasing, as Maitland and Mulford state, "a strongly needed means of hope for many Christians" (99). With their repentance, both female saints not only transform from harlots into virtuous women, but become mediators between contrasts: past and present, sin and virtue, desirable and protective hair – turning these gendered cells into a significant detail not to be neglected.

3.2.2 Saint Agnes: The Virgin Martyr

> Urere cum flammis voluisset nobile corpus,
> viribus inmensum parvis superasse timorem,
> nudaque profusum crinem per membra dedisse.
>
> *Damasi Epigrammata*[28]

> Statim autem ut expoliata est, crine resoluto, tantam desitatem capillis ejus divina gratia concessit, ut melius videretur eorum fimbriis quam vestibus tecta.
>
> *Gesta sanctae Agnes*[29]

In the previous chapter, long hair was established as a transformative step from sinner to saint. In the legend of the approximately thirteen-year-old Saint Agnes, whose *vita* is

[28] Trans.: "When he had decided to burn the noble flesh with fire, she overcame a great fear with her small strength and let loose her hair to cover her naked limbs" (White 160). For the complete Latin text see poem 40 in *Damasi Epigrammata: Accedunt pseudodamasiana aliaque ad Damasiana inlustranda idonea*, ed. Maxmilian Ihm, Anthologiae Latinae Supplementa I. (Leipzig: Teubner, 1895), pp. 43-44.

[29] Trans.: "She is disrobed immediately but her hair grows to such length that her nakedness is perfectly covered" (White 164). For the original text see *Gesta sanctae Agnes*, *Bibliotheca Hagiographica Latina*, 3 vols., 1889-1901, Subsidia Hagiographica (Brussels: Société des Bollandistes, 1949).

one of the most popular of the virgin saints, the sudden, God-given growth of her hair converts not the saint herself, but a large group of people witnessing the spectacle. The historical and textual development of her legend is well documented and, as scholars argue, originally derives from three primary sources, which at some point in history blended together to form the version of her martyrdom still known today. The earliest reference to Saint Agnes can be found in the *De Virginibus* sermon preached by Saint Ambrose in the year 377 (de'Cavalieri n.pag.; Denomy 4). Another hymn in honour of Saint Agnes appears around the year 400 in Prudentius's *Persitephanon XIV*, who is said to have composed the legend probably after his journey to Rome in 402 (Denomy 14-15). However, neither of these two early sources includes the miraculous hair growth of the later versions of Saint Agnes's legend. The earliest connection between Agnes's nudity and her hair is made on a tomb inscription composed during the reign of Pope Damasus (366-384) and consequently situated between the two other texts. The inscription states that after her tormentor has her disrobed, her naked body is covered and protected by her hair: "nudaque profusum crinem per membra dedisse" (Ihm 44; Denomy 11 n. 131; "let loose her hair to cover her naked limbs" [White 160]). Historically, the aspect of her miraculous hair growth must have been taken from the Damasus inscription and entered the Latin *Gesta sanctae Agnes*, the most famous version of the legend, dating back to the fifth century and composed by an anonymous author often referred to as Pseudo-Ambrose (Denomy 24; White 163). The legendary *Gesta* has added much to Agnes's ongoing popularity and resonance and is the basis for most of the subsequent adaptations and translations of her story, such as the *Legenda Aurea* (Kelly 54).[30] The miraculous growth of her hair has remained a part of her *vita* ever since and can be found in numerous European adaptations of her legend throughout the Middle Ages and beyond.[31]

In both the Latin and the Old English tradition, the thirteen-year-old Agnes is described as innocent and wise, "a child in body, but already aged in spirit" whose "face was beautiful [but whose] faith more beautiful" (de Voragine I: 102; "Infantia quidem computabatur in annis, sed erat senectus mentis immensa, corpore juvencula, sed animo cana, pulchra facie, sed pulchrior fide" [Graesse 113]; see also *Natale Sancte Agnetis*, Skeat I: 170). Soon she is courted by the son of the prefect, yet Agnes, who already has accepted Christ as her bridegroom and whom she calls her "lover" (de Voragine I: 102; Graesse 114; Skeat I: 171),[32] refuses the offers made by her wooer, who, lovesick and

[30] For a more detailed analysis of the textual development see Alexander Joseph Denomy, *The Old French Lives of Saint Agnes and Other Vernacular Versions of the Middle Ages* (Cambridge: Harvard UP, 1938); and Rhonda L. McDaniel, "Agnes among the Anglo-Saxons: Patristic Influences in Anglo-Latin and Anglo-Saxon Versions of the Passio of St. Agnes, Virgin and Martyr", *Writing Women Saints in Anglo-Saxon England*, ed. Paul E. Szarmach (Toronto: U of Toronto P, 2013), pp. 217-48.

[31] See for example *La vie de sainte Agnés*, Manuscript 1553, *Cataloque des manuscrits français* I. (Paris: Bibliothèque Nationale, 1868), 148-244, ll. 341-48; and Guido Battelli, *La Passione di s. Agnese*, *Fiori di Letteratura Ascetica e Mistica*, vol. 2 (Firenze: Giannini, 1921). Denomy argues that this is partially due to the fact that in 813 the Council of Tours ordered preachers to deliver their sermons in the vernacular. Soon popular compilations were adapted as well, turning the aspect of hair into an irrevocable fact (119).

[32] In particular in Ælfric's *Natale Sancte Agnetis* the traditionally eroticized relationship between Agnes and Christ is reported at length (Skeat I: 172 ff). For a scholarly discussion see Eileen

angry about Agnes's attitude and neglect, falls ill. Enraged by her determination, the prefect has her disrobed and commands her to be "taken nude to a brothel" (de Voragine I: 103; "nudam ad lupanar duci" [Graesse 115]) to be "thrown in with the harlots and handled as they are handled" (I: 102; "aut cum meretricibus scortaberis" [Graesse 114]) and to be "foully dishonoured", as the *Natale Sancte Agnetis* adds ("fullice gebysmrod" [Skeat I: 176]). As a sign of her religious steadfastness and as a proof of the almighty power of God, when she is disrobed her hair grows to such a length that she is entirely covered and her pure body is protected from the public gaze (de Voragine I: 102). With her inexplicable bodily modification, Agnes miraculously transforms the brothel and all of its prostitutes and customers into a "place of prayer" (I: 103; "locus orationis" [Graesse 115]). Arguably, Agnes's public hair growth affects the social order to a greater extent than hair does in the legends of the two Marys. While the harlot saints convert only themselves from sinners to saints, Agnes's public punishment and denunciation converts a large group of sinners to Christianity before she dies the predestined martyrical death. Even though the legends of the repentant prostitutes show the possibility of being spiritually rehabilitated, the naked hairy virgin is arguably valued higher as an instructive tool than the naked hairy hermit, since the former is a strong virginal and chaste female character right from the start. Today, Saint Agnes is regarded as the patroness of virtue, purity and modesty. Whereas the legends of Mary of Egypt and Mary Magdalene were more often used to instruct about sin and repentance, the story of Saint Agnes, according to Denomy, was, "admirably suited pedagogically" (119). He continues that the legend of Saint Agnes "should prove immensely popular, especially with the young [...] her legend and life were invaluable in instructing the youth in purity and modesty and in edifying the adult to a cultivation of these virtues" (119).

Nevertheless, the connection between the pure, naked body, the long hair that covers her, and the brothel as a place for lewd and impure behaviour generates another reading of the scene. The loss of her clothing, as Donovan notes, is "an act by which [...] Agnes' naked body [is made] public property" and is exposed unprotected to the gaze of the public (127). The short moment between undressing and redressing, in which her hair is her only bodily covering, turns her into a vulnerable woman to be gazed at – not only at her body as a whole, but particularly at her genitalia, her most private parts and the symbol of her untouched body. Consequently, at the moment in which her miraculously grown hair covers "her alike on every side" ("þœt fex hi behelede on ælce healfe gelice" [Skeat I: 178]), "better than any clothing" (de Voragine I: 103; "ut melius capillis quam vestibus tegeretur" [Graesse 115]), not only is her body shielded from the public but her genitalia are covered again, granting her privacy and intimacy. Her hair functions to preserve her virginity and protects her from "public contamination" (Donovan 127). As Donovan argues,

> The presence of long hair on a woman is normally associated with sexuality and licentiousness in late antiquity and the Middle Ages, but here [in the legend of Saint Agnes] the common convention is reversed and Agnes' hair becomes the salvations of her body, rather than an advertisement of its sinfulness. (49 n. 14)

Harney, "The Sexualized and Gendered Tortures of Virgin Martyrs in Medieval English Literature" (PhD dissertation, U of Toronto, 2008), pp. 85-150.

In addition, sending Agnes to a brothel implies the cultural ambiguity connected to loose hair. Whereas in her case it identifies a virgin, it is also directly related to the unveiled long locks worn by the prostitutes whom she is to cooperate with. While the virgin's long, unveiled hair is primarily connected to spiritual purity and biological virginity, through her nudity and the inclusion of the brothel its connection to sexuality and desire does not completely fade away. Comparable to Mary of Egypt and Mary Magdalene, her hair thus functions as a transitional contact between sin and virtue – just in a slightly different order.

Consequently, despite their textual incongruities and diverse attitudes towards sin and virtue, the legends of the saints Mary Magdalene, Mary of Egypt and Agnes share not only their continuing popularity in the postmedieval world, but also the aspect of penitence and repentance triggered through their hair. Moreover, in all three cases long hair becomes the body part through which the saint is connected to God. Either it connects them for the first time, as case studies of the transformed sinners show, or it symbolises and intensifies a preexisting spiritual and bodily relationship of the saint to God, as in the case of Saint Agnes.[33] Taking other biblical and religious texts into consideration, such as the story of Samson and Delilah (Judges 13-16), it is not the first time that a connection between God, hair and the human being has been established. In Samson's case, his physical power originates with his hair, which, according to Balabanova, is at the same time his symbolic connection to God (29). Even his name, as Cooper argues, "may well be derived from the Hebrew word *shemesh*, meaning hair" (186). When Delilah discovers the source of his power, she "made him sleep upon her knees, and lay his head in her bosom. And she called a barber, and shaved his seven locks, and began to drive him away, and thrust him from her: for immediately his strength departed from him" (Judges 16:19).[34] Cutting off his locks disconnects him from God – his source of inspiration and physical potency – leaving him weak and vulnerable until his hair has grown back. This hairy spiritual connection to God in Samson's case is also applicable to the female saints. In all three cases, hair is an instrument of transition to a higher, transcending level of spirituality – the "location of life, soul and power" (Knust 119). For the harlot saints, their conversion and repentance connects them spiritually for the first time, and as previously discussed, this alters the symbolic meaning of their hair as well. For the virgin saint, who already has a loyal relationship to God, the growth of hair implies her intense need of spiritual guidance in contemplation of defilement and martyrdom.

In conclusion, the analysis of long hair has shown that several ambiguous and sometimes contradicting definitions are related to this hairstyle – that loose, unveiled hair is both a symbol of virginity and prostitution and that hair colour mattered in constructing the saint and supported her psychological and physical transformation from sinner to saint. Furthermore, these analyses indicate that once the prostitute repents or

[33] In particular in the legend of Saint Agnes, the sudden growth of hair demonstrates God's power, which recalls of the regrowth of the breast in the legend of Saint Agatha discussed in chapter 2.

[34] "at illa dormire eum fecit super genua sua, et in sinu suo reclinare caput vocavitque tonsorem et rasit septem crines ejus et coepit abigere eum et a se repellere statim enim ab eo fortitudo discessit"

the virgin is in need of spiritual protection, the cultural conventions attributed to long hair change in their interpretations from arousing erotic desire to its original biological purpose of protecting the body against natural impacts. Long hair in hagiography demonstrates the power of repentance and serves as a tool for spiritual cleansing, but moreover it reveals God's all-encompassing authority.

3.3 Challenging Nature: Transvestite Saints and the Significance of the Haircut

They cut off their hair and are not ashamed to look like eunuchs.
Jerome[35]

The disguise of the transvestite saints, as discussed in the second chapter, often does not end with the assumption of male or unisex clothing. From Saint Eugenia, discussed in chapter 2, to the saints Euphrosyne, Margaret and Theodora and the well-known Saint Clare – all of these women not only dress as men, they also have their hair cut short. Their disguises are, so it seems, complete only when the saints additionally cut off their hair or are deliberately tonsured by other monks to enter male monastic communities (Schulenburg 155).

To pass as male, then, women had to receive a haircut, which was publicly seen as a symbol of reduced sexuality or celibacy (Rattray Taylor 71ff). For men in medieval secular society, cutting one's hair was a life-changing procedure often compared to a medical castration (Haas 12). As long hair on a man symbolized personal liberty and independence, a haircut meant a loss of status and defeat. A shaved head also indicated the submissiveness of slaves, and baldness was a certain sign of a lack of masculinity and had to be avoided (Cooper 45). In addition, those who cut their hair voluntarily were often declared outlaws of society (Bullough and Bullough 46). Matters were slightly different regarding the tonsure. The receiving of the tonsure, this holy, sacrificial haircut, was considered a voluntary submission to God and a silent agreement to lead a nonsexual life and was therefore an intentional rite upon the entrance into a distinctive religious circle.

For a woman, a haircut was generally out of the question, as Saint Paul had clarified that long hair – even if it had to be veiled – was a woman's glory (I Corinthians 3-15). A woman who cut her hair or even shaved her head deliberately was a shame in the eyes of medieval society – for the town she lived in and for her family – and had to face punishment.

The symbolic significance of female hair was discussed widely. At the Church Council of Gangra, around AD 341, canon 17 explicitly dealt with this subject and, based on Deuteronomy, forbade women from dressing as men to access male monastic communities. The bishops claimed that women who cut off "their 'natural veil' of long hair" (Brown, *Body* 288) removed the symbol "which God gave to every woman as a

[35] Jerome, Letter XXII, "To Eustochium", *Nicene and Post-Nicene Fathers*, 2nd ser., vol. VI, ed. Philip Schaff and Henry Wace (Edinburgh: T&T Clark; Grand Rapids: Eerdmans, 1892), *Christian Classics Ethereal Library*, Calvin College, Web, 17 Sept. 2016.

reminder of her subjection, thus annulling, as it were, the ordinance of subjection" (qtd. in Brown, *Body* 288).[36] As Brown states, "As late as 390, Imperial laws threatened to depose any bishop who allowed such women into his church" (*Body* 288). It was believed that "under the inspiration of their ascetic persuasion [such women acted] against the laws human and divine" (288-89) – an assumption still valid throughout the Middle Ages.

Consequently, the female haircut was unthinkable for a long time unless it was for ritualistic life transitions, as in the Jewish belief in which a future wife's hair was shortened on the day of her marriage as a symbol of submissiveness to her future husband (Balabanova 27) or if it was used as a specific form of gender-related punishment (Herrmann, *Die Folter* 170-71, 176; *Sex und Folter* 94). In Catholic belief, by contrast, a monk's tonsure remained the only socially accepted short haircut for a long time, following a strict ritual upon his entry into monastic seclusion (Balabanova 27).

From a social perspective, it is not only problematic that the female saints have their hair cut, but that many of them are tonsured deliberately (often by men) in order to enter monasteries. What function – practical and symbolic – does cutting one's hair have in women's hagiography in general? What is the status of female transvestite saints in hagiography if one considers on the one hand the challenge of cross-dressing, as previously shown in the legend of Saint Eugenia, and on the other hand that the tonsure, as God's haircut, is a sign of submission and submissiveness?

Schulenburg has argued that the "disguise [...] provided [the saints] with certain practical benefits; for example a level of protection and opportunities for a greater independence and mobility which were frequently limited because of their gender" (155). "On a symbolic level", she continues, "this 'regendering' might also be seen as a metaphor, projecting to the ultimate extreme the patristic encouragement for women to renounce their sex and become honorary males, or asexual eunuchs, when they served the Church and Christ" (155).[37] Yet is it truly a form of "greater independence and mobility" if the transvestite saints, these apparently independent virgins who successfully escape the social expectations of marriage and childbearing, again end up in the enclosure of the male monastic community? How mobile is Saint Euphrosyne, who because of her fair appearance stirs up homoerotic temptations among her brothers and is thus enclosed within her enclosure, living locked up in her cell? Rather, do not the transvestite saints' legends propose metaphorical independence in the form of personal choice, as the saints may successfully decline the submission to marriage but

[36] For canon 17 and the canons in general see also *Acta et symbola conciliorum quae saeculo quarto habita sunt*, ed. E. J. Jonkers, *Textus Minores*, vol. 19 (Leiden: Brill, 1974); and *The Seven Ecumenical Church Councils*, ed. and trans. E. J. Percival, rpt. in *Library of Nicene and Post-Nicene Fathers*, vol. 14 (Grand Rapids: Eerdmans, 1977), p. 93 ff.

[37] For further hypotheses in this direction see Joyce Salisbury, *Church Fathers, Independent Virgins* (London: Verso, 1991), pp. 90-103, pp. 106-10; John Anson, "The Female Transvestite in Early Monasticism: The Origin and Development of a Motif", *Viator* 5 (1974): 1-32; Vern Bullough, "Transvestites in the Middle Ages", *American Journal of Sociology* 79.6 (1974): 1381-94; and Bullough and Bullough, *Cross Dressing, Sex, and Gender* (Philadelphia: U of Pennsylvania P, 1993), pp. 45-73.

assent to the submission of the monastery? This also raises the question of to whom they submit in the end – God or masculinity?

Clearly, as Raymond Firth has put it,

> On the whole, [the] deliberate shaving of the head or close cutting of the hair, has taken on a ritual quality, intended to mark a transition from one social state to another, and in particular to imply a modification in the status or social condition of the person whose hair is so treated. At many periods women have cut their hair short to demonstrate if not equality with men at least a repudiation of the woman's traditional sex role. (Qtd. in Schulenburg 155; Firth 288-89; see also Firth 298)

Even though the arguments of Schulenburg and Firth are to a great extent plausible, the proposed "demonstration of equality" and the becoming of an "honorary male" facilitated by the haircut seem, at this stage of the analysis, too positive. Considering the problems of homoerotic temptation, the accusations of rape, and the exclusion from the holy communities that these holy women had to face as a result of their deliberate removal of hair, the question arises of at what cost do these women gain equality. The following subchapter will therefore take both quotes as starting points for an in-depth analysis of the legend of Saint Euphrosyne, who, comparable to Saint Eugenia, also struggles after her gender change. The chapter will try to answer the questions raised earlier by also looking at popular patterns among the transvestite saints' legends and by investigating what function masculinity still plays within the transition from woman to a female man of God.

3.3.1 Saints Eugenia and Euphrosyne: Manly Women of God

> She […] asked that they cut off her hair in the custom of males and through garments pretend that she was a young man.
>
> Saint Eugenia[38]

> But who can cut my hair? I would not wish those who have no belief in God to do it.
>
> Saint Euphrosyne[39]

The manifold roles of the transvestite saints have already been discussed in regard to the female breast in the second chapter, in which Eugenia's life has been used to exemplify

[38] "hyre fæx forcurfon on wæpmonna wysan and mid wædum gehiwodon swylce heo cniht wære". *Natale Sancte Eugenie*, Skeat I: 28; trans. Leslie A. Donovan, *Women Saints' Lives in Old English Prose* (Cambridge: Brewer, 1999), p. 69.

[39] "Ac hwa mæg me be-efesian. [Soðlice] ic nolde þœt hit þa [dydon þe nænne] geleafan nabbað to gode". *Natale Sancte Eufrasiæ*, Skeat II: 340; trans. Leslie A. Donovan, *Women Saints' Lives in Old English Prose* (Cambridge: Brewer, 1999), p. 83; see also the Latin tradition of Saint Euphrosyne in the *Patrologia Latina*: "Et quis me habet tondere? Nolebat a laico tonderi, qui non servat fidem", *PL* 73: 645C.

socially expected gender roles and the appeal but also the danger of disguising one's natural sex. In the life of Saint Eugenia, however, it is not only the metaphorical removal of the breast which is significant, as Eugenia also asks her two companions to "cut off her hair in the custom of males" (Donovan 69; "hyre fæx forcurfon on wæpmonna wysan" [*Natale Sancte Eugenie*, Skeat I: 28]). Eugenia, who already neutralizes her femininity by cross-dressing as a man, intensifies the negation of her female sex through the haircut. It becomes part of Eugenia's *rite de passage*, her transformation ceremony into becoming one of the "honorary males" (Schulenburg 155), and along with her cross-dressing marks her transition from an ordinary woman to one of the female men of God. Yet whereas gender-crossing via clothes can be performed instantly, it is the haircut which has a long-lasting influence on her outer appearance and should thus be considered the final transitory point in her metamorphosis from woman to man. She assimilates through the sacred, ritualistic performance of receiving the holy tonsure. The access to the enclosed monastic community, which was initiated through her cross-dressing and the hiding of her breasts, can be granted only with the shortening of her hair in the fashion of monks. Consequently, cutting one's hair is not only a disguise of female identity, but from a medieval point of view also a clear denial of it. This leads, as the harlot saints have shown in the desert, to a withdrawal from social life and to an ascetic lifestyle.

As already depicted in detail in chapter 2.3, the only-in-theory accepted cross-dressing and the problematic haircut cause complicated happenings in the narrative of Saint Eugenia, which at the end lead to her assassination. Yet one scene from the legend has to be taken into consideration again. As mentioned previously, while helping the sick, Eugenia also attends to Melantia, who later on accuses her of rape and thus initiates her eventual downfall. In this scene it is interesting that Eugenia, comparable to Mary Magdalene, is anointing the widow "with oil in the name of Jesus Christ" (de Voragine II: 166; "oleo perungens […] in nomine Jesu Christi" [Graesse 603]). Whereas in Mary Magdalene's case it was the sinner who anointed the Saviour's feet, here it is the cross-dressed female who anoints the female sinner. As Bullough and Bullough emphasize, society accepted women assuming male roles "as a sign of superiority to other women" (68). Thus, Eugenia in her masculine disguise is superior to the tempting, Eve-like widow and has progressed into a woman whose mind is based on reason and logic and not on emotions and sexual enticement.

With Eugenia as the analytical basis, short hair is associated with three functions in women's hagiography so far: 1) the disguise and denial of female identity, usually in order to enter a monastic community and consequently a withdrawal from social life; 2) the escape from social reality for many women (dominance of patriarchy, marriage and childbearing); and 3) the protection of virginity and bodily purity.

All of these aspects can also be found in the *vita* of Saint Euphrosyne, a saint who, if not completely fictional, may have lived in the fifth century (Donovan 79) and who is one of the few female virgin saints who is not martyred because of her vocation. In contrast to the rather active life led by Eugenia, Euphrosyne lived in monastic asceticism until her death. Even though Euphrosyne was not accused of rape and led a passive lifestyle, the allusion to homosexuality is far more obvious and, comparable to Eugenia's lesbian encounter, affects the remainder of the narrative.

According to Donovan, the earliest complete version of Euphrosyne's legend can be found in Greek sources from the seventh century (79).[40] Approximately eleven Latin manuscripts containing her story have survived in Western Europe, among them the *Vita Sanctæ Euphrosinæ* included in the *Patrologia Latina* (73: 643-52).[41] Around AD 1050 a renewed interest in her *vita* and cult may have been the result of the tenth-century Benedictine reform movement in England (80). Nevertheless, the *vita* of Saint Euphrosyne was not as widespread as the cults of the other female saints mentioned so far, which may be the reason why it is not included in the *Legenda Aurea*. When and in which source the aspect of hair was added cannot be said for sure, yet both the *Vita Sanctæ Euphrosinæ* and Ælfric's *Natale Sancte Eufrasiæ* explicitly include the aspect of hair in the process of her gender modification.

Euphrosyne grows up with a loving and caring father, who educates his daughter in faith and religion. In contrast to the other saints dealt with so far, she is even explicitly baptized. Shortly after her eighteenth birthday, her father, who wants to secure his daughter's future, starts to look for a husband for her and soon finds a suitable, wealthy candidate. Before the wedding ceremony is supposed to take place, her father takes her to a monastery, which he visits often, and asks the abbot to bless her – the turning point in Euphrosyne's life. In an interview with the abbot, Euphrosyne is overwhelmed by the ascetic lifestyle he leads and asks whether it is possible for her to join the monastic orders to avoid marriage. The brother answers that she should wed herself to Christ and adds, "Lay aside your worldly clothes also, and clothe yourself in a monk's robe" (Donovan 83; "ac fár nu to mynstre digellice and alege þine woruldlican gegyrlan and gegyre þe mid munuc-reafe" [*Natale Sancte Eufrasiæ*, Skeat II: 340]; see also *PL* 73: 646C). Thinking about which type of monastery to choose, Euphrosyne claims, "If I journeyed now to a monastery for women, my father would seek me and find me there. Then, he would take me by force for my bridegroom's sake. So, I will journey to a monastery for men where no one would expect me"[42] (Donovan 84; "Gic ic nu fare to fæmnena mynstre þonne secð min fæder me þær and me þær findað þonne nimð he me neadunga þanon for mines bryd-guman þingan ac ic wille faran to wera mynstre þaer nan man min ne wene" [Skeat II: 342]; *PL* 73: 645). With the help of the monk, she enters the monastery primarily to follow her faith, but also with the intention of avoiding the unwelcome marriage, defloration and loss of her purity. After she has received the holy blessing, her hair is sheared off and she replaces her "worldly clothes" with a monk's robe.

In addition, she not only changes her outer appearance, but also renames herself Smaragdus (Skeat II: 344; *PL* 73: 646 D). From this moment on, the pronouns within the story also change from "she" and "her" to "he" and "him" (Skeat II: 344). Interestingly, even though she discards her female identity and former life completely,

[40] See also *Bibliotheca Hagiographica Graeca*, ed. François Halkin (Brussels: Société des Bollandistes, 1957), pp. 625-26.

[41] According to Donovan, the entry in the *Patrologia Latina* dates back to the eight century (79).

[42] The statement sums up a common cultural practice at this time to place young women in cloisters until a suitable husband was found. For further explanations consult Peter Brown, *The Body and Society: Men, Women and Sexual Renunciation in Early Christianity* (New York: Columbia UP, 1988), p. 261.

her new name still indicates her femininity and her sexually pure body, as the "Smaragd" (Engl. *emerald*) was and still is associated with the female zodiacal sign of the Virgo, and the Virgo was pictured with blonde hair (Warner 374).

Euphrosyne's crossing of natural gender boundaries, performed through the haircut, is also problematic in regard to the monks' forbidden sexual temptation for her: "Because Smaragdus was so beautiful in appearance [...] whenever the brothers came to the church, they became sorely tempted by Smaragdus' fairness" (Donovan 85; "smaragdus wæs wlitig on an-syne swa oft swa ða broðra comon to cyrcan [...] and wurdon þearle gecostnode þurh his fægernysse" [Skeat II: 344]; *PL* 73: 647). Again, the haircut and the resulting denial of the female sex end in the stimulation of forbidden carnal desires – this time in a gay and not, as in Eugenia's case, in a lesbian direction. The disguise and the haircut trigger homosexual temptations, which are always brought up by others – monks and the widow – and not by the saint herself.

In contrast to Eugenia, however, there is no accusation of rape. Nevertheless, because of the disturbance among the monks, who believe her to be touched by the devil, Euphrosyne is locked away in a cell to live and pray in solitude. Even though she can now be sure that her virginity is safe, her "progress" is stopped as well. The secret flight from her home to escape from social norms, which can be considered an independent, progressive act, ends with her dependence on the monastic community, her voluntary submission to the order and, even worse, a life in solitude in an enclosed space. As Sandra Lowerre argues, "Euphrosyne living in a cell – this is precisely the state the Church Fathers wanted the woman to be: enclosed" (71). This relates to Garber's argument that masculinity and especially the Church and the Church Fathers wanted to regulate the identity and social roles of their female members (26). As a result, even though Euphrosyne evades the social expectations of femininity, her masculine disguise is accepted and tolerated only in an enclosed space. In this state of asceticism she is able to keep up her male disguise for almost forty years and her transvestite status is discovered only upon her death. According to Bullough and Bullough, "Holy women who impersonated men remained much admired, in particular if their disguise was only uncovered after their death" (51). Despite the praise, it is nature and death that finally remove the sinful temptation of the monks and transform Smaragdus back into Euphrosyne.

Returning to the arguments made by Schulenburg and Firth in the introduction to this chapter, the disguise provided by the haircut certainly gave the saints "certain practical benefits", a "level of protection" (Schulenburg 155), and truly symbolised a negation of their true sex. However, the independence these women gained through the haircut and cross-dressing is not only "frequently limited" (155), it remains merely a symbolic independence. The only independence gained was for one personal decision, namely to choose which enclosed state of life they wanted to assent to – marriage or monastery. Even if the haircut is the final step in the saints' attempt to become "honorary males" (155), the sexual and gendered equality it promises has to be paid at a high price.

3.3.2 Receiving the Holy Haircut: Patterns, Popularity and the Denial of Sexuality

> What save a little religious romance is the oft-repeated tale of the adventures of a pious woman hiding herself in a monastery with the name and in the garb of a man, accused of misconduct and proved to be innocent after her death? The heroine is called, as the case may be, Marina, Pelagia, Eugenia, Euphrosyne, Theodora, Margaret or Apollinaria. It is obvious that this was a favourite theme among pious story-tellers.
>
> Hippolyte Delehaye[43]

Within women's hagiography, there are numerous female saints whose *vitae* follow a pattern similar to that of Saint Eugenia and to a certain extent to that of Saint Euphrosyne. As Delehaye already noted during his time, the topic of a young woman escaping her social fate by hiding in a monastery was a "favourite theme among pious story-tellers" (63), and several of the older hagiographic legends correspond to such an extent that only the names of the saints differ from each other. Others, in particular later medieval female saints whose existence is not dismissed as complete hagiographic fiction but is historically proven, as is the case with Saint Clare (thirteenth century) and Saint Catherine of Siena (fourteenth century), were again influenced by the *vitae* of the earlier saints and tried to copy these saintly lifestyles.

Maitland and Mulford argue that the "reasons why these mythical or semi-mythical women disguise their gender are diverse: disguise, either from a desire to expand their own choices or to escape from limitations imposed on them from the outside is common" (127). Thus, the legends of Saints Marina, Theodora and Margaret, for example, all follow the same stylistic pattern, and all "took on maleness" in one way or the other (127). The haircut is explicitly mentioned in the life of the saints Theodora and Margaret, whereas in the legend of Saint Marina it can be assumed that she received the tonsure upon her entrance into the monastic community.[44] These saints also share several other characteristics, from adopting masculine attire to the haircut to being attributed with a masculine name, as in the legend of Saint Euphrosyne. Marina has her name changed to the masculine form Marinus (or Maryn), Margaret to Pelagius and Theodora to Theodore (de Voragine I: 324, 366; II: 232). In addition, all of these women saints are accused of misbehaving in one way or another because of their gender inversion. The assuming of male roles, as mentioned previously in chapter 2, was unofficially accepted, yet "becoming male" worked only with restrictions and limitations and had to be punished somehow. The religious steadfastness of the transvestite saints

[43] Hippolyte Delehaye, *The Legends of the Saints: An Introduction to Hagiography*, trans. V. M. Crawford (Breinigsville: Kessinger, 2009), p. 63.

[44] For the complete *vitae* see, for example, Jacobus de Voragine, *The Golden Legend: Readings on the Saints*, 2 vols., ed. and trans. William Granger Ryan (Princeton: Princeton UP, 1995), I: 324-25, I: 365-67, II: 232-33. Several scholars believe that overall it is one story; the only element which was changed was the name. Some saints such as Margaret (also known as Pelagia) and Pelagia (also known as Margaret) even share the same feast day (de Voragine I: 325, n. 1).

had to be put to the test. Therefore, in most transvestite narratives the gender crossing results in an accusation either of raping a female ward or of having committed adultery. Some even blame the female saints of being the father of a child born out of wedlock. In all cases, the gender switch leads to homoerotic implications – of women being attracted to the fair appearance of the eunuch-like monks. The legend of Saint Euphrosyne, in which men are attracted by her male appearance, seems to be an exception. Concerning the end of the narratives, the legend of Saint Eugenia seems to be singled out, as she is the only one who reclaims her womanhood to escape death. Marina, Theodora, Margaret and many more accept their fate and view their apparent misconduct as a God-given trial they have to overcome.

To exemplify these patterns among the transvestite saints' narratives, a comparison between Saint Marina, Saint Theodora and Saint Margaret will show the repetitive structures of these legends. In the legend of Saint Marina, Marina's father dresses her in men's clothes. He changes her name to Marinus and sends his disguised daughter to a monastery, where she is educated in reading and writing. When she is accused of being the father of a young woman's child, she is dismissed from the community in order to raise the child. Years later she is allowed to reenter the monastery, yet only to perform the most menial tasks, which she accepts humbly and "cheerfully" (de Voragine I: 325; "hilariter" [Graesse 353]). The same outline can be found in the legend of Saint Theodora. Akin to Marina, Theodora is also wrongly accused of fathering a child, removed from the community, and later allowed to rejoin the orders together with the child (I: 366-67). Comparable to Euphrosyne, their female identities are discovered only upon their deaths, when their brothers wash their corpses for burial. Saint Margaret, on the other hand, is, similar to Saint Eugenia, accused of having committed adultery with a nun, who is then discovered to be pregnant. Like the harlot saints, as punishment she departs to a cave outside of the town to live a hermitic life (II: 233).

The exclusion from their chosen seclusion remains until their innocence has been proven. For the majority – Eugenia can be considered an exception here – this moment does not come during their lifetime, but postmortem. Their steadfastness and virtuousness is literally discovered at the moment their (former) brothers prepare their bodies for burial and the afterlife, when the body is undressed, the masculine masquerade removed and the true sex revealed. The moment of revelation leads to various reactions, ranging from being "stupefied and frightened", as in the legend of Saint Marina (de Voragine I: 325; "stupefacti […] et perterriti" [Graesse 353]) to fear, as in the legend of Saint Theodora ("A great fear came upon all", I: 367; "Factus est igitur timor magnus super omnes" [Graesse 399]). The distress of maltreating and wrongly accusing one of God's followers, and presumably the fear of being punished by God, results in the accusers' penance and admittance that, in the case of Saint Marina, "they had grossly maltreated this handmaid of God" (I: 325; "se in Dei famulam plurimum deliquisse fatentur: currunt omnes ad tam grande spectaculum et veniam postulant ignorantiae et delicti" [Graesse 353]). As soon as these women's innocence is confirmed, each of them is praised and buried honourably (I: 325, 368; II: 233) as "a woman who somehow broke through the barriers found herself praised for having a masculine mind or in other ways following the masculine model" (Bullough and Bullough ix).

The multiple existence of identical or semi-identical hagiographic narratives dealing with cross-dressing and the resulting problems leads to some preliminary conclusions:

first, it is certain, as Delehaye has put it, that cross-dressing saints' narratives were a favourite topic among hagiographers, which seemed to satisfy an intense need among readers (63). Consequently, more stories were written, expanded and adapted, many of which are still included in hagiographical compilations and thus support the general and long-lasting popularity of these saints and their *vitae* from their literary origins in ancient or medieval times onwards. Another issue to consider is that with the increasing distribution of these narratives, the idea of leaving one's family and female identity behind in order to join a monastery was distributed as well. To what extent could this controversial topic have been used for instructing women? On the one hand, these saints' lives support the idea of the preservation of one's bodily purity despite temptations. On the other hand, these legends support the idea of "becoming male", this almost mystical concept, which is certainly praised within these stories but at the same time relativized through the obstacles placed strategically at the peak of the transvestite's success. She who decides to follow the lives of these saints has to humbly accept the temptations and accusations that either lead to her dismissal from the community or to the discovery of her true sex.

To recall Weldon, all saints dealt with in this subchapter so far have a doubtful origin or are dismissed as hagiographic fiction.[45] The question remains of whether the significance of the haircut and the resulting transvestism is limited to those stories or whether female saints with similar features exist whose existence is historically proven. The question can be answered positively as the haircut and the element of cross-dressing are featured in the legend of Saint Clare (AD 1253),[46] the foundress of the Poor Clares or Minoresses and a loyal follower of Saint Francis of Assisi, as well as in the life of Saint Catherine of Siena (AD 1380),[47] who was canonized in 1461 and was even declared a doctor of the Church in 1970 (A. Butler III: 309; II: 192-97; Farmer 96-97, 107-08).

When Saint Clare is about eighteen years old, she secretly listens to the lectures by the popular and well-known Francis of Assisi, which strengthens her idea to dedicate her life to Christ. On Palm Sunday in 1212, so it is written, she decides to leave home to

[45] Terence Weldon, "Nov 9th: Matrona/Babylas of Perge", *Queering the Church*, 9 Nov. 2010, Web, 12 Sept. 2016.

[46] The earliest written document of the life of Saint Clare is by Thomas of Celano (before 1261). A full-length reprint can be found in the *Acta Sanctorum*: *AASS* Aug. II, 739-68. It has to be noted, however, that the *Acta* itself speaks of an "auctore anonymo" (754) in the preface to the *Vita Sancta Claræ Virginis*. Thus, even though Thomas of Celano is regarded as the "anonymous author" of the earliest written account of St. Clare, it cannot be said with certainty. For a discussion of the texts' authorship as well as a translation of the earliest manuscript as presented in the *Acta* see Pascal Robinson, *The Life of Saint Clare Ascribed to Thomas of Celano* (Philadelphia: Dolphin, 1910), p. xxii ff. Another early written account of Saint Clare in English is attributed to Luke Wadding (1588-1657). The text was compiled by Francis Hendricq as *The History of the Angelicall Virgin, Glorious S. Clare* and printed at Douai in 1635.

[47] For the life of Saint Catherina of Siena see *Vita S. Catharinae Senensis*, *AASS* Apr. II, 862-969. The *Acta* includes a reprint of Raymond of Capua's (c. 1330-1399) *Legenda Major* as well as the *Legenda Minor* by Thomas Caffarini (c.1350-c. 1434). Capua was Catherine's confessor. For an English version of his work, see *The Life of Saint Catherine*, trans. George Lamb (London: Harvill, 1960).

join the community where Saint Francis stays. In a mystical ceremony, Saint Francis and his followers receive her with "lighted tapers" ("cum luminaribus receperunt", *AASS* Aug. II, 756C; Hendricq 106; Robinson 14), outside a church. Clare removes her clothes before the altar and, standing naked in front of a group of people, the brothers[48] cut off Clare's hair ("ibi manu fratrum crines deponens", 756C; see also Hendricq 106; Robinson 14; A. Butler III: 309) "of extraordinary blondness" (Maitland and Mulford 122[49]). By doing so, as Maitland and Mulford argue, they are "cut[ting] off her pride, [making] her chaste, [making] her virtuous, manly, pure and hard" (122). The scene is symbolic through and through. Not only is the haircut a sign of sexual submissiveness and thus a transitory *rite de passage* from the secular to the sacred world, but it is explicitly performed in front of an altar within God's sight and with His approval. Clare is wed to Christ in this ceremony and has to remove every indicator of vanity and therefore of femininity. Her nakedness in front of the altar, the removal of her "fine clothes" ("ornatus varios dereliquit", 756C; see also Hendricq 106; Robinson 14; A. Butler III: 309), the haircut and the re-dressing afterwards in a penitential habit fosters her metamorphosis from a common woman to a follower and moreover to a bride of Christ. The performance starts and ends with her undressing and re-dressing, but it is nevertheless the haircut that is singled out and placed as a special action between nakedness and re-dressing. As Schulenburg claims, "A number of the female virgin saints of the early Middle Ages […] adopted these [the legendary] practices of cutting off their hair as strategies of defense against marriage or sexual assault, or as a symbol of their new status as brides of Christ" (157). Her biological sex as well as her gendered constructions are no longer of any importance after the procedure and are blurred once Clare has become a female man of God. In commemoration, her "unusually blonde" and thus virginlike curls were kept as relics and can today be seen in Assisi (Maitland and Mulford 123).

In contrast to all the short-haired saints mentioned so far, the life of Saint Catherine of Siena breaks up rigid patterns. Catherine was born in 1347 in Siena, Italy, and died in 1380 in Rome at the age of thirty-three (Schneider 290; A. Butler II: 192). She left numerous letters from which it is known that she was strongly influenced by the legend of Saint Euphrosyne[50] and wanted to join a monastic community as a man if her parents would not let her devote her life to Christianity (Schneider 296). Her *vita* thus has to be viewed from a different angle. Whereas the older legends – Saints Eugenia, Euphrosyne, Marina and Theodora, among others – differ only slightly, and several can be considered adaptations of one legend under an altered name, with Saint Catherine a life is presented which was knowingly influenced by the older stories and, significantly, is historically factual. Saint Catherine adapts the older patterns, trying to be one of these praised manly women. The legend states that when Saint Catherine is about twelve years old, her parents, in particular her mother, want her to dedicate more time to her

[48] In Hendricq's *S. Clare* and Butler's *St. Clare* it is Saint Francis himself who cuts Clare's hair. See also Maitland and Mulford 123.

[49] The colour of her hair is not mentioned in any of the textual sources used for this study. However, her blonde locks are kept as relics in the Basilica di Santa Chiara in Assisi. See also Maitland and Mulford 123.

[50] See *AASS* Apr. II, 872B

appearance in order to attract a suitable husband. To please her mother she consents at first ("consensit virgo dare corporis ornatui operam", *AASS* Apr. II, 873C; see also A. Butler II: 193). Soon, however, she regrets her decision to give in to worldly vanities and even more strongly than before wants to devote her life to Christ. Because her parents still underestimate their daughter's steadfastness and insist that she find a husband, a befriended friar is summoned to question her Christian belief. Convinced of her steadfastness, he advices her to cut off her hair in order to avoid marriage ("præscindas crines capitis tui ex toto, et tunc isti forte quiescent", *AASS* Apr. II, 874D), and Saint Catherine takes scissors ("mox arripiens forfices", 874D) and cuts off her beautiful hair with joy (capillos [...] juxta caput lætanter abscidit, 874D-E; "capilli [...] pulcherrimi", 874E), which in several of her *vitae* is described to be of a golden-brown colour,[51] until her head is bare ("tonsum ex toto", 874E). In Catherine of Siena's life, certain old stylistic patterns are rearranged, which is probably attributable to her historical authenticity and therefore limits poetic licence. In contrast to the older legends, she is not blonde, which was used to indicate the virtuous state, but has brown hair, the virtuousness of which has been strengthened by it being explicitly of a golden-brown colour. According to Augusta Theodosia Drane, "Hair of this particular hue has always been held in singular esteem by the natives of Italy" and Catherine's mother "might therefore have been well content with the personal advantages which nature had bestowed on her daughter" (21). In addition, she cuts her hair herself, a central change discussed in the upcoming subchapter, and generally appears less helpless than the previously mentioned female saints and even rather emancipated, taking into consideration that Euphrosyne, for example, Catherine's idol, insecurely cries out for someone who could perform the haircut. Even though Catherine's family scolds her, her parents realize that nothing could change her opinion and let her do what she desires (*AASS* Apr. II, 875). Hence, she is also the first female saint who does not have to perform a gender switch in order to avoid marriage. Despite all of these alterations, and even if Saint Catherine can be considered the most progressive woman among the short-haired saints, it is the haircut which remains the significant trigger, the key symbolic act that marks a change in her thinking and the beginning of a new lifestyle.

Numerous examples of the impact of the haircut within women's hagiography have been provided in detail so far. Nonetheless, several loose ends remain. First of all, would a change of gender as a way to break from one's past have worked out the other way around? Since men were considered the superior gender, there was certainly no need for them to cross-dress. It would actually have meant a downgrading in social status. A man who cross-dressed as a woman was regarded as weak (Bullough and Bullough 23) because he went from a superior to a subordinate status and was not tolerated in medieval society as the female cross-dressers were. Another unanswered question is also raised by Bullough and Bullough: "If a man's cross-dressing as a

[51] See, for example, "Flavum illum capillum et aureum, jubet abicere" in John Pino's *Divæ Catharinæ Senensis Vitæ* (1505), p. 8; or "Capillos flavos quos habebat, abscidit" in *Processus contestationum super sanctitate et doctrina B. Catherinæ de Senis* in Edmond Martène and Ursin Durand, eds. *Veterum Scriptorum et Monumentorum Amplissima Collectio* (Paris, 1729), p. 1314 – the latter being the documentation of the Process of Venice held in 1411; see also "she cut off her golden-brown hair – her chief beauty" in Butler II: 193.

woman was a sign of weakness, would a woman cross-dressing as a man be regarded as having greater 'strength' than other women?" (23). With regard to the fact that these women, instead of facing their female role and social fate, fled their homes secretly and, except for Saint Catherine, could not openly declare their refusal of secular marriage and their preference for a sacred wedding to God, "strength" might not be the correct word here. These women were certainly braver than others as they stood up for their ideals in a society in which women, from a modern perspective, were often suppressed, not considered citizens, and generally thought of as the property of their fathers, brothers and husbands. They chose a lifestyle that was condemned and praised at the same time. As the legends have shown, those who cross-dressed could certainly gain a higher social status for their attempts to become male (Bullough and Bullough 53), but could also end up in complicated, life-threatening situations. Recognition of their virtuous behaviour was often granted only postmortem. These women were courageous enough to face enclosure in cells, false accusations and, most of all, the discovery of their female sex – but did they really have a greater "strength" than other common women? What about the majority of medieval women who came to terms with their fate? Is it not true "strength" to stay in the female role rather than to run away and to disguise one's personality?

Despite these questions, the analysis of patterns within these legends and their enduring popularity has shown that exactly this type of controversy between female liberation and the threat of penalty was accepted and readapted tremendously. As Schulenburg summarizes, the "Stories of female transvestite saints were [...] very popular in the medieval world, especially among monastic communities" (158), and despite the fact that these women surely questioned the traditional female role, "they were perceived [...] as especially relevant potential models for female religious" (158).

3.3.3 "But Who Can Cut My Hair?" The Function of Masculinity

> But who can cut my hair? I would not wish those who have no belief in God to do it.
>
> Saint Euphrosyne[52]

Eugenia, Euphrosyne, Clare – among the majority of the transvestite saints, the haircut is performed by men, recalling the question of whether these apparently independent, gender-bending virgins are truly independent. What types of men cut the hair and do these female saints really need a man to perform the haircut? How can it be explained that Euphrosyne is obviously helpless and does not cut her hair herself before entering

[52] Leslie A. Donovan, *Women Saints' Lives in Old English Prose* (Cambridge: Brewer, 1999), p. 83. "Ac hwa mæg me be-efesian. [Soðlice] ic nolde þœt hit þa [dydon þe nænne] geleafan nabbað to gode". *Natale Sancte Eufrasiæ*, Skeat II: 340. See also the Latin tradition of Saint Euphrosyne in the *Patrologia Latina:* "Et quis me habet tondere? Nolebat a laico tonderi, qui non servat fidem" (73: 645).

the monastery, like Saint Catherine? As other transvestite figures who do not receive the tonsure do not require a special transitional contact with a eunuch or monk, a closer look at the cultural circumstances and the specificity of the haircut itself may provide the necessary information.

Culturally, it has to be kept in mind that the Church Council of Gangra had condemned women who adopted male identities to join all-male monastic communities (Bullough and Bullough 51). Moreover, in order to secure gender boundaries, not only were women prohibited to cut off their hair, but each bishop who allowed short-haired, unveiled women to enter his church was also threatened with deposition (Coates 11; Brown, *Body* 288-89). Helping Euphrosyne and Eugenia, as well as the others, in their attempt to escape their "natural" fates therefore not only contributes to the controversial social status of short-haired (holy) women, but also turns the "hairy" performance into a complex act with fatal consequences possible for both sides.

Concerning the haircut itself, it is not just a shortening of head hair in general, but a unique, highly symbolic haircut – the tonsure, which in its original function marks the ceremonial transition into monastic seclusion. Hence, it not only reminded the monks of their avowed submission to God, but also displayed this life change publicly. For the public, the tonsure, as Cooper notes, was symbolically equivalent to castration (45), as it showed the metaphorical rejection of sexual intercourse and the resulting loss of procreation. What does the tonsure thus mean for a woman? The overall female denial of female sexuality was evaluated positively in a society strongly fighting for the ideal of virginity and bodily purity. Is the female tonsure a positive performance, because it allows the maintenance of virginity until the detection of the saints' true sex? Or can it be perceived as an action that puts their independence and "strength" (Bullough and Bullough 23) into perspective, as they have to submit again to men and to God?

First of all, it is noteworthy that whereas the heroine is usually persecuted by strong male characters, the modification from woman to man is either performed by transgender or pseudohermaphrodite men, such as eunuchs; by male members of the Church, such as bishops and monks; or by a combination of the two, since monks were often eunuchs and vice versa. In Eugenia's case the haircut is carried out by two eunuchs (*Natale Sancte Eugenie*, Skeat I: 28-29) and in Euphrosyne's case by a monk (*Natale Sancte Eufrasiœ*, Skeat II: 341-45; *PL* 73: 645), and in the legend of Saint Clare either a whole group of monks or a male saint, the ascetic Francis of Assisi, ceremonially shorten Saint Claire's hair (*AASS* Aug. II, 756C; cf. Hendricq 106). What all of these men have in common is that they lead ascetic and nonsexual, celibate lives. From a medieval perspective this turned them into outcasts, into unmanly man. Men had to be strong, powerful, and fertile. Monks and eunuchs may have been powerful within their communities and could have been high clerical officials, but none of them were regarded as strong and fertile. Moreover, eunuchs were commonly castrated and hence lacked part of their male genitalia. Furthermore, if the castration had been done prepubescence, eunuchs would be unable to assume the masculine role because their facial hair would not grow and their voices would not change, and therefore "the eunuch would no longer be recognizable as a man" (Brown, *Body* 169).[53] Comparable to the

[53] For an in-depth discussion of eunuchs and their social acceptance as well as the comparison between gender-bending female saints and eunuchism, see chapter 5.

female transvestite saints, these men, who are endowed with the power of performing the transformative element of cutting the women's hair, are themselves already modified. They have transformed themselves into rather androgynous figures, deprived of their sex and gender in one way or another, and are marginalized by society, just as the female transvestite saints are. Monks and eunuchs have opted out of society in order to assimilate themselves to a different cultural order.

Yet why is this marginalised figure required for tonsuring? The most obvious explanation is given by the haircut itself. The tonsure is a sacred act which can be implemented only by full members of the Church who are tonsured as well. As male monastic communities normally consist only of men, it is only legitimate and obvious that a man will cut the hair. That historically many women in the Middle Ages tried to join monastic communities rather than convents resulted from the fear that their relatives could remove them far more easily from a nunnery than from a monastery in order to take them back home to marry the chosen husband (Brown, *Body* 261; see also chapter 3.3.1, n. 42). As women ideally entered monasteries secretly, their transformation was also performed secretly. That his future brother was a woman may therefore have been known to the haircutter, yet the fact was, or at least seemed to be, irrelevant to many. For example, the monk in the legend of Saint Euphrosyne answers her question about whether she would be allowed to join: "Yes […] and most of all because of the Lord's command that say thus, 'he who comes to me, I will not drive him away from me'" (Donovan 82; "Gea […] swiðor for þære drihtenlican stefne þe þus cwæð þone þe me to-cymð ne drife ic hine fram me" [*Natale Sancte Eufrasiœ*, Skeat II: 338]; see also John 6:37). Nobody who seeks shelter is sent away from the community. And yet, everyone – no matter whether woman or man – who enters a monastery has to assimilate through new clothing and a hairstyle which signifies submission to God as monk or bride of Christ. The entrance to a monastic community may be voluntary, but the entrance ritual is obligatory.

Furthermore, these already transformed figures arguably serve as a mirror to women's bending of gender concepts. Eunuchs and monks and female transvestites are in many ways alike. Comparable to female transvestites, then, eunuchs and monks, both born male, modify their biological sex and their gender constructions via "castration" – in a literal and symbolic understanding of the term. A lack of facial hair, a high-pitched voice and a fair face are female rather than male attributes. The preservation of a pure body, which is not defiled by any sexual desire, is the goal of both the women and the men and both choose this lifestyle deliberately. Comparable to the performers of the haircut, the transvestite saints also represent the margins of society. Monks, eunuchs and transvestite saints categorize themselves and are categorized by society, and yet the transvestite saints are, comparable to the harlot saints, doubly marginal as they want to be and behave like men but remain women.

In addition, not only does the haircut itself indicate a transitional moment, but the haircutters also function as the transitional contact between the women and God. Thus the biological and social attributes of gender increase and decrease at the same time – from a woman to a transvestite saint to a eunuch and finally to God. The attributes increase because whereas the woman is the subordinate within medieval society, the (female) eunuch as a transgender character is neither subordinate nor superordinate. God, on the other hand, who still is widely accepted as male, represents the ultimate spiritual, masculine figure. In order to progress spiritually, women, similar to their male ascetic counterparts, wanted to achieve some kind of apotheosis, to resemble that idealized masculine persona. However, as this idealized male figure is not sexually active and "procreates" only spiritually, the socially favoured attributes of masculinity thus decrease simultaneously. Yet socially a direct comparison between women and God still remained difficult. The eunuch hence functions as a transitional figure, as a bridge between the two, as the grey zone between femininity and spiritual omniscience, which the women as well as the monks want to achieve. The notion of "becoming male" is thus omnipresent within these legends. It is enacted through the idea of cross-dressing, the haircut itself and the men who perform the haircut – even if they are emasculated men in the eyes of society. As Martha Easton summarizes, "The notion of 'becoming male' became a signifier for female spirituality; women martyrs and ascetics who had cast off the constructed characteristics of their gender progressed towards an advanced spiritual state that was described as masculine" (51).

3.4 Otherness and Ultimate Violation: The Bearded Saint

> Around those places there are women born, who have beards down to their breasts.
>
> *Wonders of the East*[54]

> Then there are other women who have boar's tusks and hair down to their heels and ox-tails on their loins. [...] Because of their uncleanness they were killed by Alexander the Great of Macedon. He killed them because he could not capture them alive, because they have offensive and disgusting bodies.
>
> *Wonders of the East*[55]

In regard to beards, sex and gender, Allen Frantzen states, "The breast is the marker of the female, the beard of the male" (76) – a statement generally correct for most human beings. However, the quotes from the *Wonders of the East* indicate that first of all, even

[54] "ða habbað beardas swa side oð heora breost", Orchard 198-99. The *Wonders of the East* can be found in three illuminated manuscripts. It appears in Late West-Saxon together with *Beowulf* in the *Cotton Vitellius A. xv*., the so-called *Beowulf* manuscript (also known as the Nowell Codex). A second manuscript, composed in Latin and Old English, can be found in the *Cotton Tiberius B.v.* A third Latin copy is preserved in the Oxford Bodleian Library. For an in-depth discussion of the texts' background see Andy Orchard, *Pride and Prodigies: Studies in the Monsters of the Beowulf-Manuscript* (Toronto: U of Toronto P, 1995).

[55] "Đonne sindon oðre wif ða habbað eoferes tucxas feax oð helan side, on lendenum oxan tægl. [...] For heora unclennesse hie gefelde wurdon fram ðam mycclan macedoniscan Alexandre. Þa he hi lifiende gefon ne mihte, þa acwealde he hi for ðam hi syndon æwisce on lichoman unweorðe". Andy Orchard, *Pride and Prodigies: Studies in the Monsters of the Beowulf-Manuscript* (Toronto: U of Toronto P, 1995), pp. 200-01.

a thousand years ago women with an enormous growth of facial hair and beards were reported to exist. Second, men, in this case Alexander the Great, were scared of them, and third these women were killed just because of their facial hair, which provided them with animallike features, atypical female characteristics and "offensive and disgusting bodies" (Orchard 201).

Today, the condition of extensive growth of hair "on parts of the body that have normally only downy, lanugo hair" is known as *hirsutism* or *hypertrichosis*, denoting a hormonal imbalance (Cooper 30; see also Leynhausen 149; Schulenburg 153). However, despite medical innovations and extensive research, even today women with beards are considered repulsive and abnormal to men and women alike. For example, in February of 2010, Gulf News reported that an Arab ambassador in Dubai had decided to "call off his wedding immediately after he discovered that his wife-to-be, who wears a niqab, was bearded and cross-eyed". The diplomat furthermore claimed that the "bride's mother deceived his mother, when she went to see his wife-to-be, by showing her pictures of the bride's sister" (Za'za')[56] and thus trying to disguise the true bride's hairy face.

Even though a thousand years apart, what the examples from the *Wonders of the East*[57] and the news article show is that despite the fact that the phenomenon of a female beard is now medically explainable, the shocking and repulsive effect of a bearded woman transcends time and borders. The only obvious difference in regard to these bearded women is that the bearded wife and her family were fully aware of her violation of female beauty standards and even unsuccessfully tried to hide her nonconformity. The bearded women presented in the *Wonders of the East* did not possess the knowledge that their outer appearance differed from other women whom Alexander the Great had met during his life. Why is the beard on a woman's face perceived as such a violation and alienation of the feminine? Why is it perceived as repulsive and as the ultimate symbol of female ugliness and yet triggers a (negative) fascination – a fascination, that for example, led to the display of bearded women in amusement parks until well into in the nineteenth century[58] – in literature and real life alike?

Several reasons why a bearded woman was and still is regarded as the Other can be found in cultural history, in which a beard was supposed to distinguish boys from men and not men from women. While beards have constantly been in and out of fashion – even Christ was at one point temporarily favoured beardless (Balabanova 119) – and

[56] Bassam Za'za', "Man Claims Fiancée Hid Beard under Niqab", *Gulf News*, 10. Feb. 2010, Web, 10 Feb. 2010. The news was distributed globally and made it to the German website of Yahoo with the title "Braut mit Bart – Ehe annuliert", *Yahoo News*, 10. Feb.2010, Web, 12 Feb. 2010. Trans: "Bride with Beard – Marriage Annulled".

[57] According to medieval geographical understanding of the world map, the East was far enough away from the European continent to be the geographical landmark for all evil, licentious, and for anti-Christian ideas and was also often used to relocate saints' legends in order to circumvent discussion. Where the East was exactly located was generally of no great importance – it was rather treated as a concept denoting "elsewhere" – away from Britain. See for example Mary B. Campbell, *The Witness and the Other World: Exotic European Travel Writing, 400-1600* (Ithaca: Cornell UP, 1988). That the news article is located in the East as well is just a coincidence.

[58] A popular example is the American and probably best-documented bearded lady, Annie Jones-Elliot (c. 1860-1902). The sensational and repulsive effect of a female beard and her blurring of gender boundaries apparently sold well (Cooper 30).

even though there has been as much "variety in beards and whiskers as in hair styles" (Cooper 94), the beard has always been a stereotypical symbol of masculinity (Haas 11). Its growth was seen as the result of a boy's increasing strength on his way to manhood (Balabanova 29). This idea supported the popular belief that hair and in particular the beard symbolizes power, and scientifically, the hair of a beard truly is the strongest hair growing on a male body (111). Consequently, throughout cultural history the beard was often treated as a "sacred token of both strength and virility", and in many cultures beards were held to such high esteem that pulling a man's beard was considered an assault on his honour (Cooper 41). Hairiness, as Cooper sums up, "has become a symbol and a proof of masculinity", and "the ability to grow a beard is a specifically male ability" (37).

If a beard is *the* symbol of masculinity, what happens if a woman, and in particular a holy woman, challenges this "marker of the male" (Frantzen 76) and this "specifically male ability" (Cooper 37) by praying explicitly for a beard to disfigure her? Does the beard on a female saint's face turn her into something superior to men, as within her person male and female features are blended together, or should it rather be interpreted as just another method of "becoming male"? In women's hagiography at least three female saints' legends exist in which the female protagonist is gifted with a beard: the Spanish saint Paula of Avila, also known as Saint Barbata – the bearded one;[59] Saint Galla of Rome;[60] and the more popular Saint Wilgefortis (*De S. Liberata alias Wilgeforte*, *AASS* Jul. V, 50-70; A. Butler III: 151), which because of the wider circulation and controversial fame of her legend will form the basis of the following analysis. All three are pictured with a beard in order to circumvent once more a common hagiographical pattern: marriage and bodily sexual defilement. This turns the beard into an interesting alteration of the gruesome "virginal strategies of disfigurement" (Schulenburg 152) and its growth into a performative act and a life-changing transitional moment, comparable to the sudden growth of hair in the legend of Saint Agnes. As seen so far, it is not unusual that many female saints become "'masculinised' through either physical or social metamorphosis" (Easton 51). However, the beard is challenging as it is "both a sign of manly identity and of womanly disgrace" (Frantzen 77) and with the growth of a beard, a woman not only questions everything culturally and socially expected to be feminine, but also shakes the foundation of masculinity and, in the case of the bearded saints, also the Church's patriarchal focus.

[59] For her legend consult *De S. Paula*, *AASS* Feb. III, 177. That the saint is still venerated and marketed nowadays is visible on the tourist information website of the region of Avila, which also provides a summary of her story: "St. Paula Barbada", *Turismo de Ávila*, n.d., Web, 5 Mar. 2014. For a critical reference to her legend see Vern Bullough, "Transvestites in the Middle Ages", *American Journal of Sociology* 79.6 (1974): 1388; and Jane Tibbetts Schulenburg, *Forgetful of Their Sex: Female Sanctity and Society, ca. 500-1100* (Chicago: Chicago UP, 1998), pp. 152-53, p. 463, n. 105.

[60] See *De S. Galla. AASS* Oct. III, 147-63. For a summary of her legend see Francis Mershman, "St. Galla", *The Catholic Encyclopaedia*, vol. 6 (New York: Appleton, 1909), 2012, Web, 12 Feb. 2013; or "Saint Galla of Rome", *CatholicSaints.Info*, 13 Feb. 2014, Web, 5 Mar. 2014. A more detailed version of her life can be found in the *Dialogues* of Gregory the Great in *Early Church Fathers – Additional Texts*, book IV, chapter 13, ed. Roger Pearse, n.d., Web, 5 Mar. 2014.

About the legend of Saint Wilgefortis, Alban Butler writers that her "story is the curiosity of hagiology"[61] and as such "hardly worth including in a collection of lives of the saints but for the fact that it has the unenviable distinction of being one of the most false and preposterous of the pseudo-pious romances by which simple Christians have been deceived or regaled" (III: 51). That the popular, rather folkloric legend of the bearded and crucified virgin is indeed a "strange cult" ("peculari cultu", Jul. V: 63F) is also attested in the *Acta Sanctorum*, which begins the discussion of *De S. Liberata alias Wilgeforte* by indicating the overall complexity of the saint's *vita* and its literary tradition, which is compared to a complex maze with many choices of paths and directions and with only a vague promise of finding an "exit" (Jul. V: 50B; "De Sancta in titulo proposita acturus vastum ingredior labyrinthum, qui tot tamque variis semitarum amfractibus est implexus, ut mihi vix ullum ex eo exitum promittere ausim").

When its cult emerged and developed in Flanders or the Netherlands sometime in the later Middle Ages (ca. fourteenth or fifteenth century[62]), the popularity of this "mysterious saint at one point nearly rivalled that of the Virgin Mary" (Friesen 1). The *vita* of Saint Wilgefortis takes place presumably in Portugal, where she was one of the seven (Farmer 538) or nine children "born at one birth" (A. Butler III: 151; "novem" [*AASS* Jul. V, 51E, 53D, 54G]; "unico partu" [Jul. V, 51E]) by the wife of a heathen king around 130 BC (Keller 368). Despite her devotion to Christ and her resolution to remain a virgin, Wilgefortis's father wants to marry her to the King of Sicily by the time she reaches puberty. In her despair, she prays to God for help and is rewarded with a "long, drooping moustache and silky, curly beard" (Bullough and Bullough 55). On her marriage day, she lifts her veil and reveals her beard to her future husband and father. Repulsed by her appearance, the suitor withdraws, and her embarrassed father kills her in a fit of rage for her misbehaviour by crucifying her (*AASS* Jul. V, 64B; A. Butler III: 151; Bullough and Bullough 55).[63] The legend of the brave virgin soon spread widely, and textual as well as artistic traces of her story were found all over Europe (Keller 368;

[61] *Hagiology* is another, uncommon term for hagiography.

[62] When exactly the literary tradition of Saint Wilgefortis emerged is still not quite clear. According to Farmer, her cult has its roots in fourteenth-century Flanders (538) and Friesen adds that "it appears likely that the English veneration of St. Uncumber originated in the Netherlandish veneration […] sometime after 1400" (59). Even though not included in popular medieval English martyrologies, a hymn in honour of Saint Wilgefortis can be found in a prayer book used by the diocese of Salisbury (1533). For the text in Latin see *AASS* Jul. V, 63F-64B. For an English translation of the prayer see Friesen (59).

[63] In other versions of her legend, it is her own father who desires to marry her because she reminds him of his dead wife (Knust 124; Friesen 118). This is not the first time a father-daughter relationship is implied to be incestuous in a religious text. A slightly similar approach can already be found in the Biblical story of Sodom and Gomorrah, for example (Genesis 19:30-38). In folklore, a similar example of implied incest and the resulting physical consequences can be found in the fairy tale *Peau d'Âne*, written in 1694 by Charles Perrault (also known as "Allerleirauh" by the Grimm brothers). Analogous to Saint Wilgefortis, the lovable, sexually attractive and feminine outer appearance is transformed either through a masculine beard or an animalistic exterior, making the protagonists not only hairier, but also rough and erotically "untouchable" (Knust 125).

Friesen). Moreover, she manifested as the encouraging patron of married women who want to free themselves from their husbands and of unlucky marriage (Bullough and Bullough 55), and praying to her was supposed to help with infertility (Knust 127). This presumed ability "to liberate those in bondage and grief" (Friesen 1) was mirrored in the multiple names given to her, including Saint Wilgefortis, as well as any translation or variation of the names Saint Uncumber or Saint Liberata,[64] which connect the saint with powerful and affirmative characteristics.[65] Interestingly, in medieval times Saint Wilgefortis was not only depicted as a steadfast virgin but was particularly loved for her deforming beard, as Friesen states:

> It was precisely the disfiguring beard that made [her] so intriguing during the fifteenth century, a period during which there was a considerable fascination with emaciated recluses and unkempt hermits [which] constituted a kind of counter-culture to the generally self-indulgent and pleasure-loving middle and upper classes. At a time when costly garments and lavish costumes were treasured and publicly displayed, the stark and shaggy depictions of destitute saints […] were particularly noteworthy [as their legends] reflected a nostalgia for an existence without cultural restraints. (52)

This nostalgia resulted in the deliberate creation of female crucifixes by re-dressing the crucified male in "unmistakeably female clothing and jewellery", and these visual "depictions were created with great sincerity, and are far from being frivolous" (2). Friesen continues, "the merging of both genders" "probably filled an emotional and spiritual need which the official patriarchal Church was failing to provide at that time, especially for women", and there "is evidence to suggest […] that both men and women were inclined to respond positively to images that embodied or otherwise represented both sexes" (2-3).

Paradoxically, exactly this early form of beyond-gender identification with Christ, who as previously mentioned was often described as female (Bynum, *Holy Feast* 272), and the cultural liberation symbolised by the beard led to the suppression and criticism of Wilgefortis's cult in the centuries thereafter. Unfortunately, "ever since the Reformation, and particularly since the Enlightenment, her veneration has been criticized and discouraged by the Catholic Church", which from then on dismissed in particular the images of the crucified bearded woman as a "grotesque and bizarre aberration of the veneration of the crucified Christ" (Friesen 1). The suppression of her cult was initiated by destroying or whitewashing her paintings and by hiding her statues in dark attics or "monastery vaults" (1). In England, even though a statue of the bearded princess can still be found in the chapel of Henry VII in Westminster Abbey,[66] among

[64] Other names connected to the legend are Kümmernis, Kumerana (Germany), Livrade (France), Liberata, Liberada (Spain, Italy, Portugal), Ontkommer (Netherlands), Regenfledis (Flanders), Uncumber (England) and many more.

[65] Wilgefortis is a blend of the Latin *virgo* and *fortis* – the strong virgin; Uncumber derives from the Germanic *ohne Kummer* ("without sorrow"); and Liberata obviously refers to the Latin *liberare* ("liberate").

[66] The chapel was begun in 1502 and more or less completed by 1512. It contains "probably the most complete series of saints in Europe" (Gardner 5; see also Friesen 59). For more detailed

others, the majority of her shrines and images were "lost due to the zeal of reformers under the reign of Edward VI" (58), and among English clerics and poets her legend was discussed sarcastically or even ridiculed.[67] Thus, by the beginning of the sixteenth century, the legend of a bearded, crucified female saint posed a challenge to the official Church, which apparently saw no other possibility than to suppress her cult and to condemn her as heretic, "unorthodox and offensive" (Friesen 7).

Taking a closer look at the legend and at the beard itself, the primary associations with the saint's facial hair are not truly offensive to any theological doctrine, but rather a repetition of yet another ever-recurrent theme in hagiography: virgin martyrs and their bodily sacrifices to maintain their virginity. Therefore, from the moment Wilgefortis prays to God for disfigurement and receives a beard shortly thereafter, the beard fulfils two performative functions. It is on the one hand a demonstration of God's power, a divine statement, comparable to the sudden growth of hair in the legend of Saint Agnes. Hence, the beards of female saints are predominantly an "awesome, divinely inspired miracle" whose disfiguring component helped to protect the saints' virginity (Friesen 112), even if the growth of a beard clearly remains an unusual alteration to the usually gruesome tradition of *virginitas deformitate defensa* discussed by Schulenburg (127-75) and others.

On the other hand, comparable to the haircut among the transvestite saints, the female beard symbolizes a break from the saint's former existence and becomes the visual bodily statement of her decision to be wedded to Christ. This is also evident in the legend of Saint Galla,[68] who after her husband's death refuses to be remarried, as carnal matrimony in her eyes "always begins with joy [...] but ends with sorrow" (A. Butler IV: 37; see *Dialogues* IV: 13). Ignoring the warning of her physicians that "unless she did marry again, [...] she would through abundance of heat, contrary to nature, have a beard like unto men: which afterward fell so out indeed", Galla casts off "her secular habit and attire" and "little regarded [her] outward deformity" (*Dialogues* IV: 13; "propinquos medici quoque illam ad secundas nuptias hortabantur, ne præ nimia ejus caliditate barbam, ut homines, emitteret" [*AASS* Oct. III, 148F]). In contrast to Wilgefortis, however, Galla is able to stay alive and to spend the rest of her life bearded in a nunnery, helping the poor.

Yet even if the growth of a beard in hagiography is a divine miracle, both legends show that by the time they circulated in Europe, the excessive female growth of facial

information about the chapel of Henry VII see Arthur Gardner, *English Medieval Sculpture* (New York: Hacker, 1973).

[67] For example, in Thomas More's work *Dialogue Concerning Heresies* (1529) in *Medieval Popular Religion, 1000-1500: A Reader*, ed. John Shinners (Peterborough: Broadview, 1997), pp. 201-02. For an in-depth discussion of the saint's influence and the treatment of her cult in England see Ilse E. Friesen, *The Female Crucifix: Images of St. Wilgefortis since the Middle Ages* (Waterloo: Wilfred Laurier UP, 2001), pp. 58-62; and David E. King, "The Cult of Saint Wilgefortis in Flanders, Holland, England in France", *Am Kreuz – eine Frau: Anfänge – Abhängigkeiten – Aktualisierungen*, ed. Sigrid Glockzin-Bever and Martin Kraatz (Münster: LIT, 2003), pp. 55-97.

[68] Whereas the life of Saint Galla in the *Dialogues* explicitly states that she was rewarded with a beard, Butler dismisses the beard as a warning given to the saint, not explaining whether she actually grew a beard (IV: 36-37). Further discussions of her beard can be found in Bullough and Schulenburg (see chapter 3.4, n. 59 in this study for full bibliographical references).

hair had already "come to be viewed as grotesque, shocking and even monstrous – an offence against the laws of aesthetics and of nature itself" (Friesen 111-12). They confirm Frantzen's argument that the female beard is a sign of "womanly disgrace" (77) and a shame for her family. For Wilgefortis's father, his bearded daughter provokes a public vilification of his high social status, and fearing the loss of his reputation, her assassination is apparently the only way out. In the legend of Saint Galla the beard itself is presented as a possible female punishment for self-determined women. Her choice to remain unmarried not only disgraces her socially, but the beard in turn becomes the visible stigma intensifying this disgrace.

The motivations for the suppression of the cult of Saint Wilgefortis are, however, more complex than just its nonconformity to aesthetics and beauty ideals. As this study will argue, the reasons for her legend to be dismissed as heretical and grotesque are instead associated with the saintly figure's attempt to "become male" and with her death, which interrogated the reapproved patriarchal structure of the official Church at the time of the Reformation. What makes the legend of Saint Wilgefortis so dangerous for theological doctrines is not her *imitatio Christi* in itself, but rather the cultural associations with the beard in conjunction with her crucifixion and the images, miniatures and paintings displaying her as a female Christ.

As the introduction to this chapter noted, whereas the tonsure was a symbol of submissiveness and sexual renunciation, the growth of a beard was connected to masculine strength and power and was thus a "specifically male ability" (Cooper 37; see also Balabanova 111). It is exactly this connection between masculinity and strength which turns the bearded saint into a powerful female figure but also into a threat to the patriarchal structure. The beard initiates Wilgefortis's symbolic transcendence from a socially subordinate woman into a superior female figure, into a manly woman who thinks "spiritual thoughts" once she abstains from men.[69] Furthermore, as the beard was commonly interpreted as "a gift of grace that enabled Christ's female followers to more closely resemble him in the process to become more Christ-like overall" (Friesen 112), Wilgefortis's facial hair equates her somewhat with Christ, turning her not only into a manly woman but even into a saviourlike figure. Therefore, even though all hairstyles create a powerful divine connection in one way or the other, it is the beard and its affirmative associations with strong masculinity, deeply rooted in the cultural understanding of the people, that leads to the fact that of all saints presented in this third chapter, the bearded saint is apotheosised the most.

While it is certainly a popular hagiographical topic that "a sanctified virile (in the sense of manly) virgin could even become a 'WomanChrist', a woman identified with Christ, once she reached the exalted status of dedicating herself fully to the *imitatio Christi*, or imitation of Christ" (Friesen 20), none of the other saints in their quest to "become male" ever question the masculinity of Christ as Wilgefortis and her painters and sculptors did. The cult of Saint Galla, even though featuring a bearded saint and thus a "WomanChrist" in her appearance and behaviour, has not experienced such protest and suppression as Wilgefortis's has. Does this have to do with the way her legend ends – in a nunnery, a suitable place for female religious, and not with her

[69] Tertullian, *De exhortatione castitatis*, ed. E. Kroymann, *Tertulliani Opera: Corpus Christianorum, Series Latina 2* (Turnhout: Brepols, 1954), pp. 1013-35, p. 1029.

crucifixion? To identify with and imitate Christ and to visually become Christ are therefore two different levels of *imitatio*. Thus, the form of her punishment and the resulting text-transcending excitement in portraying a bearded saint on the cross are arguably the true reasons why Wilgefortis's cult was perceived as grotesque and heretical and needed to be suppressed. As Knust notes, the choice of punishment was supposed to ridicule the heathen king's daughter's religious vocation by creating a picture that resembled Christ as closely as possible (126). However, by doing so, it is not only Wilgefortis who is ridiculed by the heathen king, but the official Church and their patriarchal structure as well. Painters and sculptors have intensified this criticism, as Wilgefortis on the cross looks like an effeminate Christ or "Jesus in drag", as folk singer Rebecca Clamp sings in her 2007 dedication to the virgin martyr.[70] Images and crucifixes[71] of Saint Wilgefortis frequently show God's son with breasts or at least with a swelling of his chest, which arguably turns *him* into *her* – God's daughter. Whereas in medieval times the blurring of the two traditional categorizations of sex – male and female – may have elicited positive reactions and filled a spiritual need, as Friesen has argued (29), the legend of the bearded saint also shows that as soon as the borders between the two established sexes and genders are blurred, the surrounding society responds with aggression (Leynhausen 152). It is therefore not surprising that in the centuries thereafter, in which more conservative social norms were formulated, the substitution of a woman for Christ was understood as offensive and as an open critique of the gender distribution and the traditional masculine dominance within the Bible.

Finally, a holy woman who prays for a beard to disfigure her causes trouble – textually and culturally. She poses a threat to established traditions and has to be removed or denied to keep those traditions intact. The bearded saint consequently has to die twice: first in the text to indicate the limits of her transgression into the masculine, and second, beyond the textual sphere, through the suppression and denial of her cult, as Alban Butler has done, as the crucified bearded woman challenges God's traditional maleness, questioning whether God could not have been a woman right from the start. Fortunately, her complete cultural death remained unsuccessful and thus the legend of the bearded saint which "display[s] and downplay[s] gender differences" and thereby shakes the foundation of the Church's patriarchal ideology can still "speak to us" today (Friesen 7).

[70] Rebecca Clamp, "St. Wilgefortis", 16 Aug. 2007, *YouTube*, Web, 2 Feb. 2010.

[71] See, for example, *The Nailing to the Cross of St. Kümmernis* by Leopold Puellacher, St. Veits Chapel, Telfs, Austria. A large collection of reprints of rediscovered, sometimes privately owned illustrations can be found in Ilse E. Friesen, *The Female Crucifix: Images of St. Wilgefortis since the Middle Ages* (Waterloo: Wilfred Laurier UP, 2001).

3.5 Concluding Remarks

> Die jeweilige Haartracht hat […] nicht allein beschreibende sondern oft auch motivische und damit verbunden symbolische Funktion. Sie ist dabei konventionell an bestimmte genderspezifische Deutungs- und Wahrnehmungskomplexe gebunden.
>
> Henrike Walter[72]

Hair in women's hagiography, no matter whether long, short or in the form of the beard, "connects scenarios in which power and seduction, convention and civilisation, myth and society are prominently featured" (Walter 311),[73] and it influences the way these holy women are perceived, treated and remembered within and beyond their legends. It links sinner with saint, the sacred with the secular and women with Christ. It purifies, protects and helps to progress spiritually, but it can also become a saint's punishment and initiate her prosecution. Moreover, as the analysis has specified, hair in hagiography is "attached to a complex system of gender specific interpretations" (311), ranging from the sensuality of long hair and its necessary purification through repentance to the tonsured saints who attempt to "become male" and overcome traditional female roles through the haircut. Tonsured and bearded female saints constantly question the traditional classifications of male and female, masculine and feminine. Yet the bearded saint mirrors the greatest discomfort about women who not only violate beauty ideals but also transgress traditional gender boundaries. Hair in women's hagiography may be a minor detail, but as this analysis has shown, it is a feature too powerful and at times too provocative to be ignored – it is a detail that matters.

[72] Trans.: "The individual hairstyle has not only a descriptive but often a motivic and thus symbolic function. Conventionally, it is attached to a complex system of gender specific interpretations and perceptions". Henrike Walter, "Flechten, Fell und Bärte: Genderspezifische Aspekte der Haarsymbolik im Märchen", *Haare zwischen Fiktion und Realität: Interdisziplinäre Untersuchungen zur Wahrnehmung der Haare*, ed. Birgit Haas (Berlin: LIT, 2008), p. 311.

[73] Original: "So verweist Haar auf Zusammenhänge, in denen Macht und Verlockung, Konvention und Zivilisation, Mythos und Gesellschaft eine Rolle spielen".

4 Silenced, Penetrated, Sexualized: Two Readings of Teeth, Tongues and Throats

> Cut off, cut off my feet – paths they have travelled!
> Cut off, cut off my hands – work they have completed!
> Cut out, cut out my tongue – with my heart I will pray!
> Smash, smash my mouth – with my heart, I will speak!
> Whip, crush the body – why do I need the body?
>
> St. Nikolai Velimirovich[1]

To be martyred is one thing. To be martyred as a virgin is another. Within the scope of this study, numerous female saints have been presented who are not only classified as virgins, but who had to hide or were tortured and killed just because of this way of life. The bodily focus of their *vitae* and often of their martyrdom is set, as discussed in chapter 2, predominantly on the breast or on components of the head, such as hair (see chapter 3) and the head[2] itself. This final chapter of bodily and saintly case studies intends to shift attention to yet another gender-specific treatment and maltreatment of a bodily region whose complete symbolic range seems to unfold most visibly when seeing and placing its parts in relation to each other rather than treating them as separate entities – namely the mouth and its closely connected tripartite subdivision of teeth, tongue and throat.

For example, in the legends of Saint Apollonia and Saint Febronia the torturers beat out their teeth with blows to their faces (de Voragine I: 268-69; *AASS* Feb. II, 277-82; *AASS* Jun. VII, 12-31), Saint Christina has her tongue cut out (de Voragine I: 387) and in the case of Saint Lucy a dagger is "plunged into the martyr's throat" (de Voragine I: 29; "in gutture ejus gladium immerserunt" [Graesse 32]). On the surface these may seem to be conventional practices, as all of the three treatments have been established torture methods from antiquity onwards, except for the fact that they were originally intended for adulteresses, thieves or liars (Herrmann, *Die Folter* 356) – crimes a virgin saint cannot be accused of. The fact that those particular parts of the body are subject to torture must consequently have a second meaning, at least when recalling the fact that these *vitae* were edited and modified by their authors and compilers primarily to serve educational and didactic needs and no word inserted is left to chance.

[1] Excerpt from "Hymn in Praise of Sainte Febronia" by Nikolai Velimirovich, n.d., Web, 17 Apr. 2013.
[2] The head itself, or more precisely the act of beheading, is thereby the most common method to kill the saint when it is time to end her or his martyrdom. It is also quite possible to discuss the head itself in regard to gender-specific torture as according to ancient and medieval notions the head was connected to masculinity rather than femininity. This chapter, however, intends to disregard the head for the upcoming discussion.

The following chapter aims to point out the intersections between, on the one hand, the historical and cultural symbolism as well as the torture of tongues and throats in relation to the physical silencing of rhetorically advanced women and, on the other hand, the aspect of symbolic and metaphorical defloration of virgin saints. The chapter will argue that the mouth and its tripartite components are not only treated as a "door" through which beliefs and vocation are uttered, but are also, within the female saints' legends, transformed into a symbolic vagina. Thereby the teeth play a crucial role as they function as the only visible barrier between inner and outer body, as a symbolic "hymen", which is "deflowered" in the legend of Saint Apollonia, among others, by pulling the teeth out. Within the legends of female saints, mouth and vagina, the two entrances to a woman's body, seem to be used interchangeably.

4.1 Cut Off – Cut Out: Symbolism, Torture and Common Practice

> The things which proceed out of the mouth, come forth from the heart, and those things defile a man. For from the heart come forth evil thoughts, murders, adulteries, fornications, thefts, false testimonies, blasphemies. These are the things that defile a man.
>
> Matthew 15:18-20[3]

> Metaphorical connections between the throat and the cervix/ vagina or buccal cavity and pudenda are legion in antiquity and still into the nineteenth century.
>
> Thomas Laqueur[4]

As the analysis of breasts and hair has indicated, in the Middle Ages the body was a space for numerous forms of symbolic readings and interpretations, an area for metaphorical connections of which a great number are still valid and prevailing in today's society. These metaphorical readings, however, often led to metaphorical misconceptions of body parts, depriving them of their original function and reconnecting them to a symbolic understanding to such an extent that sometimes these interpretations became firmly established in a culture's (ideological) understanding of the body. The metaphor attached to the body part was often valued higher than the biological origin and thus led to a body-metaphor relationship that influenced and affected all areas of everyday life. The influence ranged from indications within

[3] "quae autem procedunt de ore de corde exeunt et ea coinquinant hominem / de corde enim exeunt cogitationes malae homicidia adulteria fornicationes furta falsa testimonia blasphemiae / haec sunt quae coinquinant hominem […]".

[4] Thomas Laqueur, *Making Sex: Body and Gender from the Greeks to Freud* (Massachusetts: Harvard UP, 1992), p. 36. See also, for example, Ann Hanson and David Armstrong, "The Virgin's Voice and Neck: Aeschylus, *Agamemnon 245* and Other Texts", *British Institute of Classical Studies* 33 (1986): 97-100.

everyday language and an increasing number of body-related words and sayings to the invention of torture practices specially designed to punish the body part that was believed to cause people's misconduct.

Illuminating and reconstructing the mouth and its components only supports this hypothesis. Whereas in the Old Testament, mouths, lips and tongues are viewed primarily as speech organs with whose help human beings are able to articulate themselves and perform communicative tasks such as teaching, preaching, singing, and praying (Schroer 155), the New Testament introduces a metaphorical interpretation going way beyond the biological fact.

In the Gospel of Matthew, for example, it is stated that Jesus "called together the multitudes unto him [and] he said to them: Hear ye and understand. Not that which goeth into the mouth defileth a man: but what cometh out of the mouth, this defileth a man" (15:10-11).[5] As Jesus's listeners do not fully understand the purpose of his claim, he explains it further:

> Are you also yet without understanding? Do you not understand, that whatsoever entereth into the mouth, goeth into the belly, and is cast out into the privy? But the things which proceed out of the mouth, come forth from the heart, and those things defile a man. For from the heart come forth evil thoughts, murders, adulteries, fornications, thefts, false testimonies, blasphemies. These are the things that defile a man. (15:16-20)[6]

As the biblical passage indicates, the mouth at this point is no longer solely regarded as a speech organ, but suddenly as an entrance and outlet of ideological and nonideological thoughts.

Therefore, mouth and gorge were associated with a controversial role from a cultural, historical and religious perspective. On the one hand, they belonged to the upper, nobler parts of the human being, with the throat representing pride and self-confidence and the breathing gorge symbolizing the intersection of life (Schroer 61, 103). But on the other hand, the mouth – together with ears and eyes – was seen as a filter of the human body and was believed to be able to distinguish good from bad (Le Goff and Truong 84). In common belief, this system of filtration was fallible, as it was also through mouth and gorge that Satan could enter or leave the body. As Le Goff and Truong note,

> Aus dem Mund können ebenso Worte der Andacht, Frömmigkeit und des Gebets kommen wie schlüpfrige und gotteslästerliche Reden. Demnach ist der Mund ein „Riegel", die Zähne eine „Schranke", die den Fluß der Schändlichkeiten aufhalten müssen, wie sie das

[5] "et convocatis ad se turbis dixit eis audite et intellegite / non quod intrat in os coinquinat hominem sed quod procedit ex ore hoc conquinat hominem [...]".

[6] "at ille dixit adhuc et vos sine intellectu estis / non intellegitis quia omne quod in os intrat in ventrem vadit et in secessum emittitur / quae autem procedunt de ore de corde exeunt et ea coinquinant hominem / de corde enim exeunt cogitations malae homicidia adulteria fornications furta falsa testimonia blasphemiae / haec sunt quae coinquinant hominem [...]".

> Lachen nach oben spülen kann. Das Lachen ist ein „Schmutzfleck" des Mundes. An dieser Stelle muss der Körper ein Bollwerk gegen diese Höhle des Teufels sein. (84)[7]

The connection between the monstrous mouth and hell can be traced back to Anglo-Saxon England. The "representation of hell as the open jaws of a monster", as Meyer Shapiro argues, "is a typical English motive; most of the examples before the twelfth century are English" (211). The oldest example of the hell mouth, Shapiro claims, is an Anglo-Saxon ivory carving from around the year 800, displayed in the Victoria and Albert Museum in London (211, 211 n. 66).[8] Shapiro believes that the "Anglo-Saxon taste" for the depiction of hell as a gaping mouth, which is often connected to a monstrous creature, is related to northern pagan mythology such as the myth of the Crack of Doom or Odin's ferocious wolf Fenrir (211 n. 66).[9] Another example is the monstrous annihilating creature of Grendel, who wants to eat humans, in the epic *Beowulf.* In the Christian tradition, at least four scriptural places or figures of hell refer to the act of humans' souls being swallowed and consumed: the Sheol – the underworld as portrayed in the Old Testament and the Hebrew Bible – the dragon, the lion, and the leviathan, the man-eating sea monster also from the Old Testament (Schmidt 32-60; Galpern 145-46; Rossmeisl 11). "Important parallels existed between the endemic and the invading cultures (in Britain), as both Christians and pagans revelled in legends of mighty heroes battling creatures with menacing jaws", Robyn Rossmeisl notes (11). These creatures and the act of swallowing humans and eating their souls were related to the process of damnation. The vivid imagery these creatures created turned them, and consequently the mouth as well, into an alarming and threatening picture in medieval times, resulting in the hell-mouth imagery in fiction, drama and iconography (16). As Rossmeisl explains, "From its earliest appearance on a small ivory panel in the ninth century to its lurking visage in manuscripts, sculptures, paintings and finally theatre, the mouth of hell participated in a discursive process of shifting media, locations, and audiences" (13). The images of the mouth of hell soon "outgrew British shores and spread throughout continental Europe" (13). By the eleventh century the hell mouth or "gorge of hell", the literal translation of the German equivalent *Höllenschlund*,[10] was a popular image in

[7] Trans.: "Words of devotion, piety and prayer can leave the mouth as well as lewd and blasphemous talk. Consequently, the mouth is a 'lock', the teeth a 'gate', which have to withhold the river of disgracefulness, initiated by laughter. It is laughter which is a 'stain' of the mouth. At this place the body has to be a fortress against this cave of the devil".

[8] See Margaret H. Longhurst, *Catalogue of Carvings in Ivory in the Victoria and Albert Museum* (London, 1927), Part I, pl. xlv, no. 253-1867.

[9] For more information about the hell mouth see Joyce Galpern, "The Shape of Hell in Anglo-Saxon England", PhD dissertation (U of California, Berkeley, 1977); Gary D. Schmidt, *The Iconography of the Mouth of Hell: Eighth-Century Britain to the Fifteenth Century* (London: Associated University Presses, 1995); and Robyn Rossmeisl, "Encountering the Embodied Mouth of Hell: The Play of Opposition in Religious Vernacular Theatre", MA thesis (U of British Columbia, 2012).

[10] *Höllenschlund*: German compound of "hell" and "gorge" denoting the gates of hell.

paintings and illuminations[11] of the Last Judgement[12] or the Harrowing of Hell[13] and had turned into one of the most common depictions of hell in art from England to France and Italy (Baschet, qtd. in Le Goff and Truong 143[14]).

By the fourteenth century, literary references such as Dante Alighieri's famous description of hell in the *Divine Comedy* and the reinterpretation of the Leviathan[15] helped to create a more specific picture of hell and its gatekeeper, Satan (Le Goff and Truong 144-45). At the same time, the punishments which were to be faced in hell, such as hanging, dismemberment or being broken on a wheel, were differentiated more precisely, and attempts were made to set them in relation to the secular wrongdoings of the people (Baschet, qtd. in Le Goff and Truong 144-45).

Because of the widely spread representation of hell in connection with the mouth and jaw, it is not surprising that within European torture chambers, glossectomies as well as dental extractions were, in addition to other tortures involving the disfigurement of mouth and gorge, common practice. Among the most common methods was the choke pear, an instrument consisting of several segments that could be expanded in their width by turning a screw. The instrument was placed, sometimes flaming hot, into the mouth (and in some cases even into vaginas and anuses) and expanded to such an extent that the jaw or teeth could break, or in case of hot choke pears the interior of the mouth was burned terribly (Herrmann, *Die Folter* 241, 356). The choke pear was not only used as a torture method itself, but also as a form of torment preceding the removal of the tongue. Glossectomy, as Herrmann points out, was particularly used for delinquencies such as blasphemy, heresy, defamation and defying authorities, both sacred and secular (356). The methods of mutilating the tongue ranged from cutting it out to cauterization to pulling it out with hot pliers. Pliers, one of the standard and most well-known torture instruments all over the world, were also utilized for the extraction of teeth (354-55).

Reasons for the attractiveness of glossectomies and dental extractions as torture methods can easily be found. First of all, these body parts are all rather algesic and are therefore ideal for the infliction of pain. Second, because the mutilation does not kill the victim, the dismembered would be stigmatized physically and socially for the rest of his or her life. Not only would the tormented have bodily changes and restrictions, limiting his or her daily life by complicating the intake of nourishment and communication, but in particular the loss of the tongue would display his or her personal dishonour on a public scale. As people knew for which reasons tongues were removed within the judicial system, the stigma placed on the person was all-encompassing and often ended

[11] For example, a beautiful illumination can be found in the Winchester Psalter from the twelfth century, depicting an angel who locks the gates of hell with a key. Behind the "gates" two enormous animalistic mouths, belonging to scaly monsters with long sharp teeth, seem to swallow a large jumbled group of people. The manuscript and its illumination can be found in the British Library in London.

[12] See, for example, *The Last Judgment* illumination in the well-known fifteenth-century canonical book of hours *Les Très Riches Heures du Duc du Berry*, created for John, Duke of Berry by the Limbourg Brothers. Folio 34r.

[13] "Descensus Christi ad Infernos".

[14] Jérôme Baschet, *Les justices de l'au-delà: Les représentations de l'enfer en France et en Italie (XIIe-XVe siècle)* (Rome: École française de Rome, 1993).

[15] In the Middle Ages, the Leviathan became an allegory of Satan.

in social ostracism. Furthermore, from the perspective of the executioners, this visible stigmatization, this human mark of shame, demonstrated authoritative power and superiority.

Summing up so far, the mouth and its components have undergone an overarching metaphorical development. The natural, biological facts have been expanded, adding a wide range of symbolic additions. On the one hand, mouth, teeth and tongues have been identified as bodily filters and as interconnected spaces, dominating the intake and release of (non-)ideological thoughts. On the other hand, the human mind developed these ideas further, creating specially designed penalties to punish acts in which these "filters" had failed.

Leaving the idea of communication, hell, and related torture methods aside and returning to the biological origin, another strand of interpretation in regard to this tripartite area within the human body has to be noted: the belief in a connection between mouth and vagina within a woman's body, which leads to an additional gendered aspect. The idea of the transformative body as well as the interconnectivity and the interdependence of limbs, organs and body fluids was already touched upon in chapter 2, in which the connection between blood, milk and semen was traced. To recap the ancient and medieval assumptions – a woman's blood turned into breast milk after giving birth. The conversion of extra blood into milk burned up the surplus of heat and thus explained the lack of menstruation among new mothers (Laqueur 36). The interconnectivity of the throat with the menses was demonstrated, for example, by the idea that women engaging in singing were believed not to menstruate either. As Laqueur explains,

> The case of singers [...] illustrates once again the extent to which what we would take to be only metaphoric connections between organs were viewed as having causal consequences in the body as being real. Here the association is one between the throat [...] through which air flows and the neck of the womb through which the menses passes; activity in one detracts from activity in the other. (36)

Even though the idea seems unnatural and illogical to modern Western society, from antiquity until well into the nineteenth century, "metaphorical connections between the throat and the cervix/vagina or buccal cavity and pudenda are legion" (Laqueur 36-37, fig. 2). In his famous work *On the Usefulness of Parts of the Body*, the ancient scholar, philosopher and physicist Galen developed the idea that "the uvula, which hangs down at the back of the soft palate – center view as one looks into the mouth – gives the same sort of protection to the throat that the clitoris gives to the uterus" (Laqueur 37, fig. 2; see also 258 n. 59).[16] Even though Galen lived in the third century, from the eleventh century onwards Latin translations of his works appeared and underwent a renaissance among physicists, philosophers and intellectuals. As Arthur John Brock notes in his introduction to *Galen on the Natural Faculties*, together with

> [s]cholastic philosophy at the universities of Naples and Montpellier, the teachings of [...] Galen now [eleventh century onwards] assumed a position of supreme authority: from

[16] Galen, *On the Usefulness of the Parts of the Body (De Usu Partium)*, trans. Margaret Tallmadge May, 2 vols. (Ithaca: Cornell UP, 1968), 2: 622-23, 658-59, 660-61.

> [his] word, in matters scientific and medical, there was no appeal. In reference to this period the Pergamene [Galen] was referred to in later times as the "Medical Pope of the Middle Ages". (xx-xxi)

Galen's ideas about the interconnectivity of the vagina and uterus with the throat and mouth spread all over Europe and thus enable a gendered reading of the removal of tongues and teeth in women's hagiography. The intersections between mouth and vagina and the symbolic fluid exchange between the two was, with respect to ancient and medieval assumptions, an accepted relationship, opening up the possibility for a second reading of these body parts within the *vitae*.

As the historical and cultural exploration into the metaphors and traditions surrounding the mouth has shown, there are several strands of metaphorical interpretation which have evolved around this body part – all are either related to biological, religious and judicial approaches or are linked to medical or sexual assumptions. These can be narrowed down into two thematic groups, which will be analysed and set in relation with the lives of holy women in the upcoming chapter. On the one hand, most of the metaphors related to the biological, judicial and religious involve communication of some sort: from the filtration of acceptable and unacceptable discourse and the imagery of language to Satan entering the mouth if the purification mechanisms fail to the punishment of delinquencies related to communication. On the other hand, there is the idea of bodily interconnectivity, calling for a gendered reading.

4.2 "Letting Satan In…": Silencing the Saint?

> The unruly woman is the undisciplined woman. She is a renegade from the disciplinary practises which would [mould] her as a gendered being. She is the defiant woman who rejects authority which would subjugate her and render her docile. She is the offensive woman who acts out of her own interests. She is the unmanageable woman who claims her own body […]. She is the woman who cannot be silenced. She is a rebel. She is trouble.
>
> Karlene Faith[17]

In Ælfric's life of Saint Cecilia, Tiburtius, one of Saint Cecilia's questioners, claims after a lengthy discussion with her about Christianity, "[n]e þincð me þœt þu spræce mid menniscre spræce" (*Passio Sanctae Cecilie Virginis*, Skeat II: 366; "To me, you do not seem to speak in human speech" [Donovan 61]). As a result, Tiburtius "feoll […] forht to hire cneowum" (II: 366; "fell frightened at her knees" [Donovan 61]), weeps and is baptized shortly after. Cecilia's arguments, her eloquent, convincing and powerful speech, are initially a demonstration of God's power, who speaks through His believers

[17] Karlene Faith, *Unruly Women: The Politics of Confinement and Resistance* (Vancouver: Press Gang, 1993), p. 1.

as exemplified in Exodus 4:15: “Speak to him, and put my words in his mouth: and I will be in thy mouth, and in his mouth, and will shew you what you must do”.[18] However, within a gendered reading the situation portrays an independent young woman who is not afraid to speak up for her vocation and beliefs in a society in which women were supposed to be the silent, passive gender.

Among the female saints, a number of *vitae* exist, such as the legends of Saint Lucy, Saint Christina and Saint Cecilia, in which the protagonists are not only characterised as young, beautiful and devoted virgins, but as women who are intelligent, well-educated in rhetoric and religion and able to prove their arguments in a scholarly and linguistically skilled manner. All of these are – from a modern point of view – positive, maybe even affirmative human character traits. In the eyes of the saints' male questioners, tormentors, and executioners, however, these traits are characteristics that both individually and collectively lead to their martyrdom. The saints' youth and beauty turn all of them into sexual objects of male desires and are commonly the basic requirements which trigger the attention of the heathen male, who desperately tries to woo the young maidens. However, their dedication to Christianity reduces the courtship to a one-sided courtship. The virgins' refusal of their suitors for religious reasons is dishonouring for the men and their masculine egos and turns their attraction into hatred – mentally and physically – which marks the beginning of the virgins' martyrdom and deadly end. Yet next to these commonly found motives, the legends of outspoken female saints stand out, as their openly displayed intelligence only adds to the rage of their opponents. The men not only have them mutilated and murdered, but their anger is directed, in the case of the saints Christina, Cecilia and Lucy, at their organs of speech – the tongue and the throat.

Intelligence as a character trait, as Sorgo explains, is mentioned more frequently in female than male martyrologies and results in severer tortures than in the legends of less outspoken saints (83). Christina, for example, is stripped naked, beaten, bound in chains, imprisoned, has her flesh removed with hooks, her limbs broken, is stretched on a wheel, is burned and drowned – and these are only the tortures her father inflicts on her. She is also thrown into an iron cradle with oil, pitch and resin in it; her head is shaved and she is led naked through the city; she is tormented in a furnace for five days; she is put in a room with venomous animals and has her breasts[19] cut off; and finally her tongue is cut out (de Voragine I: 386-87). Why is it that female intelligence and communication leads to such an unbelievable accumulation of tortures – all of which remain unsuccessful? What incidents, actions and words trigger and follow the decision to remove the virgins' speech organs?

A first explanation is provided by Sorgo, who states that in late-Roman reasoning, the public instruction of a man by a woman was perceived as an insult to the Roman male citizen, and female intelligence was believed to support the idea of the female sex as persuasive and seductive (83). The relationship between female public instruction and insults to masculinity can be traced back to the medieval adaptations of the legends.

[18] “loquere ad eum et pone verba mea in ore eius et ego ero in ore tuo et in ore illius et ostendam vobis quid agere debeatis”

[19] The discussion of the removal of her breasts can be found in chapter 2 with regard to the symbolism of body fluids.

This chapter intends to examine the intersections between female speech and torture by taking a closer look at the communicative scenarios preceding and following the torture scenes in the legends of Saint Lucy, Saint Cecilia and Saint Christina. Can the female saint be silenced? Is she, as Karlene Faith proposes, the unmanageable, undisciplined, offensive woman who claims her own body and thus reflects a very early idea of female emancipation – even within the boundaries of Christian ideals (1)?

In the Latin tradition of Saint Lucy,[20] a *vita* well known and widely spread in medieval Europe, the female protagonist has a lengthy discussion with her accuser, Paschasius, on the significance of monotheism. When he, as governor, summons her and commands her to sacrifice to his idols, the argument unfolds in its full capacity:

> Lucy: "You obey your master's laws, and I shall obey the laws of my God. You fear your masters and I fear God. You are careful not to offend them, I take pains not to offend God. You want to please them, I wish to please Christ. Do then what you think will be of benefit to you, and I shall do what I think is good for me." Paschasius: "You have squandered your patrimony with seducers, and so you talk like a whore"; but Lucy replied, "As for patrimony, I have put it in a safe place, and never have had anything to do with any seducers of the body or of the mind." Paschasius: "Who are these seducers of the body and the mind?" Lucy: "You and those like you are seducers of the mind, because you induce souls to turn away from their Creator. As for the seducers of the body, they are those who would have us put the pleasures of the flesh ahead of eternal joys". (de Voragine I: 28)[21]

In this passage Lucy is portrayed as a young, independent woman who has made up her mind about religion and virginity and is so firm in her belief that she is able to engage strongly in the dispute and counter Paschasius in debate. Moreover, Paschasius's vulgar utterance in de Voragine's version that she has "squandered" her "patrimony with seducers" and thus "talks like a whore" (28) not only tries to degrade Lucy's pious personality but also harasses her sexually and consequently reflects the idea of the

[20] The legend of Saint Lucy is mentioned in Bede's martyrology and in Aldhelm's *Carmen de Virginitate*, among other sources. According to Donovan, she is mentioned in forty-three litanies and twenty-one calendars dating before 1100 (91). For an extensive record of her legend's origin and distribution in Europe and medieval England, consult Leslie A. Donovan, *Women Saints' Lives in Old English Prose* (Cambridge: Brewer, 1999), p. 91. For a list of the English calendars and litanies see Francis Wormald, ed., *English Kalendars Before AD 1100*, Henry Bradshaw Society 72 (London: Henry Bradshaw Society, 1934).

[21] Ad quem Lucia: tu principum tuorum decreta custodis et ego Dei mei legem custodiam. Tu prinicipes times et ego Deum timeo. Tu illos offendere non vis, et ego Deum offendere caveo. Tu illis placere desideras et ego ut Christo placeam concupisco. Tu ergo fac quod tibi utile esse cognosces et ego faciam, quod utile mihi esse perspexero. Cui Paschasius: patrimonium tuum cum corruptoribus expendisti et ideo quasi meretrix loqueris. Cui Lucia: patrimonium meum in tuto loco constitui, corruptores autem mentis et corporis nunquam scivi. Respondit Paschasius: qui sunt corruptores corporis et mentis? Lucia dixit: corruptores mentis vos estis, qui suadetis ut animae suum deserant creatorem. Corruptores vero corporis sunt, qui corporalem delectationem praeponunt epulis sempiternis (Graesse 31).

female temptress (Sorgo 83).[22] In turn, her public lecture offends Paschasius to such an extent that he angrily exclaims that "The sting of the whip will silence your lip" (de Voragine I: 28; "cessabunt verba, cum perventum fuerit ad verbera" [Graesse 31]). However, apparently unimpressed by his threat, Lucy confidently replies, "The words of God cannot be stilled" (I: 28; "verba Dei cessare non possunt" [Graesse 31]) – a reply further inciting and offending Paschasius, his masculinity, and his public reputation to the point that this marks the beginning of her brutal martyrdom – from attempted rape[23] to torture in its various degrees. Yet all of Paschasius's threats and attempts to humiliate her and make her suffer remain unsuccessful in the end. To release him from his personal desperation and misery at being unable to dominate this "handmaid of God" (de Voragine I: 28; "ancilla Dei" [Graesse 31]), witnesses to the spectacle ultimately "plunge" a dagger into her throat – unfortunately for the governor without the expected result of silencing the young woman, as she "was far from losing her speech" (I: 29; "quae nequaquam loquelam amittens" [Graesse 32]). Even though from a medical standpoint her ability to speak would have been destroyed at this point, the unsuccessful attempt to silence her leads to several preliminary conclusions. First of all, God's power is demonstrated through Lucy, whose will cannot be bent and whose strong communicative personality will remain until she decides when it is time to die – which is only after she has received the last sacraments. God speaks through the virgin and thus lifts up the female sex into a higher social position. Even without her spiritual succour, Lucy demonstrates that she is the owner of her body, which is still functioning and intact even after it has been mutilated to the extreme – a hagiographical motif which has previously been identified in other saints' legends, such as Saint Agatha's.

A similar attempt at destroying female reasoning and rhetoric – characteristics that were traditionally attributed to men (see chapter 1.2.2) – can be found in the legend of Saint Cecilia.[24] Her *vita* was one of the most venerated by the beginning of the fifth century. As Donovan explains,

> By emphasizing Cecilia's chastity within marriage, conventionally known as the *intactam sponsa* topos, this saint's legend offered medieval women a more practical possibility for achieving sanctity than the violence and refusal to marry presented in many other virgin martyr's lives. (57)

[22] In Ælfric's *De Sancta Lucia* most of the argument is omitted and mentioned solely as "hí spræcon fela oð þœt he hire swingele behét gif heo suwian nolde" (Skeat I: 214); "They argued much, until he threatened that she would be whipped, if she would not be silent" (Donovan 93).

[23] The attempted rape scene will be dealt with in the forthcoming subchapter.

[24] The legend of Saint Cecilia was venerated from the fourth century onwards and appears in Latin and Greek around the fifth century. Comparable to Saint Lucy, Cecilia was known to Aldhelm and Bede – in his eighth century martyrology as well as in his poem in praise of virginity. A detailed overview can be found in Leslie A. Donovan, *Women Saints' Lives in Old English Prose* (Cambridge: Brewer, 1999), pp. 57-58; for Bede's martyrology (which also includes the legend of Saint Lucy) see *Martyrologium: Édition Pratique des Martyrologes de Béde, de l'Anonyme Lyonnais et de Florus*, ed. Jacques Dubois and Geneviève Renaud (Paris: CNRS, 1976); or *The Complete Works of Venerable Bede in the Original Latin*, ed. J. A. Giles, vol. IV (London: Whitaker, 1843); and for Aldhelm's version (which again also includes the legend of Lucy) consult *Aldhelm: The Poetic Works*, trans. James L. Rosier and Michael Lapdige (Cambridge: Brewer, 1985).

When the young Cecilia is married to Valerian, she successfully convinces her husband to refrain from consummating the marriage and to convert to Christianity and fulfil Christian services instead. Unfortunately for both, their platonic relationship and their devotion and service to Christ do not remain secret for long, and the prefect Almachius has Valerian beheaded when he declines to offer sacrifice to the heathen gods (de Voragine II: 318-22; *Passio Sanctae Cecilie Virginis*, Skeat II: 365-77). Cecilia's social status at this point is made clear. After the death of Valerian, Almachius "made a move to get possession" of his "properties" and has Cecilia "brought before him" (de Voragine II: 322; "Tunc Almachius facultates amborum coepit inquirere et Caeciliam tamquam Valeriani conjugem coram se fecit adstare jussitque [...]" [Graesse 775-76]). Even though, in the *Legenda Aurea* but also in Ælfric's life of Saint Cecilia, the focus is predominately set on the wealth, properties and material objects Valerian has left his young widow (II: 322; Skeat II: 372), the phrasing implies that Cecilia is part of the material properties. Despite her influence and the gender equality that she achieved within the secure boundaries of matrimony, she is still viewed as a possession, as an object rather than an independent human being in the outside world of the patriarchally dominated society. However, in the following discussion between Almachius and Cecilia, which similarly to Lucy also leads to her martyrdom, Cecilia shows that she is neither the typical widow nor the typical passive woman:

> "What is your status in life?" "I am freeborn and of noble decent," she said. Almachius: "I am asking about your religion!" Cecilia: "Then your interrogation began badly, because the one question called for two answers." Almachius: "Where do your presumptuous answers come from?" "From a clear conscience and unfeigned faith!" she retorted. Almachius: "Don't you know where my power comes from?" Cecilia: "Your power is a balloon filled with wind! Prick it with a pin and it collapses, and what seemed rigid in it goes limp." Almachius: "You began with insults, and with insults you continue!" Cecilia: "You cannot speak of insults unless what is said is false! [...]" Almachius: "What makes you speak so proudly?" Cecilia: "Its not pride but constancy!" [...] Almachius: "Stop this wild talk and offer sacrifice to the gods!" Cecilia: "I don't know where you lost your eyes! What you call gods are nothing but lumps of stone [...]". (de Voragine II: 322-23)[25]

For Almachius, Cecilia's eloquent speech is not what he expected of a young widow. He finds her answers derogatory, insulting and too proud for a woman of her social standing in comparison to his powerful position as a prefect and judge, and he even

[25] "Tunc Almachius sanctam Caeciliam ad se vocans ait: cujus conditionis es? Et illa: ingenua sum et nobilis. Cui Almachius: ego te de religione interrogo. Cui Caecilia: interrogatio tua stultum sumit initium, quae duas responsiones una putat inquisitione concludi. Cui Almachius: unde tibi tanta praesumtio respondendi? At illa: de conscientia bona et fide non ficta. Cui Almachius: ignoras, cujus potestatis sim? Et illa: potestas vestra est quasi uter vento repletus, quem si acus pupugerit, omnis protinus rigor pallescit et quidquid in se rigidum habere cernitur incurvatur. Cui Almachius: ab injuriis coepisti, et in injuriis perseveras. Caecilia respondit: injuria non dicitur nisi quod verbis fallentibus irrogatur [...]. Cui Almachius: ad quid cum tanta superbia loqueris? Et illa: non est superbia, sed constantia. [...] Cui Almachius: jam depone amentiam et sacrificia Diis. Cui Caecilia: nescio, ubi oculos amiseris; nam, quos tu Deos dicis, omnes nos saxa esse videmus" (Graesse 776).

questions her mental health when he requests her to "stop her wild talk". The scene recalls the lengthy argument Lucy has with her accuser. In both incidents preceding their martyrdom, the young women protest against the patriarchal order and, of course, against heathenism. Once more, the virgin's speech needs to be silenced. She has publicly insulted a man of high rank and makes him take action to restore the social order. Cecilia is thus boiled in a hot bath for a night and a day, but as expected of the sublime saintly body, without the expected result of murdering her. Almachius then orders her to be beheaded while still bathing, yet the executioner "struck her three times in the neck but could not cut her head off", and "because the decree forbad striking a fourth blow, he left her bleeding and half dead"; and she "lived for three days, during which time she gave all her possessions to the poor"[26] (de Voragine II: 323).[27] The image of the unbroken neck and Cecilia's ability to continue teaching and speaking once again constitute a strong similarity to the legend of Saint Lucy. The virgin controls her own body, and as Constantinou claims, the important element is the soul, not the body, which is only temporary (44). Both legends once more underline the idea that no torture can harm the saint, because the body is of no importance – it is the soul which is necessary for the afterlife and which cannot be harmed by their torturer's mutilation.[28] Yet both legends also show that even though the disposal of the body is necessary for the female saint to become one with God, it is nevertheless she who decides when it is time to leave her body behind. Her voice cannot be destroyed; her firm belief (her neck) cannot be broken.

As a final case study, this chapter will take a closer look at the legend of Saint Christina.[29] Christina, so it seems, is the prototype of the "defiant woman who rejects authority which would subjugate her and render her docile" (Faith 1). She is the most rebellious one of the three case studies presented here as she, in contrast to Lucy and

[26] "Quam spiculator tribus ictibus in collo percussit, sed tamen caput ejus amputare non potuit, et quia decretum erat, ne quartam percussionem decollandus acciperet, eam semivivam cruentus carnifex dereliquit. Per triduum autem supervivens omnia, quae habebat, pauperibus tradidit et omnes [...]" (Graesse 777).

[27] The scene is similarly phrased in the Old English tradition see Ælfric *Passio Sanctae Cecilie Virginis:* "Se cwellere hí sloh þa mid his swurde æne eft and þryddan siðe ac hire swura næs forod and he forlét hí sona swa samcuce licgan forþam-þe witan cwædon þœt nan cwellere ne sceolde feower siðan slean to þonne man sloge scyldigne. Heo leofode þa þry dagas and þa geleaffullan tihte [...]" (Skeat II: 376); "The executioner struck her with his sword, once, and again, and a third time, but her neck was unbroken. He left her lying half dead, since the senators had said that, when slaying a guilty person, no executioner should strike anyone four times" (Donovan 65).

[28] For the explanation of the saintly body, consult chapter 1.2.1.

[29] For more information on the historical background, geographical accessibility and veneration of Saint Christina consult Kevin Brownlee, "Martyrdom and the Female Voice: Saint Christine in the *Cité des Dames*", *Images of Sainthood in Medieval Europe*, ed. Renate Blumenfeld-Kosinski and Timea Szell (Ithaca: Cornell UP, 1991), pp. 115-35. Another medieval legend of Saint Christina, attributed to William Paris, can be found in the *MS Arundel 168*, fols. 2r-4v. A reprint of the text together with supplementary notes can be found in Sherry L. Reames, ed., *Middle English Legends of Women Saints*, TEAMS Middle English Text Series (Kalamazoo: Medieval Institute Publications, Western Michigan U, 2003), pp. 223-48.

Cecilia, not only argues about her religious vocation, but is immediately disciplined for doing so. Not only does her father, the first out of the three tormentors she has to suffer from, punish her by imprisonment and torture, but Christina herself reacts almost aggressively to what is happening to her.

In her legend, readers are once more introduced to a beautiful young woman who is this time locked away in a tower by her father to preserve her virginity until a suitable husband is found. While encaged and watched over by serving women, Christina devotes her life to Christianity and starts believing in the Holy Trinity rather than in the multiple gods her family worships. Upon hearing the news, her father at first speaks "softly to her, seeking to win her to the cult of the gods" (de Voragine I: 386; "autem ei blandiens ad Deorum culturam eam provocabat" [Graesse 419]):

> "Daughter mine," the father responded, "don't offer sacrifice to one god only, or the others will be angry with you!" Christina: "Though you don't know it, you speak the truth, because I offer sacrifice to the Father, the Son and the Holy Spirit!" The father: "If you adore three gods, why not adore the others too?" Christina: "The three I adore are one godhead!" (I: 386)[30]

To underscore her new religious belief, Christina not only rejects her father's approach, but also actively demolishes his idols and distributes the golden and silver remains to the poor (de Voragine I: 386). As a result, her father has her beaten by twelve men "until they themselves dropped, exhausted" (I: 386; "eam jussit exspoliari et a duodecim viris caedi, adeo ut ipsi ministri deficerent" [Graesse 420]) and imprisons her in chains. As even her mother's attempt to change Christina's mind remains unsuccessful, her father orders her "flesh to be torn off with hooks and her tender limbs to be broken" (I: 386; "Tunc ille jussit carnes ejus ungulis radi et membra ejus tenera disrumpi" [Graesse 420]). At this point and in contrast to Lucy and Cecilia, Christina's legend goes beyond just leaving her female passivity and subordination behind, as she combines her words with actions. Apparently enraged herself, she picks up the pieces of her flesh and throws them into her father's face, saying, "Take that, tyrant, and eat the flesh that you once begot" (I: 386; "accipe, tyranne, et carnem a te genitam comede" [Graesse 420]). Christina is the female rebel personified. Even between all the various tortures[31] she has to endure, she continues praising God and is able to communicate her vocation to her tantalizers until her tongue is finally cut out to silence her. Comparable to Lucy, even after her tongue has been removed, Christina does not lose her "power of speech" (de Voragine I: 387; "nequaquam loquelam amittens" [Graesse 421]) and thereby actively demonstrates that Julianus, one of her torturers, cannot subjugate her. She picks up her severed flesh, in this case her cut-off tongue, and throws it into his eyes. Julianus as a result is blinded and insulted to such an extreme that, "goaded to wrath" (I: 387;

[30] "Cui pater: filia mea, ne uni Deo tantum sacrificium offeras, ne tibi alii irascantur. Cui illa: bene locutus es nesciens veritatem, offero enim sacrificium patri et filio et spiritui sancto. Cui pater: si tres Deos adoras, cur etiam alios non adoras? Cui illa: tres illi una Deitas sunt" (Graesse 419-20).

[31] For a complete list see the introduction to this chapter or consult Jacobus de Voragine, *The Golden Legend: Readings on the Saints*, 2 vols., ed. and trans. William Granger Ryan (Princeton: Princeton UP, 1995), I: 385-87.

"iratus" [Graesse 421]), he shoots two arrows through her heart, through which she "breathed forth her spirit to God" (I: 387; "illa percussa spiritum Deo tradidit" [Graesse 421]). Even though Christina is the only one of the three virgins discussed who does not decide when it is her time to die, her legend is remarkable as, in addition to her outspoken nature, she takes action. Her "resistance is even physically violent [and is] challenging commonly held stereotypes of passive femininity" (Mills, *Suspended Animation* 123). Christina is the "renegade" and she "is trouble" (Faith 1).

After showing the incidents preceding and following the destruction of the female speech organs, what conclusions can now be drawn from the legends of Saint Lucy, Saint Christina and Saint Cecilia about the intersections between female communication and their martyrdom? To recall the hypotheses made by Sorgo and Faith at the beginning of this chapter, is the outspoken female saint a threat to masculinity because she degrades her male tormentor's reputation in public and thus mirrors late-Roman beliefs (Sorgo 83)? Are the communicative saints in any way renegade women who claim their own bodies and reflect a subtle way towards female emancipation (Faith 1)? What does the torture of the female speech organs relate to?

First of all, from a medical point of view, cutting out tongues, removing teeth and lips and piercing the throat with daggers should have resulted, if not in death, at least in a dysfunction of proper speech and articulation. The torture of the mouth and its components arguably reflects the urge to silence these rhetorically eloquent, independent and almost authoritative young women, who instead of accepting the passive female role are unafraid to speak up for their vocation, discuss social and religious positions, and even dare to dissent from the social hierarchy. Whereas physical torture is intended to "disable language in the victim" (Scarry 4), the saints just discussed remain "authoritative *through* speech, interrupting [their] experiences of suffering with words addressed to [their] spectators, [their] tormentors and God" (Mills, *Suspended Animation* 123).

However, from the point of view of the masculine penetrator, the mouth, tongue and throat as bodily filters, regulating the intake and release of ideological thoughts, have failed (see chapter 4.1). Not only have they allowed a woman to speak up in public, but all of these women lecture and therefore insult their masculine opponents. The perceived failure of the filtration system consequently has to result in the punishment of the female speech organs, the body parts that have committed the crime, even though in these cases it is predominantly "just" a crime against patriarchal structures. Thereby, the removal of the tongue and the mutilation of the throat were necessary to rebalance the existing gender hierarchy. Recalling the existing belief about masculinity, femininity and the body, one then has to keep in mind that women were equated with the body but men were considered to be the head, and the head is where reason, thought, rationality and eloquent speech are located (Le Goff and Truong 47, 172-75; Schroer 93; Brown, *Body* 23). In all three cases the women presented are both more rational and logical in their arguments and instructions than their tormentors, and they also decide what is happening with their bodies – not in terms of torture and of which method is used to mutilate them, but rather when it is time to give up the human body in order to become one with Christ.

Cutting out tongues, even though it did not silence the saints presented here, was consequently a means to reestablish the existing gender hierarchy of woman below man

– even though many popular male ecclesiastical writers of the Middle Ages, such as Gregory of Tours,[32] were of the opinion that women had a special ability to transcend the naturally given weakness of their own sex, which would separate them from ordinary women and consequently "singled them out as candidates for sainthood" (Schulenburg 1). From a masculine point of view, Lucy, Christina and Cecilia were considered threatening and dangerous as their communicative nature disturbed the existing gender roles, and they had to be punished in order to redress the social balance.

Changing sides and looking at these legends from a female point of view, the systems of filtration have worked successfully. As Mills convincingly argues in regard to saints and speech,

> Such instances of debate, dissidence and verbal eloquence challenge the assumption that hagiography simply equates women with flesh. The verbal dissidence of female virgin martyrs might even have provided the circumstances for exemplary or "empowering" messages in certain contexts. (*Suspended Animation* 123)

Thus, overall, the female saint cannot be silenced, unless she decides to be silent herself.

4.3 Saintly Sexualized Bodies: Pious Pornography, Symbolic Defloration and Attempted Rape

> Invite a crowd to take their pleasure with this woman, and let them abuse her until she is dead!
>
> Saint Lucy[33]

> Saints functioned in the Middle Ages as heterogeneous figures, incorporating a body of contradictory discourses in which the lines between object-hood and subject-hood were often blurred.
>
> Robert Mills[34]

So far, the reading and analysis of female saints' lives in this study can be summarized as follows: in hagiography, the body is a significant motif, even though the ultimate goal of the saint is to dispose of the body in order to reach apotheosis. In addition, even though the entire body is subject to torture and mutilation, specific body parts are often highlighted more than others, and moreover, the interpretation of these scenes is

[32] Gregory of Tours, *Life of the Fathers*, Translated Texts for Historians, Latin Series I, trans. Edward James (Liverpool, 1985), ch. 19, p. 124.

[33] Jacobus de Voragine, *The Golden Legend: Readings on the Saints*, 2 vols., ed. and trans. William Granger Ryan (Princeton: Princeton UP, 1995), I: 29; "invitate ad eam omnem populum et tamdiu illudatur, donec mortua nuntietur" (Graesse 31).

[34] Robert Mills, *Suspended Animation: Pain, Pleasure and Punishment in Medieval Culture* (London: Reaktion, 2005), p. 122.

multifaceted and frequently contradictory.[35] The saintly legends, which deal with the martyrdom of a young virgin defending her body and soul, continuously feature sexual undertones – from the attempted rape scenes in the legend of Saint Lucy and Saint Agnes to the specific mutilation of gender-signifying body parts as in the legend of Saint Agatha. The cultural understanding of the mouth and its components and their functions within the human body as well as their claimed interconnectivity with other body parts – the female genitals – also allows for a second, gendered and sexualized reading of the female saints' *vitae*.[36] Taking the supposed interconnectivity between mouth/gorge and genitals as a starting point, this chapter wants to explore which body parts were equated with the mouth, teeth and tongue and how their cultural understanding can facilitate a sexualized reading of the legends of communicative female saints. Furthermore, the following chapter will take the supposed interconnectivity between mouth/gorge and genitals to argue that many torture scenarios can be read as role-plays of sexual penetration, in which saintly torture is presented as on the verge of pornography, or "pious pornography", as Robert Mills has called it (*Suspended Animation* 106). Sadistic fetishes – ranging from the removal of breasts to the tearing of the sides[37] – are executed on the tortured saint (Burgwinkle and Howie 34-35), and the legends try to trigger and stimulate hidden erotic fantasies.

According to the *Oxford English Dictionary*, pornography is "the printed or visual material containing the explicit description or display of sexual organs or activity, intended to stimulate sexual excitement".[38] Even though hagiography does not offer an explicit description of sexual activity as pornography does, scenes such as the attempted rape scene in the legend of Saint Lucy or the removal of breasts in the legends of Saint Christina and Saint Agatha nevertheless indicate a sexual tension within their martyrdom. It shows the sadistic sexual stimulation of a woman's body, which is performed through a painful penetration of the skin, its orifices and sensual spots, or through the threat of rape and bodily defilement. For Sorgo, the connection between pornography and hagiography means to understand a historical and textual development which started with the earliest manuscripts, with their partially erotic undertones and their cultivation of hidden sexual fantasies (17) and which are also based on the fact that most martyrical legends are the result of the fantasies and enthusiasm of male clerical writers, and thus the gender roles are noticeably defined (162).

Yet as light forms of violence, such as scratching, biting and hitting, are said to increase sexual excitement, pain and pleasure often go hand in hand, and at times no

[35] As an example, recall the contradictory strands of interpretation in the legends of longhaired saints in chapter 2.

[36] Some of my hypotheses from this chapter were recently published in Sarah Schäfer-Althaus, "Painful Pleasure: Saintly Torture on the Verge of Pornography", *Mirabilia* 18 (2014): 151-59, Web.

[37] As Sorgo writes in relation to the tearing of the sides, "Die Hüfte oder Seite umschrieben, was allgemein bekannt und gebräuchlich war, jene Körperteile, die man aus Scham nicht nennen wollte". Trans.: "The hips or the sides commonly described those body parts which one did not want to mention due to prudency". Gabriele Sorgo, *Martyrium und Pornographie* (Düsseldorf: Patmos, 1997), p. 148.

[38] "Pornography", *Oxford English Dictionary,* n.d., Web, 4 Apr. 2013.

clear boundary between pain and pleasure can be defined (136). It is, however, exactly "this conjunction of sexual pleasure within the frame – the pleasure of the woman being manipulated and restrained and the one doing this manipulating and restraining; and the pleasure of the viewer from outside the frame, both watching the scene and living it vicariously" (Burgwinkle and Howie 13) which makes a comparison between hagiography and pornography possible.

In both hagiography and pornography, the link between pain and pleasure, the staging ground for action, stimulation and penetration, is the body. As mentioned previously (see chapter 2), everything is centred on the body, its performance and the hidden codes its penetration transmits. As Burgwinkle and Howie propose in their work *Sanctity and Pornography in Medieval Culture*,

> Both [hagiography and pornography] are body focused, ostentatious, and attract attention. They produce the body as a spectacle, challenge theoretical notions about the limits of sensation and enact a process of synesthetic corporeal interaction such that the viewer believes that s/he can feel what the other is feeling or that the other is in him even more than himself. (8)

All spaces, orifices, limbs and interior and exterior organs are taken as much into the custody of the usually male tormentor (Sorgo 137) as all orifices, limbs and body parts are taken into the custody of the usually male sexual penetrator within pornography. The penetration of the body is supposed to attract the reader's attention and to explicitly sensitise him to certain body parts. To provide two examples, whereas in the legend of Saint Apollonia[39] the reader is specifically made to focus on the virgin's teeth, the emphasis in the legend of Saint Cecilia is obviously set on the martyr's throat and the unsuccessful attempt to decapitate her. Depending on the popularity of the legend, even the iconographic examples support this assumption by portraying the saints with their most significant body part – thus the display of breasts on a plate usually indicate Saint Agatha, and Saint Apollonia is commonly shown holding a pincer with one of her teeth.[40]

[39] In the legend of Saint Apollonia (AD 249), the tormentors break "out all her teeth with blows on her jaws" (Farmer 31). For the complete legend see Jacobus de Voragine, *The Golden Legend: Readings on the Saints*, 2 vols., ed. and trans. William Granger Ryan (Princeton: Princeton UP, 1995), I: 268-269; or Alban Butler, *Butler's Lives of the Saints*, 4 vols., ed. Herbert Thurston and Donald Attwater (New York: Kennedy, 1956), I: 286. Another great summary of Appolonia's life and cult can be found in "Das Martyrium der Heiligen Apollonia", Robert Uhde, *Bayerisches Zahnärzteblatt*, Jan/Feb 2009, Web, 18 Nov. 2011. In Great Britain more than fifty images of her have been counted, in particular in the areas and churches around Devon and East Anglia. Apollonia is still widely venerated as the patron saint of those who suffer from dental problems and of dentists, which has turned her into the icon of the British Dental Association and the inspiration for the name of a dentist's quarterly called *The Apollonian* in Boston, Massachusetts.

[40] For examples of images of Saint Agatha see chapter 2.2.1, n. 27. Within Germany, Apollonia's martyrdom is, for example, integrated into the "11000 Jungfrauen Altar" (1513) at the Münster in Heilbronn and into a fresco featured at the church of Saint Nikolai at Stralsund, holding her tooth in a pincer. For her distribution in English churches consult John F. Beal, "Representations of St Apollonia in British Churches", *Dental Historian* 30 (1996): 3-19.

However, whereas the breast is easily identifiable as the utmost signifier of femininity, and its unsuccessful removal opens up a complex discourse on gender and the historical and religious symbolism behind female body parts and body fluids (see chapter 2), the codes behind teeth and tongues may not be as obviously sexual. To recall the cultural understanding, from antiquity up to the nineteenth century medical scholars such as Galen[41] believed in the interconnectivity between the mouth and gorge and the female genitals. Whereas the mouth paralleled the female vagina, the tongue was equated to the clitoris, and the clitoris – though the word was not officially established until the sixteenth or seventeenth century[42] – was in turn often described as a "little tongue", a body part which belonged to one of a "woman's shameful members" (Mazzio 102). To continue this remapping of the body, the teeth are consequently transformed into a symbolic hymen, which functions as the visible barrier between outer and inner body and which, in the legends of Saint Apollonia and Saint Febronia,[43] is arguably "deflowered" by the violent removal of the teeth.

This idea of a symbolic defloration is based on the argument made by Anson, who suggested in his popular article "The Female Transvestite in Early Monasticism" that the practice of cutting off breasts is nothing but a "euphemism for the pre-execution defloration of virgins practiced to meet the Roman law that forbade the execution of virgins" (26).[44] If, in common belief, an interconnectivity between the mouth and the genital area existed, then arguably Anson's theory of defloration euphemisms in women's hagiography can be expanded to the amputation of the tongue and throat and in particular to the removal of teeth.

When one is aware of this bodily ambiguity, the legend of Saint Christina does offer a sexually motivated penetration of the virginal body. The destruction of her tongue and the removal of teeth in the legends of Saint Apollonia and Saint Febronia can therefore be seen as codes, turning the mouth into a symbolic vagina. The mouth is easier to manipulate than the actual genitals, as the virgin has to remain an intact screen on which a male audience's desires can be projected (Sorgo 70). Whereas the extraction of teeth thus grants access to the saintly, virginal female body, Christina's glossectomy even goes beyond penetration, as it can be seen as a symbolic elimination of the source of her womanhood, of the repulsive member of lust and female sexuality – the clitoris.

Within hagiography, the mouth and its components seem to be a grey zone in which the masculine torturer may exercise power and sexual domination. By deforming the

[41] Galen, *On the Usefulness of the Parts of the Body (De Usu Partium)*, 2 vols., trans. Margaret Tallmadge May (Ithaca: Cornell UP, 1968), 2: 622-23, 658-59, 660-61.

[42] There are a number of possibilities from where the original Greek word "clitoris" stems from. In the 1610s it was first used to denote the "erectile organ of female mammals" and the anatomist Mateo Renaldo Colombo (1516-1559) claimed to have discovered it. For the complete entry see "Clitoris", *Online Etymology Dictionary*, n.d., Web, 13 Sept. 2013.

[43] Saint Febronia has her cult in the Byzantine and Catholic traditions. The virgin martyr is venerated in Roman Catholicism on June 25. Butler writes that her legend is "purely fictitious", yet that during her martyrdom, before her "limbs were lopped off", "seventeen of her teeth were [...] pulled out and her breasts were cut off" (Butler II: 637). For the Latin and Greek texts see *De Sanctis Virginibus et Martyribus Febronia*, *AASS* Jun. VII, 12-31.

[44] The idea about body parts and symbolic defloration in relation to Anson's argument was previously touched upon in the analysis of the legend of Saint Agatha in chapter 2.

mouth, teeth and tongue, the masculine penetrator, this human incarnation of Satan, is able to enter the virginal body legally, with less resistance from authorities and from the saintly virgin, and above all without destroying her actual virginity. Yet the destruction also expresses a sort of masculine castration anxiety, which seems to be primarily linked to the fear of being "castrated" of his superior position in society rather than of his bodily member.

What the legends of Saint Lucy, Saint Christina and many others also have in common is that the penetrations of the virgins, these unfortunate copulation scenes, are successful only on the outside. Only the obvious, visible body parts are destroyed, yet the destruction can neither end the lives of these saints nor prevent them from being united with Jesus. Moreover, even the functions of these body parts remain intact. Christina and Lucy are still able to speak clearly, do not lose the power of speech (de Voragine I: 29, I: 387) and are not silenced after their tongues and throats are harmed.[45] The penetration removes barriers only physically, keeping the women pure spiritually. Saint Christina even picks up her "severed tongue", her "praescissuram linguae", and throws it into the face of her tormentor. And her tongue, this instrument of speech and this symbolic clitoris, takes away his eyesight (I: 387; Graesse 421). Through her activism and the mutilation of her tormentor, female reason and thought wins over male rationality, Christianity over paganism, and the male gaze, which perceived the virginal body as only a sexual object, is defeated. As this example of the body and its body parts has shown, hagiography can thus also work as a form of (subconscious) stimulation of sexual excitement, or at least it plays with erotic undertones once the historical and metaphorical codes behind the mentioned body parts have been deciphered.

Comparable to pornographic narratives, the characters within hagiography are not supposed to develop, but they need to adhere to their designated roles in order to communicate a certain fantasy and desire (Sorgo 64), which is in many cases related to sexual excitement. The torture scenarios are bound to specific rules and can be compared to sexual role-play. They can be viewed as a game in which all players – the virgin, the tormentor and the reader[46] – know exactly what role they have to play. The young maiden and the heathen men challenge and stimulate each other until the accumulation of sadistic penetrations of the virginal body ends in her death. Even though the stimulation and penetration of the virginal body is the centre of attention, the actual virginity, as scholars and frequent readers of hagiography are aware of, will remain intact, keeping the idealised sexualized phantasm of womanhood and virginal purity alive. In the end, the penetrated virgin will die sexually untouched, devoted to and joyful for the higher cause, as much as the sexually penetrated woman at the end of the most common pornographic scenarios gratefully embraces the ejaculation marking the end of the penetration.

"Invite a crowd to take their pleasure with this woman, and let them abuse her until she is dead!" (de Voragine I: 29; "invitate ad eam omnem populum et tamdiu illudatur,

[45] Another saint who is still alive after her "throat is torn out" (Butler II: 421) is Saint Theodosia. For the entire legend of Saint Theodosia (AD 745) in Latin and Greek see *De Sancta Theodosia*, *AASS* May VII, 64-85. For a summary consult Alban Butler, *Butler's Lives of the Saints*, 4 vols., ed. Herbert Thurston and Donald Attwater (New York: Kennedy, 1956), II: 420-21.

[46] For a discussion of the role of the reader within hagiography and in comparison to erotic literature, consult chapter 2.

donec mortua nuntietur" [Graesse 31]) – even the rape plot in the legend of Saint Lucy is part of the game:

> But when they tried to carry her off, the Holy Spirit fixed her in place so firmly that they could not move her. Paschasius called in a thousand men and had her hands and feet bound, but still they could not lift her. He sent for a thousand yoke of oxen: the Lord's holy virgin could not be moved. […] "What is this witchery," Paschasius exclaimed, "that makes a thousand men unable to budge a lone maiden!" "There is no witchery here," said Lucy, "but the power of Christ; and even if you add ten thousand more, you will find me still unmovable". (de Voragine I: 29)[47]

The scene underlines Lucy's steadfastness in her Christian belief and displays Paschasius's desperation in attempting to defile her body and dominate her – he even has her drenched in urine, as he believed that it would remove magical influences. Moreover, it vividly presents the game between God and the heathen in which Lucy's body becomes the match point between two masculine powers. Another reading is added by Mills, who convincingly claims that "One way of understanding these representations of objectifying violence would be to reformulate the rape-pornography reading in less victimological terms" (*Suspended Animation* 123). Doing so, "under certain circumstances, for example, it is possible to read the rape plot in hagiographic romance as an exemplary text championing the strategies of verbal and physical resistance by which rape might be countered" (123). This idea of physical and verbal resistance, which Mills identifies in regard to the legend of Saint Barbara,[48] is transferable to the *vita* of Saint Lucy as well. As Lucy herself claims, "The body is not defiled […] unless the mind consents […]. You will never be able to force my will" (de Voragine I: 28; "Cui Lucia: non inquinatur corpus nisi de consensu mentis […]. Nunquam autem voluntatem meam ad consensum poteris provocare" [Graesse 31]). Theoretically and practically, her body cannot be defiled, and physically as well as mentally she resists all the bodily punishment inflicted upon her.

In this second reading of communicative female saints it has been shown that there are stimulating, pornographic and often sadistic endeavours in female hagiographical narratives, gendering the tortured body parts such as the tongue, teeth and throat and thus supporting the development of (negative) erotic fantasies once all textual penetrations of the female body have been decoded.

[47] "Volentes autem eam trahere, tanto pondere spiritus sanctus eam fixit, ut omnino eam movere nequirent. Fecitque Paschasius mille viros accedere et manus ejus et pedes ligare, sed eam nullatenus poterant movere; tunc et cum viris mille paria boum adhibuit, sed tamen virgo domini immobilis permansit. […] Tunc dixit Paschasius: quae sunt illa maleficia, quod una puella a mille viris non moveretur? Lucia dixit: non sunt ista maleficia, sed beneficia Christi. Porro si adhuc decem millia adhibueris, aeque ut primum immobilem me videbis" (Graesse 31).

[48] For the legend of Saint Barbara see Alban Butler, *Butler's Lives of the Saints*. 4 vols., ed. Herbert Thurston and Donald Attwater (New York: Kennedy, 1956), IV: 478-89.

4.4 Concluding Remarks

> For those men we were just legs, breasts and pretty faces. Speaking up shattered their fantasy, and they responded violently to my voice.
>
> Jinan Younis[49]

"If, according to certain interpretations, saintly heroines 'function as objects and never as speaking subjects'", Mills notes, "this argument meets a challenge in those legends where the martyr's speech plays an important role" (123).[50] Outspoken female saints are different from their virginal sisters. They actively participate in their own martyrical discourse and guide the martyrical process by their speech, which insults their tormentors and at the same time converts many listeners. This chapter has portrayed the intersections between body and culture and how the multifaceted metaphors applied to certain body parts leads to a textual coding within the hagiographical text, resulting in a two-way reading of the martyrdom. On the one hand, it is used as a method, however unsuccessful, to silence rhetorically sophisticated women in a patriarchally dominated society. On the other hand, these saints' *vitae* in many aspects resemble pornographic narratives and belong to what Mills has called "pious pornography" (*Suspended Animation* 106). Once all codes have been deciphered, the legends of Saints Christina, Cecilia and Lucy allow a sexual reading which portrays scenes of attempted rape and indicates that the torture of teeth and tongues is not only used to silence these saints, but can be read as a form of symbolic defloration of those who have to remain intact – at least biologically.

[49] Jinan Younis, "What Happened When I Started a Feminist Society at School", *The Guardian*, 20 June 2013, Web, 21 June 2013.

[50] Robert Mills, qtd. in Brigitte Cazelles, *The Lady as Saint: A Collection of French Hagiographic Romances of the Thirteenth Century* (Philadelphia: U of Pennsylvania P, 1991), p. 80.

5 Gender Hybridity in Women's Hagiography

> When you meet a human being, the first distinction you make is "male or female?" and you are accustomed to the distinction with unhesitating certainty.
>
> Sigmund Freud[1]

> I shall look like a man disguised as a woman. In truth, neither sex is really mine [...]. I belong to a third sex, a sex apart, which has yet no name.
>
> Théophile Gautier[2]

Throughout this study women have been presented whose natural bodies are altered voluntarily or forcefully, who are deprived of gender-signifying body parts, hide their true selves, or have biological features associated with the opposite sex. Whereas temporarily desexed females such as Saint Agatha, short-haired and cross-dressing women such as Saint Euphrosyne and bearded saints such as Saint Wilgefortis question biological binaries, women such as Saint Eugenia, who disguised as a monk fulfils community service, and Saint Christina, who demonstrates communicative eloquence and reasonable thinking, challenge the gender presumptions of women at that time. So far, the analyses have shown that within hagiography, bodily gender hybridity is used as a common method to indicate the transcendence of the secular, passive-feminine body, particularly among female martyrs, in order to reach a higher social acceptance within the Christian community. However, in a society that historically has been trained to distinguish with "unhesitating certainty" (Freud 113) solely between two sexes, two genders and two forms of human beings, the female saints' hybridity also expands gender boundaries. This "traditional restriction to solely two genders leaves socially little space for a third form of physicality in which the restriction to man or woman is lost" (Leynhausen 152). Moreover, "once these visible boundaries between gender attributes are blurred, aggressions from the social environment can be expected" (152)[3]

[1] Sigmund Freud, "Femininity", in *New Introductory Lectures on Psycho-Analysis* (1933), rpt. in *The Standard Edition of the Complete Psychological Works of Sigmund Freud*, general ed. James Strachey (London: Hogarth and The Institute for Psycho-Analysis, 1964), vol. XXII, pp. 112-35, 113.

[2] Théophile Gautier, *Mademoiselle de Maupin*, trans. Joanna Richardson (Harmondsworth: Penguin, 1981), pp. 329-30.

[3] Original: "Sobald äußerlich die Grenzen zwischen den Gender-Attributen verschwimmen, ist in der sozialen Umwelt mit Aggressionen zu rechnen. Die tradierte Festlegung auf nur zwei Geschlechter lässt gesellschaftlich nur wenig Raum für eine dritte Form von Körperlichkeit, in der sich die Festlegung auf Mann oder Frau verliert". Maite Leynhausen, "Damen mit Bart. Zwischen sozialem Druck und ästhetischer Performanz", ed. Birgit Haas, *Haare zwischen Fiktion*

– a scenario described with impressive accuracy in respect to these saints' legends and the great variety of tortures they have to endure.

The final chapter will discuss the creation of hybridity and the effect it has on the treatment of the saint and her body. It will argue that the construction of sexual and gender transcendence follows strict patterns and is produced either through subtraction or addition of significant body parts or through the denial of a saint's true sex. The chapter will show that the female saints' hybridity not only indicates the limits of traditionally established sexual and gender binaries, but also makes room for a discussion of whether saints such as the bearded Wilgefortis and the temporarily breastless Agatha are still women in the common sense of the definition. It will question whether a classification of the female hybrid saint is possible within the range of historical and modern gender terminology. How can female saints be classified in their hybrid state – as transgender, androgynes or even as female eunuchs? Is the saintly hybrid, by moving into the realms of the *third*, a social threat to established gender hierarchies and in particular to masculinity?

Apart from hagiographical narratives, the effect of sexual and gender hybridization seems to be a frequently employed theme in the construction of the unexplainable Other in Anglo-Saxon and medieval literature, providing modern scholars with valuable insights into historical attitudes towards those who live along the margins of binary classification – presumptions which recur among the saintly gender transgressors. For example, in the *Liber Monstrorum de diversis generibus*, an Anglo-Latin catalogue listing monstrous and marvellous creatures, several entries include descriptions of cross-gendered, multisexual human beings. In its introduction the anonymous author states that he has "known a person of both sexes, who although they appeared more masculine than feminine from their face and chest, and were thought male by those who did not know, yet loved feminine occupations" (Orchard 259; "utriusque sexus cognouisse testor, qui tamen ipsa facie plus et pectore uirilis quam muliebris apparuit; et uir a nescientibus putabatur, sed muliebria opera dilexit" [258]).[4] Similar entries of odd and supposedly barbaric creatures can also be found in the *Wonders of the East*,[5] an Old English text from around AD 1000, which lists women with "beards down to their breasts" (Orchard 199; "ða habbað beardas swa side oð heora breost" [198]) and with "boar's tusks and hair down to their heels and ox-tails to their loins" (201; "ða habbað eoferes tucxas feax oð helan side, on lendenum oxan tægl" [200]). In addition, according

und Realität: Interdisziplinäre Untersuchungen zur Wahrnehmung der Haare (Berlin: LIT, 2008), pp. 148-53, p. 152.

[4] The *Liber Monstrorum de diversis generibus* exists in five manuscripts dating from the ninth or tenth centuries and was probably compiled by an Irishman or Anglo-Saxon (as evidenced by a reference to Hygelac, the Great – *Higlacus, rex Getarum*). It lists almost 120 monstrosities divided into three books and three categories (men, beasts, serpents). For the Latin and the translated versions as well as an impressive and readable discussion of its sources and textual history see Andy Orchard, *Pride and Prodigies: Studies in the Monsters of the Beowulf-Manuscript* (Toronto: U of Toronto P, 1995), chapter 4, pp. 86-115.

[5] The complete text can be found in Latin, Old English and modern English in Andy Orchard, *Pride and Prodigies: Studies in the Monsters of the Beowulf-Manuscript* (Toronto: U of Toronto P, 1995), pp. 175-203. For information on the sources and textual history of the *Wonders of the East*, see chapter 3.4, n. 54.

to the author of the *Liber Monstrorum*, "it is said to have happened often among the human race" (Orchard 259; "sed hoc frequenter apud humanum genus contigisse fertur" [258]) that people existed who could not be specifically classified as male or female, as feminine or masculine, which leads to one preliminary conclusion: it took hundreds of years until, with the development of gender theories, more categories and terms were created (*transgender*, *transsexual* or *supernumerary gender*) which tried to come to terms with and give a voice to the variety of in-between genders, sexes and identities. However, even though these classifications are relatively modern, the *Liber Monstrorum* indicates not only a medieval awareness of the existence of in-between states of human beings but also shows that already in this time period, binary thinking was favoured.

Furthermore, both manuscripts make no secret of their attitudes towards these phenomena, as their titles already indicate that these gender benders were classified as outlandish, abnormal and even monstrous. They were seen as creatures rather than human beings and the attitude towards those not easily identifiable was one of both interest and hostility. In the prologue to the *Liber Monstrorum*, the narrator notes that it was particularly asked to "answer about these [...] kinds of the world's area which strike the greatest terror of fear in humankind", that it should "record the monstrous parts of men" (255; "quae maximum formidinis terrorem humano generi incutiunt, ut de monstruosis hominum partibus describerem" [254]). One explanation for the widespread fascination with monsters and monstrous humans derived from the common belief in their necessity for the world's function and stability and thus for the natural order in the Middle Ages – even though these "monsters" sometimes simply represented people with disabilities or genetic mutations. Consequently, accounts of transsexuality[6] in the texts are placed alongside descriptions of creatures out of Greek mythology, and geographically, the catalogues are situated in the East – which was traditionally the place to "outsource" everything inexplicable in the Middle Ages.[7] As Campbell states, "The farther one got from Home, the temperate, reasonable mean, the more outlandish, *unheimlich*, became the bodies and manners of men" (65). This nonconformity with known gender behaviour and with common biological constructions of the sexes did not always end positively. In at least one described case it results in the death of the female hybrids with the justification that their extensive facial hairiness was so "offensive and disgusting" (201; "quia sunt publicato corpore et inhonesto" [180]; see also 200-01) that there was apparently no other option than killing them.

Many female saints also feature uncommon, marvellous characteristics – which in contrast to the "monsters" from the *Liber Monstrorum* and the *Wonders of the East* are

[6] For example, *Liber Monstrorum*, paragraph I.19: "Et in his incredibilibus quoddam genus utriusque sexus describitur, qui dexteram mammam uirilem pro exercendis operibus et ad fetus nutriendo sinistram habent muliebrem. Quos inter se uicibus coeundo ferunt alternis generare". Trans. I.19: "And among these incredible things there is described a certain race of joint sex, who have a right male breast for performing work and a left female breast for nourishing babies. And people say they reproduce by alternating sexual roles". Andy Orchard, *Pride and Prodigies: Studies in the Monsters of the Beowulf-Manuscript* (Toronto: U of Toronto P, 1995), pp. 270-71.

[7] The "East" thereby was a concept denoting "elsewhere" and not particularly what we consider the East or Middle East nowadays. It was a place far away from Britain and thus a convenient location for everything inexplicable.

not considered wondrous in a negative sense, but are proclaimed to be sure signs of their sanctity – even if these wondrous bodily features remain officially unexplainable. Saints are allowed, and sometimes even encouraged, to speak in tongues, to have visions, to be abnormally hairy, to smell strongly and to leak either an abnormal amount of a particular body fluid or another body fluid than biologically expected. In the case of the saints, it is precisely this inexplicability of certain phenomena deriving from the body and the creation of Otherness that makes them eligible for sainthood, yet at the same time, as described in the *Liber Monstrorum* and the *Wonders of the East*, these phenomena are also responsible for aggressive handling of their bodies by their male opponents or for other negative effects. As Mary B. Campbell writes,

> The effect of hybridization is technically inescapable in the context of describing the unknown, similitudes based on features of the known inevitably result in such perverse collages, destroying the coherence of the alien subject in order to transmit a visualizable image. (70)

Hybridization is consequently an automatic process that is initiated the moment the description of marvellous or unknown elements of the Other is attempted. Thus, hybridization is arguably a subjective construct carried out by each individual upon seeing the "alien subject" (70) in order to make sense of it and the chaos it produces within the normative and categorical thinking that Western civilization is adjusted to. Even though Western societies are at a point now where the marvellous bodies and abnormalities of numerous medieval saints are partially explainable with the help of medical terms such as *hirsutism* (extensive growth of hair) or *hyperhidrosis* (abnormal production of sweat), the reactions upon seeing a bearded woman in public is still one of unease, embarrassment and even disgust. As Salih notes, "The subject, which has neither origin nor end, comes into conflict with and defines itself against the other subjects and existing regimes" ("Introduction" 4). Consequently, as soon as traditional gender attributes are blurred, the "alien subject" is perceived as a threat to the existing social order and oftentimes faces aggressive reactions in its environment (Leynhausen 152). Within hagiographical narratives, these moments of unease, surprise, and even disgust and aggression are expressed through the male opponent, who reacts vehemently and usually life-threateningly when the female protagonist or her body suddenly behaves unexpectedly in terms of common gender norms. The reactions towards these "uncommon" physical and mental features are in turn mirrored by the tortures applied to these saints, by the removal of body parts and eventually by the murder of the saint.

Moreover, as noted previously,[8] hagiographical texts not only display a reaction within their textual frames, but they are also designed to trigger multifaceted reactions outside the text. From the male authors and compilers of the legends who translate and adapt them, adding their personal ideas and assumptions to the *vitae*, to the female and male clerical readers studying the legends who take the saints' lives as role models for their own devotional practice, to the common people who are taught how Christian behaviour should influence one's life and bodily behaviour – the authors and the

[8] For a discussion of sexual reactions towards hagiography see chapter 4.3. For the role of the reader consult chapter 2.

readership constantly have to define themselves with and in contrast to the "alien subject". Even though the "alien subject" in hagiography is an ideal the audience should aim to become and internalize, the female saint as presented throughout this study is also an ideal to frequently come "into conflict with" (Salih, "Introduction" 4), and the degree of the conflict is based on one's individual gender identity and gender assumptions. While the transvestite, the bearded and the outspoken saints are representatives of female roles that were praised for their innovative characters and their effective realization of the "becoming male" concept, they are at the same time punished for pursuing this masculine ideal and for overcoming their socially restricted femininity, which at least within the patriarchal structures results in the previously mentioned uneasiness – for masculinity rather than femininity.

Furthermore, hybridization comes with questions of identity conceptions, of the construction of the self and its (gender) identity in opposition to the Other. It touches on the problems of socially expected normativity and the limited perspective of the two gender binaries and finally ends in the complications of classification and the postulations about self-images versus hetero-images of the sex/gender hybrid. The reflected uneasiness of the tormentors upon seeing a woman behaving and looking unusual, maybe even abnormal, from their point of view directs the attention to questions still relevant nowadays: if a woman, such as Saint Agatha, loses her breast, is she still a woman? A question Herrmann answers in the negative for the Catholic Church, as "a woman without breasts is within the patriarchal structures of the Catholic Church just as little countable as a woman as a castrated man counts as a man" (*Sex und Folter* 92). If a woman grows a beard, as Galla, Paula and Wilgefortis do, is she still a woman? Recalling Frantzen's argument that "The breast is a marker of the female, the beard of the male" (76) and considering the deadly reaction of Wilgefortis's father or the vehement disapproval of her legend's general existence (A. Butler III: 151), it is another question to be answered negatively. Biologically, these questions seem redundant because (in most cases) a bearded and breastless woman is of course still considered female, yet is she still considered feminine?

When it comes to the saint's gender identity, these questions cannot be answered easily. How did a transvestite female saint perceive herself – as still a woman or rather as a (female) eunuch or even as a man? What is Saint Eugenia's self-image after cross-dressing voluntarily, and what is her perception, her hetero-image, within society? What about the way other members of her sex or the public perceive her? Is she still considered female and feminine or rather a mutilated female, a desexed female or even a desexed male? Unfortunately, for the majority of the saints presented here these questions will remain questions or can be answered only unsatisfyingly, as no insights into their perception of their personal identity are available. However, fortunately some few exceptions can be found among the transvestite saints' legends, since the disguise of their biological sex and their adaptation to the masculine gender is the focus of their *vitae*. To recall two previously analysed examples, both Saint Euphrosyne and Saint Eugenia voluntarily change their outer appearance, cut their hair and even discard their names in favour of masculine ones. Thereby they successfully enter a male monastic community and at first blend in so perfectly that none of their fellow brothers perceive them as women, but rather they "depend on a shadowy male gender category, the eunuch, the sexless male" (Frantzen 84). Consequently, even though both cause trouble later because of their fair appearances, they are at first perceived as manly. Furthermore, Eugenia's gender bending deceives not only her brothers, but also Melantia, the woman who is physically attracted to her and who accuses the saint of raping her, which leads to Eugenia's trial. The hetero-image of both saints is thus perceived as masculine rather than feminine. Upon revealing her true sexual identity, Eugenia in the *Vita Sanctæ Eugeniæ* (*PL* 73: 606-24) proclaims,

> I have not wanted to be a woman, but preserving a spotless virginity with a total effort of the soul, I have acted consistently as a man. I have not put on a senseless pretense of respectability so that as a man I might imitate a woman, but I, a woman, have acted as a man by doing as a man, by embracing boldly a virginity which is in Christ. (Qtd. in and trans. Szarmach, "Ælfric's" 153)[9]

Eugenia's self-image underlines Judith Butler's overall argument that gender identity is not "natural" or self-evident and far from stable (Salih, "Introduction" 6). Eugenia's case stresses the fragility and instability of gender identity and gender perception, which at one moment is perfectly harmonious and self-evident to the self and the other, but can in an instant turn into a delicate construct which has to be defended. To argue along the ideas of identity conception made by Stuart Hall, then, identities are not only fragile, but are "constructed within, not outside, discourse", and

> emerge within the play of specific modalities of power and thus are more the product [...] of difference and exclusion, than they are the sign of an identical, naturally constituted unity – an "identity" in its traditional meaning (that is, an all-inclusive sameness, seamless, without internal differentiation). (7)

Consequently, Eugenia's almost desperate performance of "acting consistently as a man" (Szarmach, "Ælfric's" 153) creates her singularity through "difference and exclusion" (Hall 7), but at the same time it mirrors the historical gender discourse of female bodily virginity. She has pretended to be a man only to stay virginal, to suit this metaphorical, overarching ideal of "becoming male". Hence, Eugenia's gender bending and her deliberate attempt to create a new masculine identity for herself ties in with Hall's idea about the creation of identity in general and about gender identity in particular, as this is also a product of "specific historical and institutional sites within specific discursive formations and practices, by specific enunciative strategies" (7).

Within a religious discourse, Eugenia's exclamation draws on Galatians 3:28, where it is stated that there "is neither Jew nor Greek, there is neither bond nor free: there is

[9] "nolui esse femina, sed virginitatem immaculatam tota animi intentione conservans, virum gessi constanter in Christo. Non enim infrunitam honestatis simulationem assumpsi, ut vir feminam simularem; sed femina viriliter agendo, virum gessi, virginitatem quæ in Christo est fortiter amplectendo" *Vita Sanctæ Eugeniæ* (*PL* 73: 614D) in Paul E. Szarmach, "Ælfric's Women Saints: Eugenia", *New Readings on Women in Old English Literature*, ed. Helen Damico and Alexandra Hennessey Olson (Bloomington: Indiana UP, 1990), p. 153. See also Jane Tibbetts Schulenburg, *Forgetful of Their Sex: Female Sanctity and Society, ca. 500-1100* (Chicago: Chicago UP, 1998), pp. 158-59.

neither male nor female. For you are all one in Christ Jesus".[10] Eugenia, as a consecrated virgin, has, even in her masculine disguise, turned into a *human ex voto*.[11] She is now a "bride of Christ" and thus "no longer a woman" but has become a "sacred vessel dedicated to the Lord" (Eusebius, *Homily 6.18*, qtd. in Brown, *Body* 260[12]). As such she is, at least metaphorically, considered a "sexless, gender-neutral being" (Schulenburg 128). In order to reach apotheosis the goal of the female saintly martyr is the negation of her body and thus the annihilation of her sex and gender in order to become one with God. Through the premartyrical loss or disguise of gender- and sex-defining body parts, the female saints have lost their sexual and gendered existence and are no longer able to be categorised. Therefore some scholars may argue that a saint cannot be equated to a human in the first place, that a saint is a mythical or semimythical being whose body is sublime (see chapter 1) and thus beyond any man-made categorisation, which makes a discussion about the female saint's sex and gender hybridity superfluous.

However, even though the status of sainthood may end gender questions once and for all, since sainthood itself truly is a status beyond male and female, masculine and feminine, one needs to take into consideration that the female saints are awarded sainthood only after their martyrdom. The woman within the saint loses her sexual and gendered existence only after she has died. It is her death that transforms her linguistically from a "she" into an "it". Therefore, this study argues that the displayed gender hybridity of the saints is a premartyrical, presainthood state of the saintly body. Gender is out of the equation only after the apotheosis has been accomplished and the transcendence from body to soul, woman to saint is completed. Before that, however, gender and sex are not only visible, but as the previous analyses have shown, they influence the way the saint and her body are treated in the course of her martyrdom, mirroring the historical and social expectations about femininity and the female sex. The saints' gender ambiguity is part of a countercultural movement established with "Christian conversion and its heroic demands on women who wish to escape patriarchal claims on their bodies and commit themselves to spiritual and physical unions with Christ rather than with men" (Frantzen 88). "In order to accomplish this aim", Frantzen continues, "they must cease to be either women or men, as sexual behaviour defines those categories, and pursue a life without sex" (88). Consequently, a closer look at the problems of classifying these saints according to historical and modern gender terminology and at the usually negative social outcome of hybridization for the saint seems indispensible.

Generally within hagiography, the blurring of gender boundaries follows certain rules. First of all, it is created by the subtraction of sex-defining or gender-denoting body parts, as in the legend of Saint Agatha. A second form of gender hybridity is established within the slightly larger group of those who deny their true sex and (bodily) gender identity with the help of a manly or masculine disguise, such as the saints Eugenia and Euphrosyne. The addition of gender-typifying body parts and characteristics attributed to the other sex,

[10] "non est ludaeus neque Graecus non est servus neque liber non est masculus neque femina omnes enim vos unum estis in Christo Jesu"

[11] See also chapter 1.2.2.

[12] Eusebius of Emesa, *Homily 6.18*, in *Eusèbe d'Émèse: Discours conserve en latin*, ed. E. M. Buytaert, *Spicilegium Sacrum Lovaniense* 26 (Louvain: Spicilegium Sacrum, 1953), I: 162.

as in the legend of the bearded Saint Wilgefortis and among the outspoken saints such as Saint Christina and Saint Lucy, mark the third group.

Even though the patterns surrounding the creation of hybridity are easily identifiable, the attempt to classify these saints in historical as well as modern terms[13] is challenging. Most of the saints presented throughout this study are *supernumerary genders*, are "individuals who adopt the role and many of the customs of the opposite sex" (Bullough and Bullough 3) or *transgender* figures – umbrella terms which include transvestites, cross-dressers, androgynes and many other in-between forms of gender identities. Whereas Saint Agatha's mastectomy turns her into a temporarily desexed female, as the "torture [...] temporarily refigured her bodily gender" (Frantzen 75) until her breasts are restored through prayer, finding suitable terms for the other saintly hybrids dealt with throughout this study illustrates the possibilities and limits of classification. For example, already categorized as *transvestites* and as "depend[ent] on a shadowy male gender category, the *eunuch*, the *sexless male*"[14] (84), saints such as Pelagia/us, Marina/us, Theodora/us, Eugenia and Euphrosyne, among others, seem to fulfil and to unify a number of characteristics of a diverse spectrum of gender-classifying terms – historical and modern – making it impossible to find one definite category for them. They are female *transvestites* because of their *cross-dressing* and live as *eunuchs*, indicated by their masculine clothing, their tonsure and their fair appearance and which, in the words of Athenagoras, one of the Ante-Nicene Christian apologists, "brings [one] nearer to God".[15] However, they could also be classified as *androgynous* because they do not truly belong to one gender or the other and are *asexual* to the extent that they "aspire to a male status without sex – not to a status that is ambiguously gendered, but to a male role" which is "conspicuously absent [of] sexual functions" (Frantzen 74). In addition, integrating the religious approach into the discussion, they also want to achieve a *neutrois* or *neutral-gendered* state of being. A similar complexity of suitable terminology is applicable to Saint Wilgefortis, who is neither a *desexed male* nor a *desexed female*, but rather a *pseudohermaphrodite*, in the way that she biologically combines her female sex with a male secondary sexual characteristic – the beard.[16] Consequently, the sheer endlessness of

[13] Whereas terms such as *androgyne*, *eunuch* or *hermaphrodite* can be considered historically available terms, as all three were probably coined between the high and late Middle Ages, terms such as *transsexual*, *transgender* or even *queer* in its modern sense are products of the twentieth century. The word *queer* entered the English language approximately around the 1500s and was used in the sense of strange, peculiar, eccentric – its relation to homosexuality was, however, not mentioned until 1922. For the etymology of each term see Douglas Harper, *Online Etymology Dictionary*, n.p., 2001-16, Web, 12 Nov. 2013.

[14] Emphasis added.

[15] "Nay, you would find many among us, both men and women, growing old unmarried, in hope of living in closer communion with God. [For] remaining in virginity and in the state of a eunuch brings [one] nearer to God". Athenagoras, *A Plea for the Christians*, trans. B. P. Pratten, *The Ante-Nicene Fathers*, vol. 2, ed. Alexander Roberts et al. (Edinburgh: T&T Clark; Grand Rapids: Eerdmans, 1885), ch. 33, "Chastity of the Christians with Respect to Marriage"; see also Peter Brown, *The Body and Society: Men, Women and Sexual Renunciation in Early Christianity* (New York: Columbia UP, 1988), p. 66.

[16] The phenomenon where organisms begin as female and change to male in the course of time, called protogyny, is reserved only for nonhuman organisms. See Edward M. Barrows, *Animal*

the possible combinations for each hybrid saint along with the lack of the individual saint's self-perception of her sexual and gendered identity shows that there are still limits, gaps and imprecisions in terminology despite the great variety of existing in-between and partially overlapping (bodily) gender categories.

Finally, in regard to the creation of hybridity, it also has to be taken into consideration that in comparison to the addition, subtraction and denial of gender and sex, hybridity in hagiography is not always performed voluntarily. Not all saints presented throughout the course of this study decide for themselves to become hybrids as a way to opt out of social restrictions; many are forced through torture and mutilation. Whereas Saint Agatha's breast, her utmost signifier of her femininity, is destroyed forcefully by her tormentor, Saint Wilgefortis prays to be disfigured by God in order to keep her virginity, and the saints Eugenia and Euphrosyne also decide for themselves to have their hair shortened and female features hidden. Interestingly, it seems that these self-determined transgender characters in particular are most intensely feared among hagiographical compilers. Those women who decide for themselves about their gender transgression or assimilation to the masculine, and consequently those who voluntarily move into the hybrid state, cause the greatest disturbance. These are the saints who define "an awkward gender space, awkward at least in terms of an asymmetrical gender hierarchy" (Frantzen 87) and consequently make room for the question of whether the female gender hybrid in general and the self-determined hybrid in particular is a social threat.

In "Sexual Inversions" Judith Butler explains that once sex, and as this chapter argues also gender, is seen as a fixed "principle" in the formation of identity, then sex and gender are "always positioned within a field of two mutually exclusive and fully exhaustive identities; one is either male or female [or masculine or feminine], never both at once, and never neither one of them" (66). Consequently, being classified as "both at once" or "neither one of them" places the transgendered figure on the social and sexual margins of society. In order to "qualify as legitimately human", as Butler continues, "one must be coherently sexed", as the "incoherence of sex is precisely what marks off the abject and the dehumanized from the recognizably human" ("Sexual Inversions" 67). Taking this idea further, Wilgefortis and her transvestite sisters are marginalized not only because they are women with male attributes or because they work in masculine professions, but particularly because they are "incoherently sexed". Hence, they are ostracised because they are no longer socially controllable in terms of their sexual and gendered identity. Keeping Garber's argument in mind that the "ideal scenario – from the point of view of the regulators – was one in which a person's social station, social role, gender and other indicators of identity in the world could be *read*, without ambiguity or uncertainty" (26), then the social aggression faced by the self-determined female saintly gender hybrid is the only logical result, as she places herself *voluntarily* outside of the heteronormative order. The "formation of sex" and gender "is an enactment of power" in the sense that "power works on sex [...] not only as an external constraint or repression but as the formative principle of its intelligibility"

Behavior Desk Reference: A Dictionary of Animal Behavior, Ecology, and Evolution, 2nd ed. (Boca Raton: CRC, 2001), p. 317.

(Butler, "Sexual Inversions" 64). Therefore, in a society that assumes the power to decide

> what will and will not qualify as properly sexed being […] there will be [only] two sexes, discrete and uniform, and they will be expressed and evidenced in gender and sexuality, so that any social displays of nonidentity, discontinuity, or sexual incoherence will be punished, controlled, ostracized, reformed. (65)

Taking this further, it means that Wilgefortis's death is a result of the gender and sexual discontinuity triggered through her bearded and hence unfeminine appearance, which classifies her as an incoherently sexed being. The beard on her face disqualifies her from the "norm", and the disfigured female becomes the alien subject – the social threat – who has to be removed in order to reestablish the social norm. In *The Judith Butler Reader* Salih sums up Butler's argument on the result of nonconformity of gender behaviour:

> The desire to kill someone for not conforming to the gender norms by which subjects are supposed to live means that "life" itself requires the norm, while living outside the norm involves placing oneself at risk of death – sometimes actual death, but more frequently the social death of delegitimation and non-recognition. (11 n. 58)

This confrontation with the idea of dying a "social death of delegitimation and non-recognition" is not only embedded in the life of Saint Wilgefortis, but is also detectable among the transvestite saints. Similar to Wilgefortis's disqualifying beard, the accusation of rape against Saint Eugenia and the monastic enclosure in the *vita* of Saint Euphrosyne are results of their cross-dressing and their dependence on the concept of eunuchism, which in itself already represents a male category of sexual discontinuity and an in-between state of being.

To qualify for sainthood, the majority of martyred saints – male and female alike – gracefully embrace the necessary step of ostracism and "die" a metaphorical social death in order to accomplish apotheosis later on through physical decay. Whereas the majority, however, are prosecuted and tortured predominantly because of their Christian vocation, the bearded and transvestite female saints are punished primarily because their *vitae* depend on an "awkward gender space" and "asymmetrical gender hierarchy" (Frantzen 87). Next to the mere fact that Wilgefortis, Eugenia and the others are women, this undefined gender space singles them out ambiguously. Whereas their extraordinary lives led to an indisputable popularity and positive reception among the common people, for hagiographers, scholars and clerics they were challenging. These saints' sexual and gendered incoherence turned them into frightening female characters, into nonideological women, who were self-determined protagonists and who did something or were rewarded with something that was supposed to happen only metaphorically. Thus, to rise all-accepted, all-approved and all-praised postmortem, Eugenia, Euphrosyne, Wilgefortis and the others have to face a "social death of delegitimation and non-recognition" (Salih, "Introduction" 11) that stretches far beyond the mere textual and narratological sphere into their reception and adaptation within the society and culture of the medieval and postmedieval world.

As previously mentioned, the saints' reliance on the concept of eunuchism complicates the status of the saint even further. Yet is it even possible to relate the ambiguously gendered saints to a traditionally all-male concept? Even though the concept of female eunuchism was known to ancient sources, it has remained "without much clarity" (Kuefler, "Castration" 292) how a female eunuch is defined, and yet, as Frantzen notes, the saints' gender "mobility is perfectly represented by the eunuch, the male who stands outside the patriarchal system constituted by marriage and sexual customs" and whose gender also is highly ambiguous (88).

Concerning a characterisation and definition of female eunuchism, two possibilities offer the most potential.[17] Traditionally, the term *eunuch* refers to a man who has been castrated, and if this castration has been done in prepubescence the development upon entering puberty of male hairiness or a deeper voice is eliminated.[18] Transferring the definition of the male eunuch one-to-one, then a female eunuch should be predominantly a "castrated" woman – one whose most important signifiers of femininity (breasts, genitals) have been removed. In addition, the concept of female eunuchism needs an expansion in women's hagiography, because except for Saint Agatha, whose breasts are literally cut off the body, thus turning her into a temporarily desexed female, none of the transvestite saints literally lose any of their sex-denoting body parts. In the case of hagiographical narratives, a female eunuch is therefore mostly a woman who hides her female features (body shape, breasts) and adopts the social conventions of eunuchism, in particular hairstyles (tonsure), in order to pass as a prepubescent eunuch in the general social discourse but also in exclusive communities such as all-male monasteries.

However, the idea that Saint Wilgefortis "adopts" the beard seems too abstract. Therefore, in order to include her in the concept of eunuchism, another approach to a plausible definition of the female eunuch needs to be thought of. If a male eunuch is seen as man with female features, as an effeminate male, why can a female eunuch not be a woman with male or masculine features and characteristics, which would mean a reversal of the traditional definition? As the male eunuch lacked significant bodily and social characteristics that defined ancient and medieval masculinity, this hypothesis seems plausible. Whereas the male eunuch is deprived of his testicles and the possibility of reproducing as well as of body hair, such as the beard, the female eunuch adds to her femininity (breasts, vagina) masculine attributes such as the beard, the tonsure, masculine attire, or characteristics historically defined as masculine, such as intelligence and self-determination, expressed through linguistic eloquence. Taking both possibilities of the definition into consideration for the following discussion, the question is still unanswered of why both gender hybrids, both forms of female eunuchism, face obstacles in the form of homoerotic temptations, rape accusations or crucifixion, which appear to be more than just stylistic conventions but rather a literary

[17] The following classification of what a female eunuch represents for this thesis and context is in no way related to the study *The Female Eunuch* (1970) by Germaine Greer, an Australian scholar and journalist. Her study focuses on the assumption that the family reduces women to household objects, which devitalizes them and consequently turns them into eunuchs. This has, of course, only little to do with the saints' legends, yet in order to avoid confusion the difference should be mentioned.

[18] "Eunuch", *Online Etymology Dictionary*, n.d., Web. 13 Sept. 2013.

way to punish these women's self-determination and their attempt to "become male". As "gender hierarchy begins with bodily difference and then affects social and theological relations between women and men" (Walker 78), this study argues that female gender hybridity in particular is seen as a social threat to the existing heteronormative social order and especially to masculinity.

The hypothesis that the female eunuch is regarded as a social threat recalls the general problematic position of her male counterparts within medieval society. With the increasing social and religious outcry for celibacy and asceticism, a man could be *spoken* of with esteem as a eunuch if he lived an ascetic lifestyle without having sexual intercourse (Brown, *Body* 67). From antiquity onwards, eunuchs, with their lives of sexual abstinence, were "expected to bear the mark of exceptional closeness to the spirit of God" (66). To become a pre- or even postpubescent eunuch[19] was popular in ancient and medieval societies, and even the Bible conceptualises this ideal in Matthew 19:12, stating that "there are eunuchs, who have made themselves eunuchs for the kingdom of heaven".[20] Brown writes about religiously motivated castration:

> Far from crumbling into presexual formlessness, as was the case with those castrated when young, the full-grown man who made himself a eunuch, by carefully tying his testicles, became [...] a man who wasted no vital fire on others. (*Body* 19)

Despite these apparently positive associations with eunuchism, which at first sight made eunuchs perfect candidates for the clergy, the eunuchs' gender ambiguity turned them into mysterious and "universally despised figures [through] the end of the Middle Ages and beyond" (Kuefler, "Castration" 289). As Brown illustrates, "By losing the sexual 'heat' that was held to cause his facial hair to grow, the eunuch was no longer recognizable as a man" (*Body* 169). Therefore, in a cultural system in which masculinity was the ideal, the effeminate man – the eunuch, who was expelled from both genders – "was notorious (and repulsive to many) because he had opted out of being male" (169). As Kuefler notes,

> Eunuchs occasioned unease in part because their gender ambiguity was far less easy to ignore than that of other physiologically ambiguous persons. If hermaphrodites could be assigned a male identity based on the presence and presumed function of male genitals, eunuchs could not be arbitrarily assigned a traditional gender in the same way. Their sterility meant that they could neither father children nor function as males. And the eunuch had suffered the excision, the least in part, of the external genitalia that marked maleness. (*Manly* 31)

Consequently, despite their natural maleness, eunuchs "were often portrayed as the equivalent of women in early medieval writings, and the stereotypes of their characters

[19] Kuefler notes in his essay "Castration and Eunuchism in the Middle Ages" that eunuchism was inflicted via three possibilities: the removal or disabling of the penis, the testicles or the entire genitals (285).

[20] "[...] et sunt eunuchi qui se ipsos castraverunt propter regnum caelorum [...]". Even though today scholars agree that this statement implied celibacy and avoiding marriage, many interpreted this phrase literally and castrated themselves postpubescence.

are virtually the same as those of women: carnal, voluptuous, wanton, irrational, fickle, manipulative, deceitful" (Kuefler, "Castration" 291). Prepubescent castrated men also resemble women because they retain hairless faces and bodies and develop higher-pitched voices and larger breasts. Consequently, the figure of the eunuch in itself was perceived as a social threat always on the verge of dying a "social death of delegitimation and non-recognition" (Salih, *Butler* 11). It conceptualised a challenge to everyday notions of gender classification and mirrored the true fear of masculinity – losing sexual heat and thus becoming women.

The self-determined female gender hybrids in women's hagiography represent an extreme version of this patriarchal challenge and fear. Comparable to male eunuchism, they question the "notions of the absolute divide between male and female", a problem which is not "easily erased" (Kuefler, *Manly* 19). Yet even though Wilgefortis and the transvestite saints try to disguise their gender and biological sexual identity, they have two advantages in contrast to male eunuchs: first, they do not have to opt out of being female via castration because their transformation to pass as "male" or an "effeminate male" can be performed without great difficulty. Moreover, their beards, their tonsured hair, or even their monastic enclosure already disqualifies the saints socially from femininity and female duties such as marriage and childbirth. Second, the female eunuch always has the chance, as Saint Eugenia has shown, to reclaim her femininity when needed or when her disguise is threatened and thus can move freely between both sexes and both genders. Whereas for Eugenia this is a significant form of self-determinism, to the existing patriarchal structures at that time the idea of a woman being able to switch freely between two sexes, genders and identities makes her even more threatening.

The problems caused by the saints' embodiment of an "incoherently sexed" human being are shown particularly when it comes to sexuality. Eunuchs' feminized appearance made them objects of male and female desires alike. This is shown, for example, in the monks' desire for Euphrosyne, whom they believe to be a manly eunuch because of her fair appearance, or in the legends of a number of other female transvestite saints who are desired by women, such as Saint Eugenia. "As these lives show, the eunuch is a possible sexual partner for a woman (Melantia's advances to Eugenia) or a man (the monk's attraction to Euphrosyne). These possibilities are not merely modern projections of the saints' lives but are indeed their same-sex shadows" (Frantzen 88-89). In terms of sexuality, the hardness of men also denoted their "role as sexual penetrators and sexual aggressors", whereas the softness of women reflected their "role as sexually penetrated" and their general social passivity (Kuefler, *Manly* 21). These assumptions are tested as "the confusion about eunuchs made it impossible to know whether they should be considered as men or women in the arena of sexuality, as sexual penetrators or as sexually penetrated" (34), a confusion shown in the homosexual implications that Eugenia and Euphrosyne have to face (see chapter 2.3, 3.3). This socially condemned desire must be suppressed, such as in the case of Euphrosyne, through separation from the rest of the monastic population, or it will lead to the exclusion from the monastic communities by accusing the female of raping another woman or of fathering a child. Despite the simultaneous inclusion and suppression of homosexual desire and the presence of punishment in various degrees, the association of transvestite saints with eunuchs is significant. As Walker remarks, hagiographers must "alleviate any anxiety in their male readers by stressing that the cross-dressed women unmistakably lack penises" (96). Moreover,

> Whereas those saints who claim to be eunuchs achieve a greater degree of verisimilitude by suggesting that the cross-dressed monk's beardless and more "feminine" features must result from having been castrated, the saints who are depicted as virile and are accused of sexual misdeeds take the reader's knowledge of the saint's sexual capability – defined specifically as "inability" – and amplifies the readerly pleasure through that discrepancy. (95)

Nevertheless, exclusion and imprisonment are still lighter forms of punishment than Wilgefortis's crucifixion for the possession of a beard. The movement into the bearded territory of men is arguably a greater transgression than the movement into the territory of women as objects of sexual desire. The "conflation between castration and passive homosexuality" that Matthew Kuefler identifies in his study "Castration and Eunuchism in the Middle Ages" (285) and the possibility that eunuchs may have been objects of sexual desire for both men and women perhaps suggest why the male eunuch would be more acceptable than a female counterpart.

While the cutting of hair represents a radical break from traditional feminine appearance, it does not render a woman unattractive within the medieval world. She remains an object of sexual desire, but the desire shifts instead to describing her as an attractive (near) masculine figure. The beard, in contrast, sufficiently transforms the woman into an alien figure – into the prototypical "alien subject" (Campbell 70). Other saints are approached in sensual terms, such as in the case of Euphrosyne's beauty when cross-dressed and also in the case of the long hair of several of the saints, which is an object of significant attention and sensual description. But the bearded female eunuch is visibly and militantly outside the standard sexual economy, which is a violation of the expected place of a woman. While the shared intention to avoid marriage and maintain virginity marks both the tonsured, cross-dressed saints and the bearded ones, the visibility of the beard as opposed to the disguise that the short hair affords marks the beard as a greater transgression and thus perhaps invites the extremity of the final punishment – Wilgefortis's crucifixion. When Garber writes about the necessity of constant hair removal for "the *passing* male-to-female transvestite" in contrast with "the radical drag queen who *wants* the discontinuity of hairy chest or moustache to clash with a revealingly cut dress", she highlights that the addition of hair is the trait central to creating discontinuity in the ostensibly female body (49).

The self-determined female gender hybrid and its reliance on an incoherently sexed figure overtly challenges and "questions binary thinking and introduces crisis – a crisis which is symptomatized by *both* […] overestimation *and* […] underestimation" (Garber 11). With the removal and substantial denial of femininity as well as by the adding of male attributes (metaphorically and literally),[21] these saints arguably transcend both the biological categories of male and female and the culturally established gender binaries of masculine and feminine. By doing so they create a gap that leaves space for the

[21] Whereas most body parts are "literally" removed or added, the transvestite saints form a special category: their denial of their true sex through cross-dressing only "metaphorically" subtracts their true sex from them.

possibility of the female saint as a third sex and a third gender, and this movement into the grey zone of the *third* is rebellious, thought provoking and threatening in itself, as Garber argues:

> The "third term" is *not* a *term*. Much less is it a sex, certainly not an instantiated "blurred" sex as signified by a term like "androgyne" or "hermaphrodite," although these words have culturally specific significance at certain historical moments. The "third" is a mode of articulation, a way of describing a space of possibility. Three puts in question the idea of one: of identity, self-sufficiency, self-knowledge. (11)

The third, she continues, thus "involve[s] moving from a structure of complementarity or symmetry to a contextualization, in which what once stood as an exclusive dual relation becomes an element in a larger chain" (12). The male eunuch officially exists in some senses as a *third sex*, as Kuefler describes the status of eunuchs in late Roman antiquity, but there is no mention of an equivalent position for female eunuchs (291). Because of the consistent suppression of women's desire, the understanding of it is limited in comparison. The external and obvious mutilation of the male body is quickly placed into a cultural context because defining masculinity is of greatest importance to a legal and social system that so absolutely links the masculine with dominance. In contrast, the definition of femininity is left as an absence of that which is masculine. As Luce Irigaray notes, "If the coherent subject is always sexed as masculine, then it is constructed through the abjection and erasure of the feminine" (qtd. in J. Butler, "Sexual Inversions" 68[22]). The sudden presence of an obvious marker of masculinity on a woman is thus disruptive and results in violent punishment. In a similar sense to the argument that "women are regarded as having not *sexual* but *cultural* desire" (Garber 45) for cross-dressing and that the intent to pass as a member of a privileged class makes sense, then even such a radically apparent transgression as the presence of the beard is at least culturally intelligible as a desire to be better. The bearded saints make no attempt at passing and entering into a masculine identity or seizing masculine privileges, but if one assumes the spiritual superiority of men, as emphasized by the hierarchy of the Church, then the beard is a sign of these saints' ability to be greater than other women by being more like men. Consequently, with respect to the medieval perception of gender, the female eunuch is closer to a universal gender. She is a stronger and more powerful figure than the male eunuch will ever be. However, one has to bear in mind that whereas the male eunuch was a common and tolerated gender niche within the medieval society – he was considered a *third sex* and neither man nor woman, but as something in between – the female eunuch was not.

To summarize, saintly gender hybridity reflects the time-transcending complexity of assigning a true, well-defined sexual and gendered identity to each individual labelled as "incoherently sexed" and thus living outside established Western binaries – be it in the Middle Ages or even in modern society. In addition, the legends show that the aggression that transgendered figures have to face by the social environment are deeply rooted in history, which raises the question of whether humanity will ever transcend

[22] Luce Irigaray, *This Sex Which Is Not One*, trans. Catherine Porter with Carolyn Burke (Ithaca: Cornell UP, 1985).

categorisation. And yet, the sexual and gender fluidity and hybridity of these saints, these often historically (self-)made trickster figures, show the limits and narrowness of binarity, and in order to classify them in Freudian terms "with unhesitating certainty" (113) we need to create new categories for them which allow the existence of third forms of sex and gender. Furthermore, they also question whether in our modern world we should not be beyond gender and beyond queering and hybridizing. Is not current society, which has discussed gender issues more than any other previous society, postqueer and postgender by now? As being post-anything arguably remains subjective, this study answers the question strongly in the negative. To taxonomize or not to taxonomize – that is the true difficulty here. With personal sexual identification not necessarily denoting biological identification, the labelling of anything in-between the two binaries just does not meet the specificity needed. In contrast to the medieval world, in our modern society it is clearly not about the invention of new categories any longer. It is about being more specific, precise and inclusive in our understanding and description of the *third*, the *fourth*, and the *fifth* – the large unknown of the *in-between*. The third encompasses not only one Other but a multitude of Others, some of whom, as the saints have shown, are yet to be defined.

Conclusion(s): The Gendered Body and Female Sanctity

> Der Körper hat also eine Geschichte. Der Körper ist unsere Geschichte.
>
> Jacques Le Goff and Nicolas Truong[1]

In the introduction to this study on the gendered body in women's hagiography the question was raised of why we should deal with the body and body constructions of medieval times. In answer to this, the study has shown that one should focus on the body not only because it still belongs to the greatest research gaps in history, as Le Goff and Truong have proposed (9), but because the body does have a fascinating, complex and multilayered history of its own. This history is not only dependent on the time period it is situated in, but it is primarily a history which shapes and influences while at the same time being shaped and influenced by everyday culture and its ideological and gendered presumptions about the body, and in particular about the female body.

The thesis at hand critically reflected on the complex historical, cultural, sociological and gendered constructions of the medieval female body in popular female saints' legends, because their assessment of femininity "offer[s] us an extraordinary glimpse of the past" (Schulenburg 410). Saints' *vitae* "provide us with marvellous details" in regard to women's history, women's experiences and their bodies "not found in any other sources of the period" (410) and are significant historical examples that gender mattered in medieval times.

Hagiography, as this study has shown, is a body-centred genre. The body and the female saint form a symbiosis, creating an inseparable relationship which reflects moral values, ideological and patriarchal doctrines and changing attitudes regarding the body and its treatment as well as the role of women in society and within this male-dominated genre. The longer a *vita* focuses on the body as a stylistic device and offers detailed descriptions of various, usually negative actions done to the body and specific body parts, the longer the body functions as a metaphor and the more successful the legends were in their public reception and dissemination. Besides, in the making of women saints, a large number of legends were identified as completely fictional, as created and modified by their male authors to serve the increasing demands for saints' *vitae* in the Middle Ages and to suit the taste of the hagiographers' financial sponsor – the Church. As a result, body parts in women's hagiography are placed within the narratives specifically to manifest theological and gender ideology. What is more, within hagiography only selected body parts, such as the breast, hair and hairstyles as well as the gorge and its components (teeth, tongue, throat), recur frequently, whereas others are barely or never mentioned – an observation which resulted in the outline of this study.

[1] Trans.: "The body does have a history. The body is our history". Jacques Le Goff and Nicolas Truong, *Die Geschichte des Körpers im Mittelalter* (Stuttgart: Klett-Cotta, 2007), p. 195.

Apart from explaining the significance and popularity of saints in everyday culture and the intricate author-text relation in hagiography, the study noted that the rise of Christianity not only assigned sanctity a new form of significance in everyday culture, but it also provided society with new ideas and policies regarding the body. Aside from the theological influence, the dissertation discussed the diverse theoretical framework surrounding the body – from sociological, gendered, historical and even medical perspectives. In this respect, this study argued that the body was generally understood as a performative, changeable entity – as a body in progress – divided into noble and ignoble, male and female, masculine and feminine parts. In contrast to modern gender-studies approaches, however, medieval society did not separate the *natural* from the *cultural* body and thus *sex* from *gender*. Rather, the body was perceived as a multilayered construct made up of indefinite elements (social and biological) in which *sex* influenced *gender* and vice versa. Thus the body was believed to reflect moral misbehaviour and negative characteristics in the form of bodily deformations or diseases (and vice versa) and was heavily influenced by the sexual policy and strict ideological doctrines of the growing Catholic Church.

The study of the breast has revealed that this time-transcending icon of femininity and women's sexuality, this symbol of nourishment, is treated either in cruel and misogynistic ways, as in the legends of Saint Agatha and Saint Christina, or it is hidden in order for women to opt out of social structures, as in the legend of Saint Eugenia. Despite these minor differences between the saints, the breast in all of the legends analysed in this study experiences a metamorphosis in the course of the narratives. It becomes a mediator between the saint's past and present, is offered as a space to exemplify the power struggle between God and the heathen, reflects the saint's inner change in attitude towards the necessity to depose her body in order to be sanctified and, at least in the legend of Saint Agatha, is employed symbolically and physically to outline the saint's martyrdom.

Body parts in women's hagiography thus connect "scenarios in which power and seduction, convention and civilisation, myth and society are prominently featured" (Walter 311).[2] Bodies are used as tools to demonstrate patriarchal superiority – in the form of the male torturer or in the form of God, though whereas the one destroys, the other restores. On the one hand, women saints and their usually virginal bodies are always denounced, mutilated and abused – physically and mentally – by male characters, even though, as the legends of the saints Christina, Agatha and Lucy have shown, without the intended effect of destroying the female. On the other hand, the body and its physical modification, destruction and restoration exemplify God's supremacy. Whereas in the legend of Saint Agatha, God's power is demonstrated when the breast is miraculously restored shortly after its brutal mastectomy; in the legend of Saint Agnes, God's all-encompassing authority is revealed through her sudden growth of hair, shielding her naked body from the public gaze; and in the legend of Saint Wilgefortis it is her beard which causes the same effect.

That hair is furthermore connected to a variety of ambiguous, sometimes contradicting definitions, that hair is a detail that matters, was argued in the analyses of

[2] Original: "So verweist Haar auf Zusammenhänge, in denen Macht und Verlockung, Konvention und Zivilisation, Mythos und Gesellschaft eine Rolle spielen".

long-haired and short-haired as well as bearded saints. Metaphorical insinuations range from the sensuality of long hair and its necessary metaphorical purification through repentance in the legends of the two Marys to the tonsured saints, such as Saint Eugenia and Saint Euphrosyne, who through the haircut overcome traditional roles of women. The most challenging hairstyle, however, remains the bearded female, whose legend mirrors the greatest discomfort about women who not only violate beauty ideals but also transgress traditional gender boundaries. Hair can thus purify, protect and help to progress spiritually, but as this study has explored in detail, it can also be turned into a saint's punishment and mark the starting point of her prosecution.

Arguably, then, body parts in women's hagiography are codes. They are used as euphemisms for religious and patriarchal gender ideology and for taboo topics such as sexuality. Whereas long, loose hair was within this study identified as a symbol of prostitution and of virginity, the gorge, in combination with teeth, tongues and the throat, was also interpretable in two ways: as a body part used for human speech and communication and as a metaphor for the female genitals. The violent removal of these organs of speech in the legends of the saints Christina, Lucy and Cecilia, or the destruction of teeth in the *vita* of Saint Apollonia, is consequently both: on the one hand, it is an attempt to silence rhetorically skilled and outspoken young women in a patriarchally dominated society. On the other hand, these legends permit a sexual reading, which detects scenes of attempted rape and in which the torture of teeth and tongue is arguably a form of symbolic defloration of these virginal women. Consequently, female saints' legends frequently "challenge us to ask new questions" (Friesen 7), to investigate these "controversial or unusual historical artifacts from new perspectives" (7) and to decipher the hidden body codes and subplots embedded in these *vitae*.

Originally, women saints belonged to a generation of mystic women whose lives were supposed to be spiritual guides for young women and female religious alike, exemplifying virtuous, subservient lives full of religious devotion and traditional gender conventions. However, as the analyses of breast, hair and the gorge have revealed, in spite of the fact that these *mulieres sanctae* were supposed to display a consistent ideological orthodoxy, many legends presented in the course of this study feature unorthodox women who challenge the essentiality of gender by "breaking with normal social values" (Riches and Salih 5). Female saints' legends repeatedly portray "individuals [who] could move on occasion between genders or adopt the attributes of another" (4). They describe women who are "'masculinised' through either physical or social metamorphosis" (Easton 52), who display a permeability of sex and gender and advertise the possibility to transcend one's natural sex – an attempt for which these women were at the same time praised and punished, honoured and vehemently denied in the Middle Ages and beyond. In fact, bodily gender hybridity, as this thesis has argued, is used as a common method to indicate the transcendence of the secular, passive-feminine body, particularly among female martyrs, in order to reach a higher social acceptance within the Christian community. Moreover, as the final chapter has discussed, the creation of sexual and gender hybridity in hagiography follows strict patterns: it is either achieved through the subtraction or addition of gender-signifying body parts, the saint's disguise and subsequent denial of her true sex, or by employing traditionally masculine characteristics. Ideally, according to the writings of the Church Fathers, women could overcome the frailty and fallibility of the female sex by renouncing any form of sexual activity and by devoting their lives fully to the ideals of the Christian community – acts for which these women were generally praised and honoured. However, as the analyses of the legends of Saint Eugenia and Saint Wilgefortis, for example, have shown, by expanding existing gender boundaries and questioning the limits of traditional binary structures, women saints not only move into the territory of men, but furthermore into the realms of the *third*, into what Judith Butler has called the "incoherently sexed" ("Sexual Inversions" 67). They often voluntarily place themselves outside the dualistic understanding of man and woman, male and female, feminine and masculine. They appear in the forms of transvestites or female eunuchs and by doing so, these saints create not only a "screen for potentially dangerous ideas" (Reames, "Artistry" 199), but also become a "serious threat to male order or authority" (Schulenburg 2) – a threat which had to be punished, ostracised or even removed to restore the social order.

Consequently, the legends of women who are described as former prostitutes, as female cross-dressers, as bearded or as questioning the existing gender norms of the time in any other way display a rich variety of "cultural symbols of gendered images", which reproduce "the ecclesiastical or patriarchal morality of the period" (Schulenburg 407) in regard to women, femininity and the female body. It is precisely these saints' interrogation of the essentiality of sex and gender binaries which makes their legends still relevant today, as they imply that assigning a true, well-defined sex and gender for each individual whom society has classified as "incoherently sexed" is a complexity that transcends time – a discourse still significant in modern discussions of gender, reminding us that the "remembrance of the past" is never completely "disassociated from the present" (Chazelle et al. 3).

That sanctity and saints' lives are still an undeniable part of our contemporary present was also noticeable when, in April of 2014, Pope John Paul II and Paul XVII were declared saints by the Vatican in a public ceremony. The mass held at the Piazza San Pietro in Rome was attended by more than 800,000 pilgrims, 1,000 bishops and 6,000 priests, and more than 90 governmental and social delegations as well as kings, queens and presidents were said to be present.[3] The ceremony, which was live-streamed all over the world and followed by millions of people, indicated two important facts: first, the significance of saints has not come to an end. Saints are still a global phenomenon whose popularity endures even in our society, which has become increasingly sceptical of religion. However, the ceremony also implied that there are still disproportionate numbers of male and female saints and that women's paths to sainthood, despite the overall claim of spiritual egalitarianism, is still not an easy one.[4] In the making of woman saints, it thus seems necessary to further engage critically with the process of canonization and to continue "our 'nimbus count' according to gender", as Schulenburg has phrased it (412). In this respect, the question arises of how today's cases of female sainthood differ from their ancient and medieval sisters. Are modern

[3] "ZDF Spezial: Die Heiligsprechung", *ZDF Mediathek*. 24 Apr. 2014, Web, 29 July 2014.

[4] The last woman to be beatified was Mother Teresa (Teresa of Calcutta) in 2003. A second miracle was attributed to her by Pope Francis in December 2015. She was recently sanctified, only eighteen years after her death, in September of 2016. See further "Mutter Teresa wird heiliggesprochen", *Zeit Online*, 15 Mar. 2016, Web, 20 Mar. 2016.

candidates for sainthood still "rule-breakers" and "flouters of boundaries", as Petroff notes (161)? Do they still challenge the essentiality of gender, as the saints Agatha, Eugenia, Wilgefortis and Christina have done, or do they rather return to the orthodox virtues of patience, poverty, chastity and obedience?

Thus, despite the in-depth analyses of women saints and their bodies presented in this study, several loose ends remain whose analyses would have gone beyond the scope of this study. Yet these loose ends propose stimulating perspectives and new starting points for future research in regard to sanctity, bodies and gender. Apart from a comparative investigation of sainthood in medieval and modern times, the complexity of historical hagiographical narratives and their attitudes towards women and the body make us wonder, for example, how women are perceived if they are solely part of a male saint's life and how much their treatment differs, if at all, from those who have individual entries in the martyrologies. One example from this study would be the case of Saint Eugenia, who in de Voragine's *Legenda Aurea* does not have a separate entry but is presented as part of the legend of the male saints Protus and Hyacinthus (II: 165-67). Interestingly, Eugenia does not remain a mere subplot embedded in a heroic account of male sanctity, but instead the legend includes a twist, turning both men into helpmates for the virgin. The question thus arises of whether Eugenia's presence in the legend of two male saints is an exception or whether similar constructions exist in hagiography in which this side-by-side depiction of male and female saints is supposed to function as an explicit contrast between the masculine ideal and the woman's attempt to "become male". Could this inevitable comparison be yet another means to further denunciate women, restricting them to the role of the Other "who must be marginalized and contained" (Schulenburg 408)?

To propose gender egalitarianism, at least in academic research, another fruitful perspective for future research could be a closer investigation of gender, masculinity and the body in male saints' lives. Does the treatment of the body in male saints' *vitae* also allow for conclusions in regard to masculinity and gender as is possible in women's hagiography? What are potential interpretations in regard to male sanctity and masculinity as well as in terms of male-to-male communication when men are tortured and denounced by other men? How are men and their bodies generally presented in hagiography and iconography alike, and are certain body parts described and tortured more frequently than others, as in women saints' *vitae*?

What all of these examples show is that gender matters – then and now. It influences, controls and categorizes both present and historical attitudes towards men, women and their bodies. It is in this context that Riches and Salih note that "gender affects sanctity" as "sanctity affect[s] gender" (5). And the body? "The body does have a history" (Le Goff and Truong 195). It is our history.

Bibliography

1 Abbreviations

AASS *Acta Sanctorum*
PL *Patrologia Latina*

2 Biblical Citations

Biblical references are used in accordance with the *Douay-Rheims Bible* (OT 1609/10, NT 1582)

Genesis 1:27-28
Genesis 2:20-23
Genesis 19:30-38
Exodus 4:15
Deuteronomy 22:5
Judges 13-16
Judges 16:19
Song of Solomon 8:10
Matthew 15:10-11
Matthew 15:16-20
Matthew 15:18-20
Matthew 19:12
Matthew 26:41
Luke 7:36-50
Luke 7:37-38
John 6:37
I Corinthians 11:3-15
I Corinthians 11:3
I Corinthians 11:9
I Corinthians 11:15
Galatians 3:28
Ephesians 5:22-23
I Timothy 2:11-13
I Timothy 2:15

3 Primary Sources

Acta et symbola conciliorum quae saeculo quarto habita sunt. Ed. E. J. Jonkers. *Textus Minores*. Vol. 19. Leiden: Brill, 1974. Print.

Acta Martyrum et Sanctorum. Ed. Paul Bedjan. 7 vols. Paris: Otto Harrassowitz, 1890-97. Print.

Acta S. Agathæ. AASS Feb. I, 621-24. Print.

Acta Sanctorum. 68 vols. to date. Ed. J. Bollandus et al. 1643-. Print.

Ælfric's Lives of Saints. Trans. and ed. Walter W. Skeat. 2 vols. London: Oxford UP, 1881-1900. Print. The Early English Text Society Original Series.

Aldhelm. *Carmen De Virginitate. Aldhelm: The Poetic Works*. Trans. Michael Lapidge and James L. Rosier. Cambridge: Brewer, 1985. Print. 95-167.

———. *Carmen De Virginitate. Aldhelmi Opera.* Ed. R. Ehwald. Berlin: Monumenta Germaniæ Historica, 1919. 325-471. Print. Auctores Antiquissimi 15.

———. *De Virginitate. Aldhelm: The Prose Works*. Trans. Michael Lapidge and Michael Herren. Cambridge: Brewer, 1979. 49-132. Print.

———. *De Virginitate. Aldhelmi Opera*. Ed. R. Ehwald. Berlin: Monumenta Germaniæ Historica, 1919. 209-323. Print. Auctores Antiquissimi 15.

Ambrose. *Expositionis in Evangelium secundum Lucum libri X. Patrologiae Cursus Completus: Series Latina*. Vol. 15. Ed. Jacques-Paul Migne, Paris: Garnieri Fratres, 1887. Print.

———. *De institutione virginis*. *PL* 16: 319-47. Print.

Aretaeus. "Causes and Symptoms of Chronic Diseases." *The Extant Works of Aretaeus the Cappadocian*. Trans. F. Adams. London: Sydenham Society, 1856. Print.

Aristotle. *Generations of Animals*. Trans. A. L. Peck. London: Heinemann, 1943. Print. Loeb Classical Library.

Athenagoras. *A Plea for the Christians*. Trans. B. P. Pratten. *The Ante-Nicene Fathers*. Vol. 2. Ed. Alexander Roberts et al. Edinburgh: T&T Clark; Grand Rapids: Eerdmans, 1885. *Christian Classics Ethereal Library*. Calvin College. Web. 17 Sept. 2016.

Augustine. *Confessions*. *PL* 32: 659-868. Trans. Rex Warner. New York: Mentor, 1963. Print.

Battelli, Guido. *La Passione di s. Agnese*. *Fiori di Letteratura Ascetica e Mistica*. Vol. 2. Firenze: Giannini, 1921. Print.

Bede. *The Complete Works of Venerable Bede in the Original Latin*. 8 vols. Ed. J. A. Giles. London: Whitaker, 1843. Print.

———. *A History of the English Church and People*. Trans. Leo Sherley-Price. Rev. R. E. Latham. New York: Penguin, 1968. Print.

———. *Martyrologium*. *Édition Pratique des Maryrologies de Béde, de l'Anonyme Lyonnais et de Florus*. Eds. Jacques Dubois and Geneviève Renaud. Paris: CNRS, 1976. Print.

Bernard of Clairvaux. *The Works of Bernard of Clairvaux*. 2 vols. Trans. Kilian Walsh. Kalamazoo: Cistercian, 1976. Print.

Biblia Sacra Vulgata. 5th edition. Ed. Robert Weber and Roger Gryson. Stuttgart: Deutsche Bibelgesellschaft, 2007. Print.

Bibliotheca Hagiographica Graeca. Ed. François Halkin. Brussels: Société des Bollandistes, 1957. Print.

Bibliotheca Hagiographica Latina Manuscripta. Ed. Société des Bollandistes, Université Catholique de Louvain. 1998. Web. 12 Nov. 2013.

Bokenham, Osbern. *A Legend of Holy Women*. Trans. Sheila Delany. Notre Dame, IN: U of Notre Dame P, 1992. Print.

———. *Legendys of Hooly Wummen*. Ed. Mary S. Serjeantson. London: Oxford UP, 1938. Print. Early English Text Society Original Series 206.

Caxton, William. *The Golden Legend or Lives of the Saints as Englished by William Caxton*. 7 vols. Ed. F. S. Ellis. Great Britain: Constable, 1900. Temple Classics.

Ps. Clement. *Ad virgines*. *Patrologia Graeca* 1: 350-452.

———. *Two Epistles Concerning Virginity*. Trans. B. P. Pratten. *The Ante-Nicene Fathers*. Vol. 8. Ed. Alexander Roberts et a'. Edinburgh: T&T Clark; Grand Rapids: Eerdmans, 1885. *Christian Classics Ethereal Library*. Calvin College. Web. 17 Sept. 2016.

Damasi Epigrammata: Accedunt pseudodamasiana aliaque ad Damasiana inlustranda idonea. Ed. Maxmilian Ihm. Leipzig: Teubner, 1895. Print. Anthologiae Latinae Supplementa I.

De'Cavalieri, Pio Franchi. *S. Agnese nella tradizione e nella leggenda.* Rome: Römische Quartalsschrift für christliche Altertumskunde und Kirchengeschichte, 1899. Print.

De Voragine, Jacobus. *The Golden Legend: Readings on the Saints*. 2 vols. Ed. and trans. William Granger Ryan. Princeton: Princeton UP, 1995. Print.

———. [Jacobi a Voragine]. *Legenda aurea, vulgo Historia lombardica dicta*. 2nd ed. Ed. Theodor Graesse. Lipsiae [Leipzig]: Librariae Arnoldianae, 1850. Print.

De Sancta Clara Virgine. *AASS* Aug. II, 739-68. Print.

De Sancta Julia. *AASS* May V, 168-72. Print.

De Sancta Theodosia. *AASS* May VII, 64-85. Print.

De Sanctis Virginibus et Martyribus Febronia. *AASS* Jun. VII, 12-31. Print.

De S. Apollonia. *AASS* Feb. II, 277-82. Print.

De S. Galla. *AASS* Oct. III, 147-63. Print.

De S. Liberata alias Wilgeforte. *AASS* Jul. V, 50-70. Print.

De S. Maria Ægyptiaca. *AASS* Apr. I, 68-90. Print.

De S. Paula. *AASS* Feb. III, 177. Print.

Divæ Catharinæ Senensis Vitæ. Ed. John Pino. 1505. Print.

Eusebius of Emesa. *Homily 6.18*. *Eusèbe d'Émèse: Discours conservés en latin*. Ed. E. M. Buytaert. Louvain: Spicilegium Sacrum, 1953. Print. Spicilegium Sacrum Lovaniense 26.

Galen. *De Usu Partium*: *On the Usefulness of the Parts of the Body*. Trans. Margaret Tallmadge May. Ithaca: Cornell UP, 1968. Print.

Gesta sanctae Agnes. *Bibliotheca Hagiographica Latina*. 3 vols. 1889-1901. Brussels: Société des Bollandistes, 1949. Print. Subsidia Hagiographica 6.

Gilte Legende. 3 vols. Ed. R. F. S. Hamer. Oxford: Oxford UP, 2006. Print. The Early English Text Society Original Series 315, 327, and 328.

Gregory of Tours. *Life of the Fathers*. Trans. Edward James. Liverpool: Liverpool UP, 1985. Print. Translated Texts for Historians, Latin Series I.

Gregory the Great. *Dialogues*. *Early Church Fathers – Additional Texts*. Ed. Roger Pearse. N.d. Web. 5 Mar. 2014.

The History of the Angelicall Virgin, Glorious S. Clare. Ed. Francis Hendricq. Douai, 1635. Print.

Jerome. *Epistulae*. Ed. Jerôme Labout. 8 vols. Paris: Belles Lettres, 1949-63.

———. *Letters*. *PL* 22: 325-1197. Print.

———. "Letter XXII: To Eustochium." *Nicene and Post-Nicene Fathers*. 2nd ser. Vol. VI. Ed. Philip Schaff and Henry Wace. Edinburgh: T&T Clark; Grand Rapids: Eerdmans, 1892. *Christian Classics Ethereal Library*. Calvin College. Web. 17 Sept. 2016.

———. "Letter XLVIII [XLIX]: To Pammachius." *Nicene and Post-Nicene Fathers*. 2nd ser. Vol. VI. Ed. Philip Schaff and Henry Wace. Edinburgh: T&T Clark; Grand Rapids: Eerdmans, 1892. *Christian Classics Ethereal Library*. Calvin College. Web. 17 Sept. 2016.

———. "Letter CVII: To Laeta." *Nicene and Post-Nicene Fathers*. 2nd ser. Vol. VI. Ed. Philip Schaff and Henry Wace. Edinburgh: T&T Clark; Grand Rapids: Eerdmans, 1892. *Christian Classics Ethereal Library*. Calvin College. Web. 17 Sept. 2016.

The Life of Saint Catherine. Trans. George Lamb. London: Harvill, 1960. Print.

The Life of Saint Clare Ascribed to Thomas of Celano. Trans. and ed. Pascal Robinson. Philadelphia: Dolphin, 1910. Print.

More, Thomas. *Dialogue Concerning Heresies*. 1529. *Medieval Popular Religion, 1000-1500: A Reader*. Ed. John Shinners. Peterborough: Broadview, 1997. 201-02. Print.

Paris, William. *Life of St. Christina*. *Middle English Legends of Women Saints*. Ed. Sherry L. Reames. Kalamazoo: Medieval Institute Publications, Western Michigan U, 2003. 223-48. Print. TEAMS Middle English Text Series.

Passio S. Christinæ Virginis et Martyris. *AASS* Jul. V, 524-28. Print.

Patrologiae Cursus Completus: Series Latina. 221 vols. Ed. Jacques-Paul Migne. Paris: Garnieri Fratres, 1844-91. Print.

Philo. *On the Creation*. Trans. and ed. F. H. Colson and G. H. Whittaker. London: William Heinemann, 1963. Print.

———. *Questions and Answers on Genesis*. Trans. and ed. Ralph Marcus. London: William Heinemann, 1961. Print.

Plutarch. *Praecepta conjugalia*. *Plutarch's Moralia*. Vol. 2. Trans. and ed. F. C. Babbitt. Cambridge: Harvard UP, 1971. Print. Loeb Classical Library.

Processus contestationum super sanctitate et doctrina B. Catherinæ de Senis. *Veterum Scriptorum et Monumentorum Amplissima Collectio*. Ed. Edmond Martène and Ursin Durand. Paris, 1729. Print.

Roger of Wendover. *Flowers of History: Comprising the History of England from the Descent of the Saxons to A.D. 1235*. 2 vols. Trans. J. A. Giles. London: Bohn, 1849. Print.

Seinte Katerine: Re-Edited from MS Bodley 34 and the Other Manuscripts. Ed. S. R. T. O. d'Ardenne and E. J. Dobson. London: Oxford UP, 1981. 2-130. Print.

The Seven Ecumenical Church Councils. *Library of Nicene and Post-Nicene Fathers*. Vol. 14. Trans. and ed. E. J. Percival. Grand Rapids: Eerdmans, 1977. Print.

The South English Legendary: Edited from Corpus Christi College Cambridge MS 145 and British Museum MS Harley 2277: With Variants from Bodley MS Ashmole 43 and British Museum MS Cotton Julius D. IX. 3 vols. Ed. Charlotte D'Evelyn and Anna J. Mill. London: Oxford UP, 1956. Print. Early English Text Society Original Series 235, 236, and 244.

SS. Proti et Hyacinthi: qui errant eunuchi S. Eugeniæ. Ed. J. A. Giles. *The Complete Works of Venerable Bede in the Original Latin*, Vol. IV. London: Whitaker, 1843. 122. Print.

Tertullian. *De exhortatione castitatis*. Ed. E. Kryomann. *Tertulliani Opera: Corpus Christianorum, Series Latina 2*. Turnhout: Brepols, 1954. 1013-35. Print.

Verne, Simon. *Sainte Eusebie, abbesse, et ses quarante compagnes martyres à Marseille*. Marseille: Imprimerie Marseillaise, 1891. Print.

La vie de sainte Agnés. Manuscript 1553. *Cataloque des manuscrits français I*. Paris: Bibliothèque Nationale, 1868. Print.

Vita Sanctæ Eugeniæ. *PL* 73: 605-24. Print.
Vita Sanctæ Euphrosynæ Virginis. *PL* 73: 643-52. Print.
Vita Sanctæ Mariæ Ægyptiacæ. *PL* 73: 671-901. Print.
Vita S. Catharinæ Senensis. *AASS* Apr. II, 862-969. Print.

4 Secondary Sources

Angenendt, Arnold. *Heilige und Reliquien. Die Geschichte ihres Kultes vom frühen Christentum bis zur Gegenwart*. München: Beck, 1994. Print.

———. "Sühne durch Blut." *Frühmittelalterliche Studien* 18 (1984): 437-67. Print.

Anson, John. "The Female Transvestite in Early Monasticism: The Origin and Development of a Motif." *Viator* 5 (1974): 1-32. Print.

Bakhtin, Mikhail. "The Grotesque Image of the Body and Its Source." *Rabelais and His World*. Trans. Helene Iswolsky. Bloomington: Indiana UP, 1984. Rpt. in *The Body: A Reader*. Ed. Mariam Fraser and Monica Greco. New York: Routledge, 2005. 92-95. Print.

Balabanova, Svetlana. *...Aber das Schönste an ihr war ihr Haar, es war rot wie Gold...: Haare im Spiegel der Kultur und Wissenschaft*. Ulm: Universitätsverlag Ulm, 1993. Print.

Baer, Richard A., Jr. *Philo's Use of the Categories of Male and Female*. Leiden: Brill, 1970. Print.

Barrows, Edward M. *Animal Behavior Desk Reference: A Dictionary of Animal Behavior, Ecology, and Evolution*. Boca Raton: CRC, 2001. Print.

Bartlett, Robert. *Why Can the Dead Do Such Great Things? Saints and Their Worshippers from the Martyrs to the Reformation*. Princeton: Princeton UP, 2013. Print.

Baschet, Jérôme. *Les justices de l'au-delà: Les représentations de l'enfer en France et en Italie (XIIe-XVe siècle)*. Rome: École française de Rome, 1993. Print.

Beal, John F. "Representations of St. Apollonia in British Churches." *Dental Historian* 30 (1996): 3-19. Print.

Berg, Charles. *The Unconscious Significance of Hair*. London: Allen & Unwin, 1951. Print.

Bernau, Anke, Ruth Evans, and Sarah Salih, eds. *Medieval Virginities*. Cardiff: U of Wales P, 2005. Print.

Biller, Peter, and A. J. Minnis. *Medieval Theology and the Natural Body*. York: York Medieval P, 1997. Print. York Studies in Medieval Theology I.

Blamires, Alcuin. "Paradox in the Medieval Gender Doctrine of Head and Body." *Medieval Theology and the Natural Body*. Ed. Peter Biller and A. J. Minnis. York: York Medieval P, 1997. 13-30. Print. York Studies in Medieval Theology I.

"Blonde." *Online Etymology Dictionary*. N.d. Web. 13 Aug. 2012.

Bock, Gisela. *Frauen in der europäischen Geschichte: Vom Mittelalter bis zur Gegenwart*. Munich: Beck, 2000. Print.

Boureau, Alain. *La légende dorée*. Paris: Edition du Cerf, 1984. Print.

———. *The Myth of Pope Joan*. Trans. Lydia G. Cochrane. Chicago: U of Chicago P, 2001. Print.

"Braut mit Bart – Ehe annulliert." *Yahoo News*. 10 Feb. 2010. Web. 12 Feb. 2010.

Brock, Arthur John, ed. and trans. *Galen on the Natural Faculties*. London: Heinemann, 1916. Print.

Brown, Peter. *The Cult of the Saints: Its Rise and Function in Latin Christianity*. Chicago: U of Chicago P, 1981. Print. Haskell Lectures on History of Religion.

———. *The Body and Society: Men, Women and Sexual Renunciation in Early Christianity*. New York: Columbia UP, 1988. Print.

Brownlee, Kevin. "Martyrdom and the Female Voice: Saint Christine in the *Cité des Dames*." *Images of Sainthood in Medieval Europe*. Ed. Renate Blumenfeld-Kosinski and Timea Szell. Ithaca: Cornell UP, 1991. 115-35. Print.

Brundage, James A. *Law, Sex and Christian Society in Medieval Europe*. Chicago: U of Chicago P, 1987. Print.

Bryer, Robin. *The History of Hair: Fashion and Fantasy down the Ages*. London: Wilson, 2000. Print.

Bullough, Vern L. "Cross Dressing and Gender Role Change in the Middle Ages." *Handbook of Medieval Sexuality*. Ed. Bullough and James A. Brundage. New York: Garland, 1996. 223-42. Print.

———. "Transvestites in the Middle Ages." *American Journal of Sociology* 79.6 (1974): 1381-94. Print.

Bullough, Vern L., and Bonnie Bullough. *Cross Dressing, Sex and Gender*. Philadelphia: U of Pennsylvania P, 1993. Print.

Bullough, Vern L., and James A. Brundage. *Handbook of Medieval Sexuality*. New York: Garland, 2000. Print.

———. *Sexual Practices and the Medieval Church*. Amherst, New York: Prometheus, 1994. Print.

Burgwinkle, William, and Cary Howie. *Sanctity and Pornography in Medieval Culture: On the Verge*. Manchester: Manchester UP, 2011. Print.

Burrus, Victoria. *The Sex Lives of Saints: An Erotics of Ancient Hagiography*. Philadelphia: U of Philadelphia P, 2004. Print.

Butler, Alban. *Butler's Lives of the Saints*. Ed. Herbert Thurston and Donald Attwater. 4 vols. New York: Kennedy, 1956. Print.

———. *Butler's Lives of the Saints*. Rev. Michael Walsh. New York: Harper Collins, 1991. Print.

Butler, Judith. "Bodies That Matter: On the Discursive Limits of 'Sex.'" *The Body: A Reader*. Ed. Mariam Fraser and Monica Greco. New York: Routledge, 2005. 62-65. Print.

———. *The Judith Butler Reader*. Ed. Sarah Salih with Butler. Oxford: Blackwell, 2004. Print.

———. "Revisiting Bodies and Pleasure." *Theory, Culture and Society* 16.2 (1999): 11-20. Print.

———. "Sexual Inversions." *Feminist Interpretations of Michel Foucault*. Ed. Susan Hekman. Philadelphia: U of Pennsylvania P, 1996. 59-75. Print.

Bynum, Caroline Walker. *Fragmentation and Redemption: Essays on Gender and the Human Body in Medieval Religion*. New York: Zone, 1991. Print.

———. *Holy Feast and Holy Fast: The Religious Significance of Food to Medieval Women*. Berkeley: U of California P, 1987. Print.

Campbell, Mary B. *The Witness and the Other World: Exotic European Travel Writing, 400-1600.* Ithaca: Cornell UP, 1988. Print.

Cazelles, Brigitte. *The Lady as Saint: A Collection of French Hagiographic Romances of the Thirteenth Century*. Philadelphia: U of Pennsylvania P, 1991. Print.

Chazelle, Celia, Simon Doubleday, Felice Lifshitz, and Amy G. Remensnyder, eds. *Why the Middle Ages Matter: Medieval Light on Modern Injustice*. Abingdon: Routledge, 2012. Print.

Clamp, Rebecca. "St. Wilgefortis." *YouTube*. 16 Aug. 2007. Web. 2 Feb. 2010.

"Clitoris." *Online Etymology Dictionary*. N.d. Web. 13 Sept. 2013.

Coates, Simon. "Scissors or Sword? The Symbolism of a Medieval Haircut." *History Today* 49.5 (1990): 7-13. Print.

Constantinou, Stavroula. *Female Corporeal Performances: Reading the Body in Byzantine Passions and Lives of Holy Women*. Uppsala: Uppsala Universitet, 2005. Print. Acta Universitatis Upsaliensis. Studia Byzantina Upsaliensia 9.

Cooke, Alexander. *Pope Joan*. London: Blunt and Baring, 1610. Print.

Cooper, Wendy. *Hair: Sex, Society, Symbolism*. New York: Stein and Day, 1971. Print.

Crane, Susan. *The Performance of the Self*. Philadelphia: U of Pennsylvania P, 2002. Print.

Delehaye, Hippolyte. *The Legends of the Saints: An Introduction to Hagiography*. 1905-06. Trans. V. M. Crawford. Breinigsville: Kessinger, 2009. Print.

———. "Sanctus: Essai sur le culte de saints dans l'antiquité". Brussels: Société des Bollandistes, 1927. Print. Subsidia Hagiographica 17.

Delooz, Pierre. *Sociologie et Canonisations*. Collection scientifique de la faculté de droit de l'Université de Liège, no. 30. Liège, 1969. Print.

———. "Towards a Sociological Study of Canonized Sainthood in the Catholic Church." Trans. Jane Hodgkin. *Saints and Their Cults: Studies in Religious Sociology, Folklore and History*. Ed. Stephen Wilson. Cambridge: Cambridge UP, 1983. 189-216. Print.

Denomy, Alexander Joseph. *The Old French Lives of Saint Agnes and Other Vernacular Versions of the Middle Ages*. Cambridge: Harvard UP, 1938. Print.

D'Evelyn, Charlotte. Rev. of *Die englische Heiligenlegende des Mittelalters*, by Theodor Wolpers (Tübingen, 1964). *Speculum* 42 (1967): 213-17. Print.

Drane, Augusta Theodosia. *The Life of Saint Catherine of Siena and Her Companions*. London: Burns and Oats, 1887. Print.

Donovan, Leslie A. *Women Saints' Lives in Old English Prose*. Cambridge: Brewer, 1999. Print.

Douglas, Mary. "The Two Bodies." *Natural Symbols: Explorations in Cosmology*. 3rd ed. New York: Routledge, 1996. Rpt. in *The Body: A Reader*. Ed. Mariam Fraser and Monica Greco. New York: Routledge, 2005. 78-81. Print.

Duby, Georges. *The Three Orders: Feudal Society Imagined*. Trans. Arthur Goldhammer. Chicago: U of Chicago P, 1980. Print.

Dyas, Dee. *Images of Faith in English Literature 700-1500: An Introduction*. London: Longmans, 1997. Print.

Easton, Martha. "Pain, Torture and Death in the Huntington Library *Legenda Aurea*." *Gender and Holiness: Men, Women and Saints in Late Medieval Europe*. Ed. Samantha Riches and Sarah Salih. Abingdon: Routledge, 2002. 49-64 Print.

Eilberg-Schwartz, Howard. "The Spectacle of the Female Head." Introduction. *Off with Her Head: The Denial of Women's Identity in Myth, Religion, and Culture.* Ed. Eilberg-Schwartz and Wendy Doniger. Berkeley: U of California P, 1995. 1-13. Print.

Elliot, Alison Goddard. *Roads to Paradise: Reading the Lives of Early Saints*. Hanover: UP of New England, 1987. Print.

Erickson, Carolly. *The Medieval Vision: Essays in History and Perception*. New York: Oxford UP, 1976. Print.

"Eunuch." *Online Etymology Dictionary*. N.d. Web. 13 Sept. 2013.

Faith, Karlene. *Unruly Women: The Politics of Confinement and Resistance*. Vancouver: Press Gang, 1993. Print.

Farmer, David Hugh. *Oxford Dictionary of Saints*. 5th ed. Oxford: Oxford UP, 2004. Print.

Firth, Raymond. *Symbols: Public and Private*. Ithaca: Cornell UP, 1973. Print.

Fisher, A. L. "Women and Gender in Palladius' *Lausaic History*." *Studia Monastica* 33 (1991): 23-50. Print.

Foucault, Michel. *Discipline and Punish: The Birth of the Prison*. Trans. Alan Sheridan. New York: Vintage, 1977. Print.

Fouracre, Paul. "Merovingian History and Merovingian Historiography." *Past and Present* 127 (1990): 3-38. Print.

Frantzen, Allen J. *Before the Closet: Same Sex Love from "Beowulf" to "Angels in America."* Chicago: U of Chicago P, 1998. Print.

Fraser, Mariam, and Monica Greco, eds. *The Body: A Reader.* New York: Routledge, 2005. Print.

Freud, Sigmund. "Femininity." *New Introductory Lectures on Psycho-Analysis*. 1933. Rpt. in *The Standard Edition of the Complete Psychological Works of Sigmund Freud.* Vol. XXII. Ed. James Strachey. London: Hogarth and The Institute for Psycho-Analysis, 1964. 112-35. Print.

Friesen, Ilse E. *The Female Crucifix: Images of St. Wilgefortis since the Middle Ages*. Waterloo: Wilfred Laurier UP, 2001. Print.

Galpern, Joyce. "The Shape of Hell in Anglo-Saxon England." Diss. U of California, Berkeley, 1977. Print.

Garber, Marjorie. *Vested Interests: Cross-Dressing and Cultural Anxiety*. New York: Routledge, 1997. Print.

Gardner, Arthur. *English Medieval Sculpture*. New York: Hacker, 1973. Print.

Gautier, Théophile. *Mademoiselle de Maupin*. Trans. Joanna Richardson. Harmondsworth: Penguin, 1981. Print.

Glucklich, Ariel. "Sacred Pain and the Phenomenal Self." *The Harvard Theological Review* 91.4 (1998): 389-412. Print.

———. "Self and Sacrifice: A Phenomenological Psychology of Sacred Pain." *The Harvard Theological Review* 92.4 (1999): 479-506. Print.

Goodich, Michael. "Biography 1100-1350." *Historiography in the Middle Ages*. Ed. Deborah Mauskopf Delyannis. Leiden: Brill, 2003. 353-58. Print.

Görlach, Manfred. *Studies in Middle English Saints' Legends*. Heidelberg: Winter, 1998. Print.

Goulemot, Jean Marie. *Forbidden Texts: Erotic Literature and Its Readers in Eighteenth Century France*. Trans. James Simpson. Philadelphia: Pennsylvania UP, 1995. Print.

Grantley, Darryll, and Nina Taunton. *The Body in Late Medieval and Early Modern Culture*. Aldershot: Ashgate, 2000. Print.

Grimm, Jacob, and Wilhelm Grimm. “Allerleirauh.” *Die schönsten Kinder- und Hausmärchen. Spiegel Online*. 9 Sept. 2011. Web. 2 Feb. 2012.

Greer, Germaine. *The Female Eunuch*. New York: McGraw-Hill, 1970. Print.

Grosz, Elizabeth. “Refiguring Bodies.” *Volatile Bodies*. Bloomington: Indiana UP, 1994. Rpt. in *The Body: A Reader*. Ed. Mariam Fraser and Monica Greco. New York: Routledge, 2005. 47-51. Print.

Gulley, Allison. “Suffering and Salvation: Birthing Pains in Ælfric’s Life of Agatha.” *Medieval Perspectives* 17.1 (2002): 105-20. Print.

Haas, Birgit, ed. *Haare zwischen Fiktion und Realität: Interdisziplinäre Untersuchungen zur Wahrnehmung der Haare*. Berlin: LIT, 2008. Print.

Hall, Stuart. “Who Needs ‘Identity.’” *Identity: A Reader*. Ed. Paul du Gay, Jessica Evans, and Peter Redman. London: Sage, 2005. 15-30. Print.

Hanson, Ann, and David Armstrong. “The Virgin’s Voice and Neck: Aeschylus, *Agamemnon 245* and Other Texts.” *British Institute of Classical Studies* 33 (1986): 97-100. Print.

Harney, Eileen. “The Sexualized and Gendered Tortures of Virgin Martyrs in Medieval English Literature.” Diss. U of Toronto, 2008. *TSpace*. Web. 4 Feb. 2016.

Harper, Douglas. *Online Etymology Dictionary*. N.p., 2000-16. Web. 12 Nov. 2013.

Hastrup, Kirsten. “The Semantics of Biology: Virginity.” *Defining Females: The Nature of Women in Society*. Ed. Shirley Ardener. New York: Wiley, 1978. 49-65. Print.

Head, Thomas. *Hagiography and the Cult of Saints*. Cambridge: Cambridge UP, 1990. Print.

Heck, Andreas. “Farbpsychologie und Symbolik.” *Farbcodes*. Filmakademie Baden-Württemberg, 2002. Web. 1 May 2010.

Heffernan, Thomas. *Sacred Biography: Saints and Their Biographers in the Middle Ages*. Oxford: Oxford UP, 1988. Print.

Herrmann, Horst. *Die Folter: Eine Enzyklopädie des Grauens*. Frankfurt: Eichborn, 2004. Print.

———. *Sex und Folter in der Kirche: 2000 Jahre Folter im Namen Gottes*. München: Bassermann, 2011. Print.

Hirschfeld, Magnus. *Die Transvestiten: Eine Untersuchung über den erotischen Verkleidungstrieb mit umfangreichem casuistischen und historischem Material*. Leipzig: Spohr, 1910. Print.

Honegger, Thomas, ed. *Riddles, Knights and Cross-Dressing Saints*. Bern: Lang, 2004. Print.

Hughes, Kathleen. *Early Christian Ireland*. Ithaca: Cornell UP, 1972. Print

Irigaray, Luce. *This Sex Which Is Not One*. Trans. Catherine Porter with Carolyn Burke. Ithaca: Cornell UP, 1985. Print.

Kay, Sarah. “The Sublime Body of the Martyr: Violence in Early Romance Saints’ Lives.” *Violence in Medieval Society*. Ed. Richard W. Kaeuper. Woodbridge: Boydell, 2000. 3-20. Print.

Keller, Hiltgart L. *Reclams Lexikon der Heiligen und biblischen Gestalten: Legende und Darstellung in der bildenden Kunst*. Stuttgart: Reclam, 2001. Print.

Kelly, Kathleen Coyne. *Performing Virginity and Testing Chastity in the Middle Ages*. London: Routledge, 2000. Print.

King, David E. "The Cult of Saint Wilgefortis in Flanders, Holland, England in France." *Am Kreuz – eine Frau: Anfänge – Abhängigkeiten – Aktualisierungen*. Ed. Sigrid Glockzin-Bever and Martin Kraatz. Münster: LIT, 2003. 55-97. Print.

Klein, Melanie. *The Selected Melanie Klein*. Ed. Juliette Mitchell. New York: Free, 1987. Print.

Klinger, Elmar, Stephanie Böhm, and Theodor Seidl, eds. *Der Körper und die Religion: Das Problem der Konstruktion von Geschlechterrollen*. Würzburg: Echter, 2000. Print.

Knust, Christine. "'Allen sinen lip bedecktent die loecke': Zur Symbolik der Haare in Heiligenlegenden und Heiligendarstellungen des Mittelalters." *Haare zwischen Fiktion und Realität: Interdisziplinäre Untersuchungen zur Wahrnehmung der Haare*. Ed. Birgit Haas. Berlin: LIT, 2008. 115-34. Print.

Kuefler, Matthew. "Castration and Eunuchism in the Middle Ages." *Handbook of Medieval Sexuality*. Ed. Vern L. Bullough and James A. Brundage. New York: Garland, 1996. 279-306. Print.

———. *The Manly Eunuch: Masculinity, Gender Ambiguity and Christian Ideology in Late Antiquity*. Chicago: U of Chicago P, 2001. Print.

Kunze, Konrad. *Studien zur Legende der heiligen Maria Aegyptiaca im deutschen Sprachgebiet*. Berlin: Erich Schmidt, 1969. Print.

Laqueur, Thomas. *Making Sex: Body and Gender from the Greeks to Freud.* Massachusetts: Harvard UP, 1992. Print.

Lasareff, Victor. "Studies in the Iconography of the Virgin." *Art Bulletin* 20.1 (1938): 26-65. Print.

Leach, Edmund. "Magical Hair." *Myth and Cosmos: Readings in Mythology and Symbolism*. Ed. John Middleton. Austin: U of Texas P, 1967. 77-108. Print.

Le Goff, Jacques, and Nicolas Truong. *Die Geschichte des Körpers im Mittelalter.* Stuttgart: Klett-Cotta, 2007. Print.

———. *Une Histoire du Corps au Moyen Âge*. Paris: Levi, 2003. Print.

Lensing, Irmgard. *Die Altenglischen Heiligenlegenden*. Heidelberg: Winter, 2010. Print.

Lewis, Charlton T., and Charles Short, eds. *A Latin Dictionary*. 1879. Oxford: Oxford UP, 1980. Print.

Lewis, Katherine J. "Margery Kempe and Saint Making in Later Medieval England." *A Companion to "The Book of Margery Kempe."* Ed. John H. Arnold and Katherine Lewis. Cambridge: Brewer, 2004. 195-216. Print.

Leynhausen, Maite. "Damen mit Bart. Zwischen sozialem Druck und ästhetischer Performanz." *Haare zwischen Fiktion und Realität. Interdisziplinäre Untersuchungen zur Wahrnehmung der Haare*. Ed. Birgit Haas. Berlin: LIT, 2008. 148-53. Print.

Lifshitz, Felice. "Beyond Positivism and Genre: Hagiographical Texts as Historical Narrative." *Viator* 25 (1994): 95-113. Print.

Lipp, Wolfgang. "Körper, Körpersymbolik und Gesellschaft." *Der Körper und die Religion: Das Problem der Konstruktion von Geschlechterrollen*. Ed. Elmar Klinger, Stephanie Böhm, and Theodor Seidl. Würzburg: Echter, 2000. 9-26. Print.

Long, Mary Beth. "Corpora and Manuscripts, Authors and Audience." *A Companion to Middle English Hagiography*. Ed. Sarah Salih. Cambridge: Brewer, 2006. 47-69. Print.

Longhurst, Margaret H. *Catalogue of Carvings in Ivory in the Victoria and Albert Museum*. London, n.p. 1927. Print.

Lowerre, Sandra. "To Rise beyond Their Sex: Female Cross-Dressing Saints in Caxton's *Vitas Patrum*." *Riddles, Knights and Cross-Dressing Saints*. Ed. Thomas Honegger. Bern: Lang, 2004. 55-94. Print.

Maitland, Sarah, and Wendy Mulford. *Virtuous Magic: Women Saints and their Meanings*. London: Mowbray, 1998. Print.

Marshall, Claire. "The Politics of Self-Mutilation: Forms of Female Devotion in the Late Middle Ages." *The Body in Late Medieval and Early Modern Culture*. Ed. Darryll Grantley and Nina Taunton. Aldershot: Ashgate, 2000. 11-22. Print.

Matchar, Emily. *Homeward Bound: Why Women Are Embracing the New Domesticity*. New York: Simon and Schuster, 2013. Print.

Mazzio, Carla. "Sins of the Tongue in Early Modern England." *Modern Language Studies* 28.4 (1998): 93-124. Print.

McDaniel, Rhonda L. "Agnes among the Anglo-Saxons: Patristic Influences in Anglo-Latin and Anglo-Saxon Versions of the *Passio* of St. Agnes, Virgin and Martyr." *Writing Women Saints in Anglo-Saxon England*. Ed. Paul E. Szarmach. Toronto: U of Toronto P, 2013. 217-48. Print.

McLane, Janice. "The Voice on the Skin: Self-Mutilation and Merleau-Ponty's Theory of Language." *Hypatia* 11.4 (1966): 107-18. Print.

McLaughlin, Mary Martin. "Survivors and Surrogates: Children and Parents from the Ninth to the Thirteenth Centuries." *History of Childhood*. Ed. Lloyd DeMause. New York: Psychohistory P, 1974. 115-18. Print.

Mecklin, John M. *The Passing of the Saint: A Study of a Cultural Type*. Chicago: U of Chicago P, 1941. Print.

Meiss, Millard. *Painting in Florence and Siena after the Black Death*. New York: Harper, 1964. Print.

Mershman, Francis. "St. Galla." *The Catholic Encyclopedia*. Vol. 6. New York: Appleton, 1909. N. pag. *New Advent*, 2012. Web. 12 Feb. 2013.

Miles, Margaret R. *A Complex Delight: The Secularization of the Breast 1350-1750*. Berkeley: U of California P, 2008. Print.

———. "God's Love, Mother's Milk." *The Christian Century* 125.2 (2008): 22-26. Print.

Milliken, Roberta. *Ambiguous Locks: An Iconology of Hair in Medieval Art and Literature*. Jefferson: McFarland, 2012. Print.

———. "Neither 'Clere Laude' nor 'Sklaundre': Chaucer's Translation of Criseyde and Sensual and Holy Locks: A Study of Hair in Women's Hagiography." Diss. U of Toledo, 1995. Print.

Mills, Robert. *Suspended Animation: Pain, Pleasure and Punishment in Medieval Culture.* London: Reaktion, 2005. Print.

———. "Violence, Community and the Materialisation of Belief." *A Companion to Middle English Hagiography*. Ed. Sarah Salih. Cambridge: Brewer, 2006. 87-103. Print.

Mulder-Bakker, Anneke B. “Saints without a Past: Sacred Places and Intercessionary Power of Saints’ Lives from the Low Countries.” *Inventions of Saintliness*. Ed. Mulder-Bakker. London: Routledge, 2002. 38-57. Print.

Mullen, Robert F. “Holy Stigmata, Anorexia and Self-Mutilation: Parallels in Pain and Imagining.” *Journal for the Study of Religions and Ideologies* 9.25 (2010): 91-110. Print.

“Mutter Teresa wird heiliggesprochen.” *Zeit Online*. 15 Mar. 2016. Web. 20 Mar. 2016.

The New Catholic Encyclopaedia. 15 vols. New York: McGraw Hill, 1967. Print.

Niermeyer, J. F. *Mediae Latinitatis Lexicon Minus*. Leiden: Brill, 1957. Print.

Orchard, Andy. *Pride and Prodigies: Studies in the Monsters of the Beowulf-Manuscript*. Toronto: U of Toronto P, 1995. Print.

Perrault, Charles. “Peau d’Âne.” *Les Contes de ma Mère l’Oye*. 1697. Print.

Petroff, Elizabeth Alvilda. *Body and Soul: Essays on Medieval Women and Mysticism*. Oxford: Oxford UP, 1994. Print.

“Pornography.” *Oxford English Dictionary*. N.d. Web. 4 Apr. 2013.

Rattray Taylor, Gordon. *Kulturgeschichte der Sexualität*. Frankfurt am Main: Fischer, 1977. Print.

Reames, Sherry L. “Artistry, Decorum and Purpose in Three Middle English Retellings of the Cecilia Legend.” *The Endless Knot: Essays on Old and Middle English in Honor of Marie Borroff*. Ed. M. Teresa Tavormina and R. F. Yeager. Cambridge: Brewer, 1995. 177-99. Print.

———. *The Legenda Aurea: A Reexamination of Its Paradoxical History*. Madison: U of Wisconsin P, 1985. Print.

———, ed. *Middle English Legends of Women Saints*. Kalamazoo: Medieval Institute Publications, Western Michigan U, 2003. Print. TEAMS Middle English Text Series.

Richardson, Ernest C. *Materials for a Life of Jacopo da Varagine*. New York: Wilson, 1935. Print.

Riches, Samantha. “Hagiography in Context: Images, Miracles, Shrines and Festivals.” *A Companion to Middle English Hagiography*. Ed. Sarah Salih. Cambridge: Brewer, 2006. 25-46. Print.

Riches, Samantha, and Sarah Salih. *Gender and Holiness: Men, Women and Saints in Late Medieval Europe*. Abingdon: Routledge, 2002. Print.

Ripperberger, Helmut, and William Granger Ryan, eds. and trans. *The Golden Legend of Jacobus de Voragine*. New York: Longmans, 1941. Print.

Rossmeisl, Robyn. “Encountering the Embodied Mouth of Hell: The Play of Oppositions in Religious Vernacular Theater.” MA thesis. U of British Columbia, 2012. *UBC Theses and Dissertations*. Web. 7 June 2013.

Rousselle, Aline. *Porneia: On Desire and the Body in Antiquity*. Trans. Felicia Pheasant. New York: Blackwell, 1988. Print.

Ryan, William Granger. Introduction. *The Golden Legend: Readings on the Saints*. By Jacobus de Voragine. 2 vols. Ed. and trans. William Granger Ryan. Princeton: Princeton UP, 1995. xiii-xviii. Print.

“Saint Galla of Rome.” *CatholicSaints.Info*. N.d. Web. 13 Feb. 2014.

Salih, Sarah, ed. *A Companion to Middle English Hagiography*. Cambridge: Brewer, 2006. Print.

———. Introduction. *The Judith Butler Reader.* Ed. Salih with Judith Butler. Oxford: Blackwell, 2004. 1-17. Print.
———. "Performing Virginity: Sex and Violence in the Katherine Group." *Constructions of Widowhood and Virginity in the Middle Ages*. Ed. Cindy L. Carlson and Angela Jane Weisl. New York: St. Martin's, 1999. 95-112. Print.
Salisbury, Joyce E. *Church Fathers, Independent Virgins*. London: Verso, 1991. Print.
Scarry, Elaine. *The Body in Pain: The Making and Unmaking of the World.* Oxford: Oxford UP, 1985. Print.
Schäfer-Althaus, Sarah. "Painful Pleasure: Saintly Torture on the Verge of Pornography." *Mirabilia* 18 (2014): 151-59. Web. 13 Sept. 2016.
———. "The Significance of Hair in Women's Hagiography." MA thesis. U of Paderborn, 2010. Print.
Schmidt, Gary D. *The Iconography of the Mouth of Hell: Eighth-Century Britain to the Fifteenth Century*. London: Associated University Presses, 1995. Print.
Schneider, Roswitha. "Katharina von Siena als Mystikerin." *Frauenmystik im Mittelalter*. Ed. Peter Dinzelbacher and Dieter R. Bauer. Ostfildern: Schwabenverlag, 1985. 290-313. Print.
Schroer, Sylvia. *Die Körpersymbolik der Bibel.* Darmstadt: Wissenschaftliche Buchgesellschaft, 1998. Print.
Schulenburg, Jane Tibbetts. *Forgetful of Their Sex: Female Sanctity and Society, ca. 500-1100*. Chicago: U of Chicago P, 1998. Print.
Shapiro, Meyer. "Cain's Jaw-Bone That Did the First Murder." *The Art Bulletin* 24.3 (1942): 205-12. Print.
Shinners, John, ed. *Medieval Popular Religion, 1000-1500: A Reader*. Peterborough: Broadview, 1997. Print.
Sorgo, Gabriele. *Martyrium und Pornographie.* Düsseldorf: Patmos, 1997. Print.
"St. Paula Barbada." *Turismo de Ávila*. N.d. Web. 5 Mar. 2014.
Synnott, Anthony. "Hair: Shame and Glory." *The Body Social: Symbolism, Self and Society*. London: Routledge, 1993. 103-27. Print.
Szarmach, Paul E. "Ælfric's Women Saints: Eugenia." *New Readings on Women in Old English Literature*. Ed. Helen Damico and Alexandra Hennessey Olson. Bloomington: Indiana UP, 1990. 146-57. Print.
———. *Writing Women Saints in Anglo-Saxon England.* Toronto: Toronto UP, 2013. Print.
Talbot, Alice-Mary, ed. *Holy Women of Byzantium: Ten Saint's Lives in English Translation*. Washington, DC: Dumbarton Oaks Centre Studies, 1996. Print. Byzantine Saints' Lives in Translation.
Turner, Bryan. *The Body and Society: Explorations in Social Theory*. Oxford: Blackwell, 1984. Print.
———. *The Body and Society*. 2nd ed. London: Sage, 1996. Print.
———. "Social Fluids: Metaphors and Meanings of Society." Online abstract. *Body & Society* 9 (2003): 1-10. *Sage Journals*. Web. 12 Sept. 2016.
Turner, Victor. *The Ritual Process*. Harmondsworth: Penguin, 1969. Print.
Uhde, Robert. "Das Martyrium der Heiligen Apollonia." *Bayerisches Zahnärzteblatt*. Jan/Feb. 2009. Web. 18 Nov. 2011.
Vauchez, André. *Sainthood in the Later Middle Ages*. Trans. Jean Birrell. Cambridge: Cambridge UP, 1997. Print.

Velimirovich, Nikolai. “Hymn in Praise of Sainte Febronia.” *Santafebronia.* N.d. Web. 17 Apr. 2013.
Von Beit, Hedwig. *Symbolik des Märchens. Versuch einer Deutung*. Bern: Francke, 1981. Print.
Walker, Jonathan. “The Transtextuality of Transvestite Sainthood; Or, How to Make the Gendered Form Fit the Generic Function.” *Exemplaria* 15 (2003): 73-110. Print.
Walter, Henrike. “Flechten, Fell und Bärte. Genderspezifische Aspekte der Haarsymbolik im Märchen.” *Haare zwischen Fiktion und Realität: Interdisziplinäre Untersuchungen zur Wahrnehmung der Haare*. Ed. Birgit Haas. Berlin: LIT, 2008. 311-29. Print.
Warner, Marina. *From the Beast to the Blonde: On Fairy Tales and Their Tellers*. London: Chatto & Windus, 1994. Print.
Weldon, Terence. “Nov 9th: Matrona/Babylas of Perge.” *Queering the Church*. 9 Nov. 2010. Web. 12 Sept. 2016.
White, Cynthia. *The Emergence of Christianity*. Westport: Greenwood, 2007. Print.
Wilson, Elizabeth A. *Neural Geographies: Feminism and the Microstructure of Cognition*. New York: Routledge, 1998. Print.
Winstead, Karen A. *Virgin Martyrs: Legends of Sainthood in Late Medieval England.* Ithaca: Cornell UP, 1997. Print.
Wood, Clement. *The Woman Who Was Pope*. New York: Faro, 1931. Print.
Worcestre, William. *Itineraries*. Ed. John H. Harvey. Oxford: Clarendon, 1969. Print.
Wormald, Francis, ed. *English Kalendars Before AD 1100*. London: Henry Bradshaw Society, 1934. Print. Henry Bradshaw Society 72.
Younis, Jinan. “What Happened When I Started a Feminist Society at School.” *The Guardian*. 20 June 2013. Web. 21 June 2013.
Za’za’, Bassam. “Man Claims Fiancée Hid Beard under Niqab.” *Gulf News*. 10 Feb. 2010. Web. 14 Feb. 2010.
“ZDF Spezial: Die Heiligsprechung.” *ZDF Mediathek*. 24 Apr. 2014. Web. 29 July 2014.